Hidden Rhythms in Prophecy

*How Astronomical Cycles
Interpret Prophecies In
Daniel, Jeremiah And Ezekiel*

Ron Bublitz

Hidden Rhythms in Prophecy

Copyright © 2016 by Ronald M. Bublitz.

All rights reserved. No portion of this book may be reproduced in any form without the written permission of the copyright owner, except for brief excerpts quoted in critical reviews.

All Scripture quotations in this book, except those noted otherwise, are from the ESV Bible® (The Holy Bible, English Standard Version®), copyright © 2001 by Crossway Bibles, a publishing ministry of Good News Publishers.
Used by permission. All rights reserved.

Cover design: Ron Bublitz

ISBN: 978-0-9951997-0-5

For my father.
He introduced me to Biblical prophecies
and
we spent many hours discussing them.

CONTENTS

Introduction

The Hebrew Calendar

Chapter 1
Calendrical Concepts in the Bible — 9

Chapter 2
The Calendar at the Exodus — 17

Chapter 3
Calendar of Creation Week — 24

Chapter 4
Ancient Calendars — 26

Chapter 5
The Jewish Calendar — 28

Chapter 6
Discovering the Original Calendar — 34

Chapter 7
Reconstructing the Original Calendar — 44

Gabriel's 70 Weeks Recorded by Daniel

Chapter 8
The Interpretations by Anderson and Hoehner — 70

Chapter 9
Changing a Comma into a Period Changed Everything — 75

Chapter 10
How Many Are There? — 93

Chapter 11
Who Gave the Command? — 96

Chapter 12
The 7 Weeks — 107

Chapter 13
The 62 Weeks — 111

Chapter 14
The 1 Week — 122

The Birth and Sacrifice of Jesus Christ

Chapter 15
    The Year of Christ's Birth   144

Chapter 16
    The Year of Christ's Sacrifice   173

Eclipse Event Signs

Chapter 17
    Feasts of the LORD   209

Chapter 18
    The Blood Moon Phenomenon   211

Chapter 19
    Eclipse Event Signs   214

Chapter 20
    Eclipse Event Signs of the Recent Past   216

Chapter 21
    Eclipse Event Signs of Jesus Christ   233

Chapter 22
    Eclipse Event Signs of the Babylonian Exile   241

Chapter 23
    Eclipse Event Sign for Creation Week   248

Rhythms of the Future

Chapter 24
    Eclipse Event Signs for Gabriel's 1 Week   257

Chapter 25
    Days of the Lord   266

Chapter 26
    The 430 Day Prophecy of Ezekiel   267

Chapter 27
    Other Significant Numbers in Daniel   277

Appendix

Bibliography

Index

Introduction

"That can't be right!", I exclaimed and let the ebook reader settle on the cushion next to me. I had just downloaded the English Standard Version (ESV) of the Bible in order to look it over. Up until then, I wasn't aware that the translation had even existed. I was attending a new church in 2009 and it was their translation of choice. I began surfing through favorite passages, evaluating how each was translated and comparing them with what I was familiar with.

A good passage to evaluate had come to mind – I needed to look up the Prophecy of the 70 Weeks in the book of Daniel. Years before, when I had first heard the passage interpreted, it was one of the most amazing examples of the accuracy of God's word that I knew of. If a new translation did not get this passage right, then I knew there was something wrong.

The prophecy consists of three periods of time – Daniel refers to them as Weeks. Most scholars say that they are Weeks of years, not seven day weeks. I remembered that the first two Weeks – of 7 and 62 – are taken together as a unit and multiplied by the number of days in a "prophetic year." There were biblical reasons why this special 360-day year was used. Then the total number of days was converted back to our modern calendar. Starting from the specific date of a decree to rebuild Jerusalem and going forward the calculated number of days, this ended exactly on the day of Palm Sunday of the year that Jesus Christ presented Himself as Messiah, the Anointed One, in Jerusalem. It was truly amazing.

I navigated to Daniel Chapter 9 and began to read. That's when I came to verse 25, which shocked me:

> "Know therefore and understand that from the going out of the word to restore and build Jerusalem to the coming of an anointed one, a prince, there shall be seven weeks. Then for sixty-two weeks it shall be built again with squares and moat, but in a troubled time."

Wait. This version had a definite split between the first two sets of Weeks. The way it was written, there was no way to combine them into one time period. The "anointed one" now shows up at the end of the first 7 Weeks. That went against the interpretation I was familiar with. This translation had gotten it wrong.

This began the journey of research and discovery culminating in this book. During the following flurry of research, I discovered why the ESV had translated the passage the way it had – and it was not wrong after all. In addition, my research included such areas as the original Hebrew, the Aramaic Peshitta, traditional scholarly interpretations, textual criticism, chronology of the Babylonian Exile, the life of Jesus Christ, eclipses, astronomy, calendar systems and modern fulfilled prophecy with a brief stop in plant physiology. I was overwhelmed at what began to take shape. I want to share these amazing discoveries with you over the next pages.

This is not an introduction to prophecy. When writing this book, I assume the reader already has a familiarity with the overall history of ancient Israel/Judah (from 700 BC to 70 AD) and has investigated the common interpretations of the 70 Weeks Prophecy in Daniel and the 430 Day Prophecy in

Ezekiel. It would also be useful to be familiar with the Feast Days celebrated in the Jewish calendar and what they represent. However, I will begin by laying a foundation with basic concepts. Each new layer will then be added on top and soon an intricate clockwork throughout history will become evident.

Part 1 will investigate the ancient Hebrew calendar, how it differed from the modern calendar and if it can be reconstructed.

Part 2 will delve into the 70 Weeks Prophecy that Gabriel gave to Daniel. Traditional assumptions will be reevaluated and an alternative interpretation will be presented that makes use of the common definition of a year.

Part 3 will examine various aspects of the chronology of the birth and the sacrifice of Jesus Christ.

Part 4 will present the phenomenon of eclipses which coincide with Jewish Feast Days. This will tie together all the previous discussions.

Part 5 presents patterns that already exist for the future. Ezekiel's 430 Day enigmatic prophecy will be thoroughly explored. The significance of the numbers 2300, 1290 and 1335 will be presented.

I assume that my reader is a good Berean.

Acts 17:11

Part 1

The Hebrew Calendar

Overview

After I read the 70 Weeks Prophecy of Daniel as translated in the English Standard Version (ESV), I began an intense period of investigation. This led me to various diverse areas of study and things quickly became quite overwhelming. Over a period of time the fog began to dissipate and some fascinating observations became clear. However, I do not feel that presenting the information in the order that it was investigated would be very helpful. Instead, I first want to drill down to the essential simple concepts.

A basic foundation will be laid down. Each subsequent piece will then be considered and verified as it is layered on. The common traditions and assumptions will be presented and evaluated. In this manner, the previously "hidden" patterns start to become visible. However, this means that what some people would consider tedious has to be presented first. Patience is required in order to work through various technical details.

I'll start by laying out what the Bible says about the calendar. The account of the Exodus of Israel contains God's instructions for their new calendar system and how they were to order their year. The history and changes to the modern Jewish calendar will then be described. Finally, I will explore whether the ancient calendar can be accurately reconstructed.

Chapter 1

Calendrical Concepts in the Bible

WHAT CONSTITUTES A DAY

The most basic aspect of a calendar is to describe what constitutes a day. Various cultures begin their day at different points in the cycle of light and dark. As it is the first act of Creation in the Genesis 1 account, determining the start of the day is important to understand correctly.

> "And God said, "Let there be light," and there was light. And God saw that the light was good. And God separated the light from the darkness. God called the light Day, and the darkness he called Night. And there was evening and there was morning, the first day." (Genesis 1:3-5)

As the earth rotates about its axis, the portion facing the light source is called Day and that facing away is called Night. Notice that this had nothing to do with the Sun since it did not exist at this point and wouldn't for several more days. God creates the cycle in a certain order: evening, then morning; darkness, then light.

To become more familiar with this concept, think of an ongoing wave representing the amount of visible light to a viewer. The earth's horizon is the midpoint between the top of the crest where there is maximum light and the bottom of the trough where there is maximum darkness. The moon's light is not considered since that is reflected light.

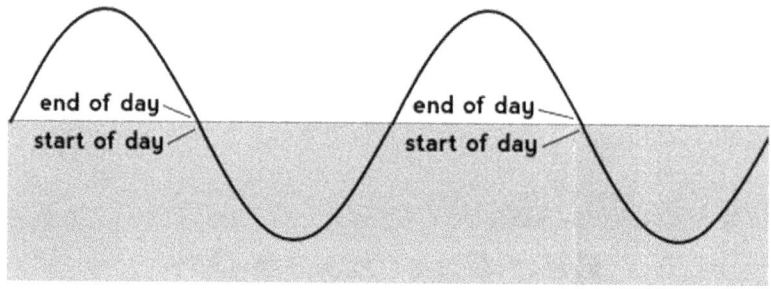

The concept of a complete Day starts as the horizon bisects the downward slope of the amount of light. The Day begins with the period that is below the horizon line. It is followed by the period that is above the horizon as the light increases again. These two ordered periods together make up a Day. God says the evening portion is first, then the morning portion.

The modern Day based on the Roman/Greek calendar system starts at midnight which, conceptually, is the midpoint between sunset and sunrise. The abbreviations of A.M. (ante meridiem) and P.M. (post meridiem) are used which mean "before noon" and "after noon." This division of time is according to the highest point of the sun in the sky during the daylight hours at the viewer's longitude. Originally, this was determined by observing the shifting shadows on a sundial. Alternatively, starting the Day at midnight was determined with an astrolabe by observing certain stars in the night sky as they passed the same longitude line.[1]

Compare this with God's system where the observable action of the light (the sun) setting below the horizon is used as a definite mark in time to start the new Day.

The sun, moon and stars as the sources of light, were created later in the Creation Week, on the fourth day.

> "And God said, "Let there be lights in the expanse of the heavens to separate the day from the night. And let them be for **signs and for seasons, and for days and years**, and let them be lights in the expanse of the heavens **to give light upon the earth**." And it was so. And God made the two great lights—the greater light to rule the day and the lesser light to rule the night—and the stars. And God set them in the expanse of the heavens to give light on the earth, to rule over the day and over the night, and to separate the light from the darkness. And God saw that it was good. And there was evening and there was morning, the fourth day." (Genesis 1: 14-19) [emphasis added]

There are five reasons stated for the existence of the sun, moon and stars:

- separation of day from night
- signs
- seasons
- days
- years

Let's explore what "signs" and "seasons" mean. First, "signs" is translated from the Hebrew word "oth" (Strong's #226). This is defined as "a signal (literally or figuratively), as a

---

1 [Sachau] p. 7

flag, beacon, monument, omen, prodigy, evidence, etc. -- mark, miracle, (en-)sign, token." These signs would include the cycles of the interaction between the sun and moon with the earth. There seem to be particular arrangements of their orbital positions in space that are special marks in time - conjunctions. These conjunctions are visible as the two types of eclipse – lunar and solar. This is not to imply that every conjunction is significant – only certain ones. This will be explored much more fully in Part 5.

The word translated as "seasons" is "moed" (S#4150) and is defined as an "appointed time, place, or meeting." Seasons in this case, are not the four seasons of spring, summer, autumn and winter that immediately come to mind. This particular use for the heavenly bodies was as a signal for the proper time for Israel to celebrate the Feast Days.

> "You shall keep the Feast of Unleavened Bread. Seven days you shall eat unleavened bread, as I commanded you, **at the time appointed** in the month Abib, for in the month Abib you came out from Egypt." (Exodus 34:18) [emphasis added]

The same word "moed" translated as seasons in Genesis is translated here as "at the time appointed." God's command to celebrate at the proper time leads directly to the structure of the Hebrew calendar which will be detailed very shortly.

WHAT CONSTITUTES A WEEK

The concept of the week is a grouping of seven cycles of units of time. Usually we consider a week as consisting of seven days – or seven cycles of dark and light as has just been discussed. There is no corresponding astronomical cycle which coincides with this period of seven.

The Creation Week is God imposing this seven period cycle on the days and therefore on the calendar. It becomes such a fundamental concept in the Judeo-Christian tradition that it drives our cycles of work and worship. In fact, this is a command of God recorded in the Old Testament:

> "Six days shall work be done, but on the seventh day is a Sabbath of solemn rest, a holy convocation. You shall do no work. It is a Sabbath to the Lord in all your dwelling places." (Leviticus 23:3)

The Hebrew week did not include names for the weekdays. They were referred to as "the first day," "the second day," etc. However, the seventh day did have a special name – the Sabbath. Compare this with our Greco/Roman/Germanic tradition which tie the weekdays to astronomy and the names of gods/planets.

A few chapters later in Leviticus 25, another definition of a week is given. This is a week of years – or a grouping of seven years. This week gave structure to Israelite practices of law and agriculture. It also seems to be a key component in God's structure for judgement and for prophecies dealing with time.

What Constitutes a Month and Year

The Hebrew month is based on the phases of the moon. Specifically, the start of the month is related to the timing of the new moon phase. The Hebrew word for month is "chodesh" (S#2320) and is defined as "new moon, month." This is from a root word "chadash" (S#2318) defined as "to renew, repair." Another Hebrew word used for month is "yerach" (S# 3391) defined simply as "month." The root word for this is "yareach" (S#3394) defined as "moon."

The Old Testament requirement that sacrifices are to be made on each new moon shows the great significance of the new moon phase. The word "month" in the following passages is the Hebrew word "chodesh."

> "At the beginnings of your months, you shall offer a burnt offering to the Lord." (Numbers 28:11a)

> "The contribution of the king from his own possessions was for the burnt offerings: the burnt offerings of morning and evening, and the burnt offerings for the Sabbaths, the new moons, and the appointed feasts, as it is written in the Law of the Lord."
> (2 Chronicles 31:3)

The Bible gives two sets of names for the months. Prior to the Babylonian exile (circa 600 BC), the Bible records only four names of the twelve. During the exile, the population adopted the Babylonian month names.

Before the Babylonian exile, these names are mentioned:

1st	Abib	Exodus 13:4
2nd	Ziv	I Kings 6:1
7th	Ethanim	I Kings 8:2
8th	Bul	I Kings 6:38

After the Babylonian exile, these are used:

1st	Nisan	Esther 3:7
2nd	Iyyar	

3rd	Sivan	Esther 8:9
4th	Tammuz	
5th	Av	
6th	Elul	Nehemiah 6:15
7th	Tishri	
8th	Kheshvan	
9th	Kislev	Nehemiah 1:1
10th	Tebeth	Esther 2:16
11th	Shebat	Zechariah 1:7
12th	Adar	Esther 3:7

The Hebrew year consisted of a cycle of twelve months:

> "This is the number of the people of Israel, the heads of fathers' houses, the commanders of thousands and hundreds, and their officers who served the king in all matters concerning the divisions that came and went, month after month throughout the year..." (I Chronicles 27:1)

Over the next verses in I Chronicles 27:2-15 there is a listing of twelve months and the divisions that were assigned to each month. I Kings describes a similar arrangement:

> "Solomon had twelve officers over all Israel, who provided food for the king and his household. Each man had to make provision for one month in the year." (I Kings 4:7)

Their year, as a grouping of twelve complete cycles of the moon phases, was not the same as the year with which we are familiar. Our Gregorian calendar year is based on one complete orbit of the earth around the sun.

The length of each Hebrew month alternated between twenty-nine or thirty days. This was due to the fact that from New Moon to New Moon is an average of 29.5 days (synodic month). Therefore:

29.5 days per month x 12 months = 354 days in a year

Compare this with the length of the solar year (or tropical year) which is the time period between the same point between two identical seasons; roughly 365.242 days. A discrepancy in year length obviously causes some issues after several years pass and some other correction needed to take place. The solution was the addition of an extra month, or intercalary month, every few years. This practice is not mentioned in the Bible, however. The topic will be investigated in a later section.

Chapter 2

The Calendar at the Exodus

At the time of the Exodus, God gave the Hebrew people detailed instructions about the construction of their new calendar and for what purposes it should be used. The modern Jewish calendar is still based on these same basic principles but has been modified so that it is now a purely calculated and fixed calendar. Originally, the calendar depended on observations of the moon for the start of each month and on the state of the winter barley harvest to correctly begin the year.

BIBLICAL INSTRUCTIONS FOR THE CALENDAR

The instructions on how to begin a new year were given at the time of the Exodus: "The Lord said to Moses and Aaron in the land of Egypt, "This month shall be for you the beginning of months. It shall be the first month of the year for you."" (Exodus 12:1-2)

Correctly determining the beginning of the year was essential for the celebration of the "Feasts of the Lord" at the proper time. The first feast of the new year was Passover:

> "These are the appointed feasts of the Lord, the holy convocations, which you shall proclaim at the time appointed for them. In the first month, on the fourteenth day of the month at twilight, is the Lord's Passover." (Leviticus 23:4-5)

The next feast was the Feast of Unleavened Bread which occurred starting one day following Passover:

> "Then Moses said to the people, "Remember this day in which you came out from Egypt, out of the house of slavery, for by a strong hand the Lord brought you out from this place. No leavened bread shall be eaten. Today, in the month of Abib, you are going out. And when the Lord brings you into the land of the Canaanites, the Hittites, the Amorites, the Hivites, and the Jebusites, which he swore to your fathers to give you, a land flowing with milk and honey, you shall keep this service in this month. Seven days you shall eat unleavened bread, and on the seventh day there shall be a feast to the Lord." (Exodus 13:3-6)

Six months later was another grouping of feasts:

> "You shall observe the Feast of Weeks, the firstfruits of wheat harvest, and the Feast of Ingathering at the year's end." (Exodus 34:22)

The timing for when the feasts were to occur was very specific:

> "Three times in the year you shall keep a feast to me. You shall keep the Feast of Unleavened Bread. As I commanded you, you shall eat unleavened bread for seven days at the appointed time in the month of Abib, for in it you came out of Egypt. None shall appear before me empty-handed. You shall keep the Feast of Har-

vest, of the firstfruits of your labor, of what you sow in the field. You shall keep the Feast of Ingathering at the end of the year, when you gather in from the field the fruit of your labor. Three times in the year shall all your males appear before the Lord God." (Exodus 23:14-17)

"You shall keep the Feast of Unleavened Bread. Seven days you shall eat unleavened bread, as I commanded you, at the time appointed in the month Abib, for in the month Abib you came out from Egypt." (Exodus 34:18)

"Observe the month of Abib and keep the Passover to the Lord your God, for in the month of Abib the Lord your God brought you out of Egypt by night." (Deuteronomy 16:1)

The "month of Abib", the start of the year, became very important to determine correctly so that the feasts could be celebrated at the proper time and in the proper manner. "Abib" is a Hebrew word describing a state of ripeness of the barley harvest; "abib" (S#24) defined as "fresh, young ears."

"(The flax and the barley were struck down, for the barley **was in the ear** and the flax was in bud. But the wheat and the emmer [type of wheat] were not struck down, for they are late in coming up.)" (Exodus 9:31) [emphasis added]

The phrase "was in the ear" is translated from "abib." This was the state of the winter barley crop. It had flowered and the heads of grain were just newly formed and were still green and were not yet ripe. The start of the year was at the time of a new moon during the period when the barley was in the state of "abib." What is the significance of the barley?

"And the Lord spoke to Moses, saying, "Speak to the people of Israel and say to them, When you come into the land that I give you and reap its harvest, you shall bring the sheaf of the firstfruits of your harvest to the priest, and he shall wave the sheaf before the Lord, so that you may be accepted. On the day after the Sabbath the priest shall wave it.'" (Leviticus 23:9-11)

"And you shall eat neither bread nor grain parched or fresh until this same day, until you have brought the offering of your God: it is a statute forever throughout your generations in all your dwellings." (Leviticus 23:14)

This is the Feast of Firstfruits and was to be the first harvest of the ripe barley offered on the day after the Sabbath occurring within the week of the Feast of Unleavened Bread. Ripe barley had to exist at this point in order for the priest to be able to wave it. Also, the people could not eat bread or grain until this offering was done so it was essential for them to know when the winter barley would be ripe enough.

The Feast of Unleavened Bread always occurred on the 15th day of the first month. During this seven-day feast period, the weekly Sabbath could fall on any one the days depending on the order of days of a year. Since Firstfruits was the day after the Sabbath, the first possible date of Firstfruits was the 16th of the month if the Sabbath occurred on the 15th. Ripe barley had to be available by the 16th of the first month so there had to be evidence of green heads at the beginning of that month. The barley had to be "abib" since it takes about two weeks from just after flowering and observing the first evidence of head development for it to be in the first harvestable state.

Reconstructing the Calendar at the Exodus

Given the instructions described in the previous section and noting the dates given in the narrative in Exodus, it is possible to determine the day order of the first month of their calendar. Passover occurred on the 14th of the first month. The Israelites left Egypt on the next day, on the 15th.

> "They set out from Elim, and all the congregation of the people of Israel came to the wilderness of Sin, which is between Elim and Sinai, **on the fifteenth day of the second month** after they had departed from the land of Egypt." (Exodus 16:1) [emphasis added]

The date of this incident takes place on the 15th of the second month. The people had journeyed for a month and were beginning to grumble for lack of food. God tells Moses that He is going to rain bread from heaven and provide meat for food. Moses instructs Aaron to call the people together for a holy assembly.

> "Then Moses said to Aaron, "Say to the whole congregation of the people of Israel, 'Come near before the Lord, for he has heard your grumbling.'" And as soon as Aaron spoke to the whole congregation of the people of Israel, they looked toward the wilderness, and behold, the glory of the Lord appeared in the cloud." (Exodus 16:9-10)

The people are informed that the next day (starting at twilight) they would have meat and that in the morning they would have bread. They were to collect food for the following six days but the seventh day was to be a Sabbath.

> "On the sixth day they gathered twice as much bread, two omers each. And when all the leaders of the congre-

gation came and told Moses, he said to them, "This is what the Lord has commanded: 'Tomorrow is a day of solemn rest, a holy Sabbath to the Lord...'" (Exodus 16:22-23)

This means that the 15th and the 22nd (seven days later) were Sabbaths in the second month. From this information, the calendar day order for the first and second months can be worked out.

Su	M	Tu	W	Th	F	Sa	Su	M	Tu	W	Th	F	Sa
					1	2	3	4	5	6	7	8	9	10
11	12	13	14	15	16	17	18	19	20	21	22	23	24
			Passover										
25	26	27	28	29	30	1	2	3	4	5	6	7	8
9	10	11	12	13	14	15	16	17	18	19	20	21	22
						Assembly before start of manna & quail

Passover would have occurred on a Wednesday. The first day of the first month would have been a Thursday. This particular arrangement of days of the month on these days of the week would not be the same the next year. It would not return to this same pattern for a number of years.

Interestingly, there are records of a Jewish sect who considered the day of Wednesday of such importance that they made sure to celebrate Passover on that day of the week every year. This is recorded in the writings of a moslem scholar named Al-Biruni circa 1000 AD.

> "Abu-'lsa Alwarrak speaks in his Kitab-Almakalat of a Jewish sect called the Maghribis, who maintain that the feasts are not legal unless the moon rises in Palestine as a full moon in the night of Wednesday, which follows after the day of Tuesday, at the time of sunset. Such is their New-Year's Day. From this point the days and

months are counted, and here begins the rotation of the annual festivals. For God created the two great lights on a Wednesday. **Likewise they do not allow Passover to fall on any other day except on Wednesday.** And the obligations and rites prescribed for Passover they do not hold to be necessary, except for those who dwell in the country of the Israelites.

All this stands in opposition to the custom of the majority of the Jews, and to the prescriptions of the Thora [Torah]."[2] [emphasis added]

---

2 [Sachau] p. 278

Chapter 3

Calendar of Creation Week

Although the time of the Exodus contains the first explicit instructions for God's calendar of appointed days, the Creation Week is actually when time started and the calendar came into existence. The days consisted of periods of night and day and this cycle can be charted:

	Day 1	Day 2	Day 3	Day 4	Day 5	Day 6	Day 7	Day 1
Daylight	1	2	3	4	5	6	7	1
Night	1	2	3	4	5	6	7	1

The first few days existed on their own; there was nothing to connect them with – they were just cycles of dark and light. Only after the fourth day when the sun, moon and stars were created were the days connected with a way of determining months and years. At that point, the calendar actually began. God's instructions state that the New Moon phase is the start of each new month. Therefore, it stands to reason that the moon as created on the fourth day was in the "new moon" phase. Creation of the heavenly bodies was complete by the end of that fourth day so the very first day of the very first month of the calendar would have been the start of the fifth day, i.e. Thursday.

Compare the start of the very first month and year on a Thursday with the start of the first month and year of the Exodus which also occurred on a Thursday. Is this significant? Store this cycle "coincidence" away for now and we'll come back to it later.

Chapter 4

Ancient Calendars

Up to this point, only a single year has been described. Some issues emerge once multiple years pass. The difference between the 354-day lunar year and the 365 1/4-day solar year has already been identified. A year based solely on the phases on the moon (12 x 29.5 days) is not in sync with the solar year. The beginning of each year would occur earlier and earlier. However, Deuteronomy 16:1 commands that the Passover must be kept in the month of Abib. We have discovered that this is a description of a certain state of the winter barley harvest. But the Bible does not mention that the year will get out of sync or contain instructions as to how it should be recalibrated. This leads some to assume that originally the length of the year was different.

A simple observation of the current cycle lengths shows that they are indeed close:

Moon	(a little less than 360)
29.5 days x 12 =	354 days

Earth	(a little more than 360)
solar year	365.242 days

There is intriguing evidence that multiple ancient cultures had years consisting of 360 days. Velikovsky's research into the calendars of ancient cultures investigated this thoroughly even though his conclusions are disputable. The ancient calendars of the Indians, Persians, Babylonians, Assyrians, Egyptians, Greeks, Romans, Mayans, Peruvians and Chinese all had 360-day years. The Greek writings of Hippocrates, Aristotle, Cleobulus, and Philochorus all cite years containing 360 days.[3] The evidence shows that some time around 700 BC, they all had to modify their calendars for some undiscovered reason.[4]

For example, the moslem scholar Al-Biruni (circa 1000 AD) described the need for the Magi, followers of Zoroaster, to add five additional days to their year around 600 BC.

> "But afterwards when Zoroaster appeared and introduced the religion of the Magi, when the kings transferred their residence from Balkh to Persis and Babel and occupied themselves with the affairs of their religion, they ordered new observations to be made, and then they found that the summer-solstice preceded by five days the beginning of the year, which was the third year after intercalation."[5]

These new observations by the various cultures led them to modify their calendar and add recalibration rules to match the observable solar year. Some added days to every year and some collected them together and added an extra month every few years. The latter method is what the Jewish calendar adopted in order to keep in sync with the solar cycle.

---

3 [Heath] p. 285
4 [Wong]
5 [Sachau] p. 220

Chapter 5

The Jewish Calendar

DETERMINING THE START OF THE MONTH

The earliest discovered Hebrew calendar is a limestone tablet from the tenth century BC. Known as the Gezer Calendar, it was excavated in 1908 and displays the year split into twelve months with the agricultural activities that occur in each one.[6] The tablet is from the era of the first temple built in the reign of King Solomon. Calendar decisions at this time were at the sole discretion of the Levites in Jerusalem.

During the era of the second temple (circa 530 BC until AD 70), the Great Sanhedrin oversaw the decisions for the calendar. They would hold a special court called the "Beth Yaazek" on the thirtieth day after the first day of the month. They would declare the start of a new month based on the testimony of two witnesses. These witnesses would give evidence that they had seen the first sliver of the moon's crescent after the new moon phase.

---

6 [Albright]

The new month was decided at the phase of the new moon when the earth, moon and sun are in line – they were in conjunction. However, the actual phase of the new moon could not be seen so they had to wait until they saw the very first signs of the moon's light after this phase. Since the lunar cycle is 29.5 days long, a month could have either twenty-nine or thirty days. They met on the thirtieth day and heard from any available witnesses. If the witnesses were credible, then that day was declared the first day of the new month – the previous month declared as having twenty-nine days. If there were no witnesses at that time, then the next day was declared the first day – the previous month declared as having thirty days. They could go three consecutive months without hearing from witnesses (i.e. months made up of thirty days). But then, the following month had to be determined by calculation. A year could consist of no more than eight and no fewer than four "full" months (i.e. thirty days).

These were the questions of the witnesses:

1. whether the moon was east or west of the sun

2. whether the moon was north or south of the western point (sunset)

3. what was the moon's altitude and azimuth

4. what was the direction of the moon's crescent horns

5. what was the width of the crescent[7]

The moon has a predictable relationship with the sun. At conjunction they are in line. From that point, the moon will travel increasingly eastward through the sky through its phases – roughly 12.2 degrees per day. When waxing, it will "appear at the eastern horizon after sunrise, and will set at the western horizon after sunset; the reverse being the case with the waning

---

7 [Feldman] p. 181

moon"[8] The moon is visible after the conjunction when its crescent has nine degrees of elongation. It rotates at half a degree per hour and therefore has a period when it cannot be seen for eighteen hours on either side of the conjunction. Since the moon reflects the sun's light, the horns of the moon's crescent always point away from the sun when the moon is waxing, and towards the sun when waning. Stern explains further,

> "In addition, the new moon is only visible at a specific time of the day: between sunset and moonset. At this stage of the moon's orbit, the interval between sunset and moonset is often not more than a half an hour. It is only in this short period of time, when the sun is 'isolated' from the moon and deep enough below the horizon, that the sky becomes sufficiently dark for the thin moon crescent to become visible against its background."[9]

The Sanhedrin also added a series of rules which could postpone the first day of the month so that certain preparation days for the feast would not fall on a weekly Sabbath. They based this concept on the time of the giving of Manna during the Exodus. The Israelites would collect Manna for six days and on the sixth day they would collect a double portion so that the Sabbath during the following day could be observed.

DETERMINING THE START OF THE YEAR

In order to keep the year of the twelve month moon cycles in sync with the solar year, they added an extra month after a certain number of years had past. Each year would "lose" roughly eleven days and so after two to three years, an extra month was needed to keep in sync – an

---

8 [Feldman] p. 181
9 [Stern] p. 100

intercalation. Their year actually had two beginnings. The first in the month of Abib, later renamed Nisan, was the beginning of the religious year. The seventh month, Tishri, was the start of the civil year. The intercalated month was added just prior to the first month of Nisan. Eventually, as they transitioned into a completely calculated calendar an additional requirement was added based on the vernal equinox (our March 20/21 as the start of spring). This rule stated that if the vernal equinox falls after what would be Nisan 16, then a leap month should be added for that year.

> "R. Huna b. Abin sent an instruction to Raba: When you see that the cycle of Tebeth extends to the sixteenth of Nisan, declare that year a leap year and have no scruples, since it is written, Observe the month [Hodesh] of Abib, which signifies, See to it that the Abib of the cycle should commence in the earlier half [Hodesh] of Nisan." (Babylonian Talmud - Rosh Hashanah 21A)

> "Our Rabbis taught: a year may be intercalated on three grounds: on account of the premature state of the corn crops; or that of the fruit trees; or on account of the lateness of the 'tekufah' [literally 'cycle,' 'season']. Any two of these reasons can justify intercalation, but not one alone. All, however, are glad when the state of spring-crop is one of them." (Babylonian Talmud – Sanhedrin 11A)

Several surrounding cultures noticed that the solar year and the lunar year would sync over a nineteen year period or after 235 lunar cycles if seven additional leap months would be added over that period. This is called the "metonic cycle" and the additional months occur in years: 3, 6, 8, 11, 14, 17, 19.

CHANGES TO THE CALENDAR

After 70 AD with the destruction of the temple, there was no longer any central religious body that could determine decisions for the calendar. As the Jewish people dispersed, it was very difficult to get witnesses for the state of the barley harvest in Judea. The calendar could no longer rely on observation but became a completely fixed calendar. However, this fixed calendar has become increasingly inaccurate over the centuries. Stern's research states:

> "The observance of Passover before the equinox, widespread in the fourth century, contrasts with our findings for the first century, when Passover appears to have occurred considerably later, sometimes over a month after the equinox."[10]

Circa 270 AD, the following description of the Jewish calendar was written:

> "And this [i.e. the rule of the equinox] is not our own reckoning, but it was known to the Judeans long ago even before the Messiah and it was carefully observed by them. One can learn it from what is said by Philo, Josephus, (and) Musaeus, and not only by these, but also by both of the Agathobuli, who are still more ancient and are surnamed the teachers. One can learn it also from what is said by the excellent Aristobulus...When these (writers) explain questions concerning the Exodus, they say that it is necessary that all alike sacrifice Passover after the vernal equinox, in the middle of the first month; and this occurs when the sun passes through the first sector of the solar, or as some of them call (it), the zodiacal cycle." (Anatolius ap. Eusebius, Ecclesiastical History, 7. 32. 16-17)

---

10 [Stern] p. 70

At some point before 1178 AD, the Jewish calendar shifted the start of the month by observation to completely relying on the calculated lunar conjunction. These calendar rules are commonly attributed to Hillel II (359 AD) but no surviving document exists to this effect.

The numbering of the first year, Anno Mundi ("from the creation of the world") was set to the equivalent calendar year of 3761 BC. This is attributed to Seder Olam Rabbah of Rabbi Jose ben Halfta (circa 160 AD). During this time there was an ongoing disagreement between the Karaites and the Rabbanites. The Karaites wanted to continue to set the year by observation and objected to the use of the nineteen year metonic cycle. The Rabbanites claimed that the fixed calendar rules were handed down all the way from Adam; or at least from Moses.[11]

---

11 [Goldstein] p. 32

Chapter 6

Discovering the Original Calendar

The modern Jewish calendar has been in its present form for over a millennium. The current calendrical method does not follow the calendar as determined when first introduced in Exodus and most likely was not even the same as that in the first century AD. The realization suddenly hits that this is problematic when people use modern Jewish calendar dates to try and pin down specific ancient timing connecting a certain weekday with a certain numbered day of the month. But what other options are there?

When trying to determine the correct method, we will examine two areas: the calendars used by the ancient surrounding cultures and whether the life cycle of winter barley can give any clues as to why it was used.

AL-BIRUNI

The fascinating ancient text "Vestiges of the Past" was authored by the moslem scholar named Al-Biruni from around 1000 AD. The purpose of his work is described this way:

"Containing, as it does, all the technical and historical details of the various systems for the computation of time, invented and used by the Persians, Sogdians, Chorasmians, Jews, Syrians, Harranians, and Arabs, together with Greek traditions, it offers an equal interest to all those who study the antiquity and history of the Zoroastrian and Jewish, Christian and Muhammadan religions."[12]

In his section detailing how the Jewish calendar was constructed, Al-Biruni describes three existing methods of intercalation (*Ordines Intercalationis*); that is, various methods for adding leap months to the calendar which existed when he wrote his volume. Each method is described as a "Mahzor" or cycle.

1. The Jews from the Syrian area would take their numbered year (Era Adami) and divide it by 19. The following remainders would be leap years:

    2, 5, 7, 10, 13, 16, 18

2. The Jews from a different region would take their numbered year (Era Adami), subtract 1 and then divide it by 19. The following remainders would be leap years:

    1, 4, 6, 9, 12, 15, 17

3. He claims the most common method, based on the Babylonian year was to take the numbered year (Era Adami), subtract 2 and then divide by 19. The following remainders would be leap years:

    3, 5, 8, 11, 14, 16, 19[13]

When examining all three of these methods, one realizes that they are all describing the same cycle of intercalation.

---

12 [Sachau] Preface
13 [Sachau] p. 65

The result of subtraction just moves the metonic cycle one or two years previous.

How does this method of intercalation compare with the modern Jewish method? Al-Biruni includes what he calls a "Table of Kebioth." This is something like a Rosetta stone for calendar calculations. In the table, Era Adami is defined as 3,448 years from Adam to Era Alexandri (the reign of Alexander the Great). Era Alexandri is defined as beginning twenty-six years after Alexander the Great's birth in 356 BC. Al-Biruni states that when Alexander entered Jerusalem, he forced them to base the start of their year from that point forward.[14] Then investigating further, Era Adami is actually another name for Anno Mundi (modern Jewish era).[15]

The end result is that the Table of Kebioth allows a conversion between the modern Jewish era dates and Julian calendar dates and Era Alexandri dates.

$$\text{Year 1 Era Alexandri} = 330 \text{ BC} = 3448/3449 \text{ Era Adami/AnnoMundi}$$

The metonic cycle sequence used in the modern Jewish calendar is: 3, 6, 8, 11, 14, 17, 19. This numerical sequence is the same as that listed in the Al-Biruni's Table of Kebioth. Now a comparison can be done with the three Mahzor cycles listed previously. What one notices is that the modern metonic cycle has been shifted one year later from that which Al-Biruni says was used in ancient times (even ancient before him). To be clear, order of the numerical cycle of years is the same but the actual year that it is applied to has been shifted.

---

14 [Sachau] p. 32
15 [Sachau] p. 155

This shift of metonic cycles means that some years would have a different starting month as compared with the solar year. When converting dates to Julian/Gregorian dates (our calendar is solar year based), this would result in dates that could be a month off from where they actually historically occurred. For example, consider the year 3449 AM.

Using modern Jewish method:

3449 / 19   =   remainder 10

The cycle instructions *say not* to add a leap month.

Using Mahzor 1 method:

3449 / 19   =   remainder 10

The cycle instructions *do say* to add a leap month.

According to the Modern Jewish method, Nisan 1 would correspond to sometime in March while using the more ancient Mahzor method, Nisan 1 would correspond to sometime in April, a full month later.

BABYLONIAN CHRONOLOGY

A very valuable chronological resource exists that has used available archaeological information to reconstruct the calendar dates for the Babylonian, Persian and Seleucid periods. This resource is the "Babylonian Chronology."

The authors speculate that the intercalations used during the Babylonian period began within the reign of Nabonassar (circa 747 BC). The calendar of this time intercalated either in the spring or in the autumn before settling on a fixed pattern.[16] Up until about 600 BC, the intercalations are wildly erratic – some years occurring in spring and some occurring in

---

16 [Parker] p. 1-5

autumn. Interestingly, after 600 BC when the Jewish exile to Babylon begins, the intercalations are shifted almost completely from autumn to spring, which is the start of the religious year for the Jews. This period also marks the beginning of the final fixed intercalation pattern which does not change over the subsequent centuries. Is this evidence of the rise of Daniel's influence as he becomes the head of the Magi in the Babylonian kingdom? This group of astrologers was in charge of determining the calendar for the regional empire.

The Babylonian calendar metonic cycle sequence converted to Anno Mundi years would be:

1, 4, 7, 9, 12, 15, 18[17]

This cycle is shifted one year ahead of that used in the modern Jewish calendar.

COMPARING THE FIXED METHODS

We have now seen several metonic cycle sequences which were used in ancient calendars. There is enough information in order to create a chart for comparison. The chart focuses on the years between 8 BC and 35 AD since this period will be more fully examined in subsequent chapters.

---

17 [Parker] p. 45

Year (BC/AD)	AM (Tishri as start)	Modern Jewish (Hillel II)	Table of Kebioth (Albiruni)	First Ordine (AlBiruni) (minus 0)	Babylonian Chronology
8	3753			•	
7	3754	•	•		
6	3755				•
5	3756			•	
4	3757	•	•		
3	3758				•
2	3759			•	
1	3760	•	•		
1	3761			•	•
2	3762	•	•		
3	3763				•
4	3764			•	
5	3765	•	•		
6	3766				•
7	3767			•	
8	3768	•	•		
9	3769			•	•
10	3770	•	•		
11	3771				•
12	3772			•	
13	3773	•	•		
14	3774				•
15	3775			•	
16	3776	•	•		
17	3777				•
18	3778			•	
19	3779	•	•		
20	3780			•	•
21	3781	•	•		
22	3782				•
23	3783			•	
24	3784	•	•		
25	3785				•
26	3786			•	
27	3787	•	•		
28	3788			•	•
29	3789	•	•		
30	3790				•
31	3791			•	
32	3792	•	•		
33	3793				•
34	3794			•	
35	3795	•	•		

Table 1: Comparing the fixed intercalation methods from 8 BC to 35 AD showing which years have leap months added

Although each method's use of its particular metonic sequence will keep the years in sync with the solar year, it is not clear which is the actual intercalation cycle used during the period of years in question. It can be assumed that the modern method (Hillel II) was not used during this time. It is then quite evident that if this current method of intercalation is relied on by biblical chronologists for determining accurate dates for this era, significant differences would result in the numbered days of the month and their associated weekdays.

Two other possibilities exist: the Babylonian Chronology which includes calendar dates based on archaeological records of surrounding cultures and the intercalation method which Al-Biruni claims was used in the Syrian locale of this period. Since the instructions for the original Hebrew calendar included observation of the winter barley, does examination of this subject make the choice of methods any more clear?

BARLEY LIFE CYCLE

The original Hebrew calendar was based on observable phenomenon. However, calculations were eventually introduced as a means of verification. This is where botany and astronomy meet. Let's investigate the life cycle of barley and become familiar with exactly what the observation of its development meant.

There are two types of barley: summer barley and winter barley. Winter barley is planted in the autumn and is the earliest maturing grain in the spring time. It is known to be the fastest growing of the winter grains with roots traveling over six feet deep in the ground. This type of barley can handle both weather and soil extremes having the highest soil salinity and pH tolerance of all the cereal crops.[18]

It is not just that winter barley can survive colder winter weather, but it requires it. There is a period of "vernalization." This is one of two internal "switches" which must be "flipped on" in order for the process of flowering and the production of grain to start. The second "switch" is what is called "photoperiod." Barley is a "long day" plant having a requirement for a certain number of daylight hours. The plant starts its growth phase in vernalization waiting until a certain number of "cold" hours have been met. During this time it hugs the ground with a very flat (prostrate) growth habit. Its growing tip is near the soil surface which reduces the risk of damage from this period of colder weather.[19]

Once the required number of cold hours have been reached, it enters a phase where it is affected by the length of day; waiting for a day with a certain number of daylight hours. When this is met, the reproductive phase switches on and the rate of development drastically increases.[20] After meeting these two internal requirements, the barley enters a two week optimal flowering window.[21] In Israel, located at roughly 31 degrees latitude, wild barley flowers for a two week period in early to mid March. Just ten degrees further north (i.e. in Spain), the winter barley flowering occurs in mid April.[22] These particular characteristics of barley can be relied on as an extremely precise calendar trigger point which is specific to a relatively small geographic region.

---

18 [GreenCoverSeed]
19 [Edwards] p. 35
20 [Edwards] p. 36
21 [Edwards] p. 51
22 [Lister] p. 1097

After flowering, two phases of grain development begin: cell division and grain filling. Cell division starts after the fertilization process and continues for fourteen to thirty days depending on the variety of barley, the environmental conditions and the position in the head of grain. The process of grain filling begins five to ten days after fertilization and continues until the grain is fully ripe and depends mainly on temperature and moisture conditions. Physiological maturity occurs between forty to fifty days after flowering; in Israel, this would be from mid to late April. The outward sign is a loss of green colouring and the grain's loss of moisture is very rapid during this stage – the period of optimal barley harvest. However, barley is still harvestable a few weeks before this time as well. The seed embryo development inside each grain is complete roughly twenty-five days after flowering; on average shortly after the vernal equinox.[23]

The photoperiod requirement is extremely important in determining the start of the plant's reproduction phase and when abib barley would occur. Although weather and environmental conditions have a part to play, it is this internal "switch" that determines the flowering phase based on the amount of daylight hours experienced. This requirement is consistent and predictable every year as the short days of winter gradually lengthen approaching the longer days of spring. The result is a relatively short time frame of two weeks occurring on average two to three weeks before the vernal equinox. Formation of green ears of grain would be evident immediately following, around one week before the vernal equinox – the barley being in a state of abib.

This is a possible explanation of why the vernal equinox rule would have been developed, which was eventually added to the calendar requirements. When observing the winter bar-

---

23 [Edwards] p. 59

ley growth cycle, it is consistent with abib occurring around the time of the equinox. However, relying on the equinox, an unwavering astronomical event, is not consistent with the biblical instructions to wait to observe abib, introducing variability based on the environmental conditions of temperature and precipitation. The main purpose of the biblical instructions is that there should be harvestable barley by the time it was required at the Firstfruits offering.

Chapter 7

Reconstructing the Original Calendar

Taking into account the previous discussions, it is now possible to reconstruct the probable ancient calendar over a set number of years. The same range of years between 8 BC and 35 AD will be considered. It should be noted that these results are not verifiable without ancient records but the calendar is consistent with the biblical instructions. Determining these various dates becomes necessarily complex and precise. However, accuracy is needed in order to convert the start of the ancient year between Julian/Gregorian equivalent calendar dates.

The first step when determining when the start of the year, or Nisan 1, could have occurred is to determine the start of a set of surrounding months. This consists of a group of three months for each year in question. The start of each month depends on the date of the new moon phase during that period. Moon phases have been worked out very accurately for the past (and the future for that matter) and are available on reputable astronomy websites. I have used this as my source:

http://astropixels.com/index.html

It must be recognized that the further back one looks from the present time, the more error is introduced into the calculations. However, this margin of error is only within an hour.

At this point a quick explanation is required as to the difference between the Julian year and Gregorian year. It is very important to be specific which calendar system is being used when comparing dates. Our modern Gregorian year was introduced in 1582 AD. The older style Julian year used previously consisted of a year length of 365.25 days which, when compared with the actual length of the year of 365.2425 days, had allowed the calendar to become inaccurate over the centuries. The Gregorian calendar method corrected for this discrepancy and also added additional modern leap year rules. Therefore, any dates before 1582 AD have to specify which calendar system is being used.

The source table for moon phases uses the Julian year calendar system. The vernal equinox does not occur on March 20/21 in that calendar. A full featured calendar date converter will allow dates to be converted between the systems.

http://www.tarekmaani.com/LunchCOnverter.html

https://www.fourmilab.ch/documents/calendar/

46 Hidden Rhythms in Prophecy

	Month A				Month B				Month C			
	New Moon				New Moon				New Moon			
	(UT Julian)	Week day	Jerusalem (UT+2)	Julian	(UT Julian)	Week day	Jerusalem (UT+2)	Julian	(UT Julian)	Week day	Jerusalem (UT+2)	Julian
8 BC	02/10 10:19	M	02/10 12:19	1718541.9	3/12 3:35	W	05:35	1718571.6	4/10 18:50	TH	20:50	1718601.3
			Jerusalem (@ +18)	Julian			Jerusalem (@ +18)	Julian			Jerusalem (@ +18)	Julian
			02/11 6:19	1718542.7			03/12 23:35	1718572.4			04/11 14:50	1718602.0
	Ideal Month Start	Week day		Julian	Ideal Month Start	Week day		Julian	Ideal Month Start	Week day		Julian
	02/12	W		1718543.2	03/14	F		1718573.2	04/12	SA		1718602.2
	New Moon				New Moon				New Moon			
	(UT Julian)	Week day	Jerusalem (UT+2)	Julian	(UT Julian)	Week day	Jerusalem (UT+2)	Julian	(UT Julian)	Week day	Jerusalem (UT+2)	Julian
7 BC	3/1 3:31	SU	05:31	1718925.6	3/30 20:16	M	22:16	1718955.3	4/29 12:15	W	14:15	1718985.0
			Jerusalem (@ +18)	Julian			Jerusalem (@ +18)	Julian			Jerusalem (@ +18)	Julian
			03/01 23:31	1718926.4			03/31 16:16	1718956.1			04/30 8:15	1718985.8
	Ideal Month Start	Week day		Julian	Ideal Month Start	Week day		Julian	Ideal Month Start	Week day		Julian
	03/03	TU		1718927.2	04/01	W		1718956.2	05/01	F		1718986.2
	New Moon				New Moon				New Moon			
	(UT Julian)	Week day	Jerusalem (UT+2)	Julian	(UT Julian)	Week day	Jerusalem (UT+2)	Julian	(UT Julian)	Week day	Jerusalem (UT+2)	Julian
6 BC	2/18 7:00	TH	09:00	1719279.8	3/19 21:28	F	23:28	1719309.4	4/18 12:50	SU	14:50	1719339.1
			Jerusalem (@ +18)	Julian			Jerusalem (@ +18)	Julian			Jerusalem (@ +18)	Julian
			02/19 3:00	1719280.5			03/20 17:28	1719310.1			04/19 8:50	1719339.9
	Ideal Month Start	Week day		Julian	Ideal Month Start	Week day		Julian	Ideal Month Start	Week day		Julian
	02/20	SA		1719281.2	03/21	SU		1719310.2	04/20	TU		1719340.2
	New Moon				New Moon				New Moon			
	(UT Julian)	Week day	Jerusalem (UT+2)	Julian	(UT Julian)	Week day	Jerusalem (UT+2)	Julian	(UT Julian)	Week day	Jerusalem (UT+2)	Julian
5 BC	2/7 17:33	M	19:33	1719634.2	3/8 4:45	W	06:45	1719663.7	4/6 16:51	TH	18:51	1719693.2
			Jerusalem (@ +18)	Julian			Jerusalem (@ +18)	Julian			Jerusalem (@ +18)	Julian
			02/08 13:33	1719635.0			03/09 0:45	1719664.4			04/07 12:51	1719694.0
	Ideal Month Start	Week day		Julian	Ideal Month Start	Week day		Julian	Ideal Month Start	Week day		Julian
	02/09	W		1719635.2	03/10	F		1719665.2	04/08	SA		1719694.2

Reconstructing the Original Calendar 47

	Month A				Month B				Month C			
	New Moon (UT Julian)	Week day	Jerusalem (UT+2)	Julian	New Moon (UT Julian)	Week day	Jerusalem (UT+2)	Julian	New Moon (UT Julian)	Week day	Jerusalem (UT+2)	Julian
4 BC	02/25 18:33	SU	12/30 20:33	1720018.3	3/27 3:59	TU	05:59	1720047.7	4/25 13:38	W	15:38	1720077.1
			Jerusalem (@ +18)	Julian			Jerusalem (@ +18)	Julian			Jerusalem (@ +18)	Julian
			02/26 14:33	1720019.0			03/27 23:59	1720048.4			04/26 9:38	1720077.8
	Ideal Month Start	Week day		Julian	Ideal Month Start	Week day		Julian	Ideal Month Start	Week day		Julian
	02/27	TU		1720019.2	03/29	TH		1720049.2	04/27	F		1720078.2
3 BC	New Moon (UT Julian)	Week day	Jerusalem (UT+2)	Julian	New Moon (UT Julian)	Week day	Jerusalem (UT+2)	Julian	New Moon (UT Julian)	Week day	Jerusalem (UT+2)	Julian
	2/15 11:01	F	13:01	1720373.0	3/16 19:57	SA	21:57	1720402.3	4/15 3:49	M	05:49	1720431.7
			Jerusalem (@ +18)	Julian			Jerusalem (@ +18)	Julian			Jerusalem (@ +18)	Julian
			02/16 7:01	1720373.7			03/17 15:57	1720403.1			04/15 23:49	1720432.4
	Ideal Month Start	Week day		Julian	Ideal Month Start	Week day		Julian	Ideal Month Start	Week day		Julian
	02/17	SU		1720374.2	03/18	M		1720403.2	04/17	W		1720433.2
2 BC	New Moon (UT Julian)	Week day	Jerusalem (UT+2)	Julian	New Moon (UT Julian)	Week day	Jerusalem (UT+2)	Julian	New Moon (UT Julian)	Week day	Jerusalem (UT+2)	Julian
	2/5 1:30	W	03:30	1720727.6	3/6 12:18	TH	14:18	1720757.1	4/4 20:44	F	22:44	1720786.4
			Jerusalem (@ +18)	Julian			Jerusalem (@ +18)	Julian			Jerusalem (@ +18)	Julian
			02/05 21:30	1720728.3			03/07 8:18	1720757.8			04/05 16:44	1720787.1
	Ideal Month Start	Week day		Julian	Ideal Month Start	Week day		Julian	Ideal Month Start	Week day		Julian
	02/06	TH	03/11 4:00	1720374.2	03/08	SA		1720758.2	04/06	SU		1720787.2
1 BC	New Moon (UT Julian)	Week day	Jerusalem (UT+2)	Julian	New Moon (UT Julian)	Week day	Jerusalem (UT+2)	Julian	New Moon (UT Julian)	Week day	Jerusalem (UT+2)	Julian
	2/24 0:27	TU	02:27	1721111.5	3/24 11:48	W	13:48	1721141.0	4/22 20:31	TH	22:31	1721170.4
			Jerusalem (@ +18)	Julian			Jerusalem (@ +18)	Julian			Jerusalem (@ +18)	Julian
			02/24 20:27	1721112.3			03/25 7:48	1721141.7			04/23 16:31	1721171.1
	Ideal Month Start	Week day		Julian	Ideal Month Start	Week day		Julian	Ideal Month Start	Week day		Julian
	02/25	W		1721112.2	03/26	F		1721142.2	04/24	SA		1721171.2

48 Hidden Rhythms in Prophecy

1 AD

Month A

New Moon (UT Julian)	Week day	Jerusalem (UT+2)	Julian
02/12 8:05	SA	12/30 10:05	1721465.8
		Jerusalem (@ +18)	Julian
		02/13 4:05	1721466.6
Ideal Month Start	Week day		Julian
02/14	M		1721467.2

Month B

New Moon (UT Julian)	Week day	Jerusalem (UT+2)	Julian
3/13 20:49	SU	22:49	1721495.4
		Jerusalem (@ +18)	Julian
		03/14 16:49	1721496.1
Ideal Month Start	Week day		Julian
03/15	TU		1721496.2

Month C

New Moon (UT Julian)	Week day	Jerusalem (UT+2)	Julian
4/12 9:19	TU	11:19	1721524.9
		Jerusalem (@ +18)	Julian
		04/13 5:19	1721525.6
Ideal Month Start	Week day		Julian
04/14	TH		1721526.2

2 AD

Month A

New Moon (UT Julian)	Week day	Jerusalem (UT+2)	Julian
2/1 5:01	W	07:01	1721819.7
		Jerusalem (@ +18)	Julian
		02/02 1:01	1721820.5
Ideal Month Start	Week day		Julian
02/03	F		1721821.2

Month B

New Moon (UT Julian)	Week day	Jerusalem (UT+2)	Julian
3/2 22:47	TH	00:47	1721849.4
		Jerusalem (@ +18)	Julian
		03/03 18:47	1721850.2
Ideal Month Start	Week day		Julian
03/04	SA		1721850.2

Month C

New Moon (UT Julian)	Week day	Jerusalem (UT+2)	Julian
4/1 14:58	SA	16:58	1721879.1
		Jerusalem (@ +18)	Julian
		04/02 10:58	1721879.9
Ideal Month Start	Week day		Julian
04/03	M		1721880.2

3 AD

Month A

New Moon (UT Julian)	Week day	Jerusalem (UT+2)	Julian
2/19 22:56	M	00:56	1722203.5
		Jerusalem (@ +18)	Julian
		02/20 18:56	1722204.2
Ideal Month Start	Week day		Julian
02/21	W		1722204.2

Month B

New Moon (UT Julian)	Week day	Jerusalem (UT+2)	Julian
3/21 15:26	W	17:27	1722233.1
		Jerusalem (@ +18)	Julian
		03/22 11:26	1722233.9
Ideal Month Start	Week day		Julian
03/23	F		1722234.2

Month C

New Moon (UT Julian)	Week day	Jerusalem (UT+2)	Julian
4/20 7:45	F	09:45	1722233.8
		Jerusalem (@ +18)	Julian
		04/21 3:45	1722234.6
Ideal Month Start	Week day		Julian
04/22	SU		1722233.2

4 AD

Month A

New Moon (UT Julian)	Week day	Jerusalem (UT+2)	Julian
2/9 4:16	SA	06:16	1722557.8
		Jerusalem (@ +18)	Julian
		02/10 0:16	1722558.5
Ideal Month Start	Week day		Julian
02/11	M		1722559.2

Month B

New Moon (UT Julian)	Week day	Jerusalem (UT+2)	Julian
3/9 17:49	SU	19:49	1722587.2
		Jerusalem (@ +18)	Julian
		03/10 13:49	1722588.0
Ideal Month Start	Week day		Julian
03/11	TU		1722588.2

Month C

New Moon (UT Julian)	Week day	Jerusalem (UT+2)	Julian
4/8 8:30	TU	10:30	1722616.9
		Jerusalem (@ +18)	Julian
		04/09 4:30	1722617.6
Ideal Month Start	Week day		Julian
04/10	TH		1722618.2

Reconstructing the Original Calendar

Month A

5 AD	New Moon (UT Julian)	Week day	Jerusalem (UT+2)	Julian
	02/27 3:04	F	12/30 5:04	1722941.6
			Jerusalem (@ +18)	Julian
			02/27 23:04	1722942.4
	Ideal Month Start	Week day		Julian
	03/01	SU		1722943.2

6 AD	New Moon (UT Julian)	Week day	Jerusalem (UT+2)	Julian
	2/16 17:57	TU	19:57	1723296.2
			Jerusalem (@ +18)	Julian
			02/17 13:57	1723297.0
	Ideal Month Start	Week day		Julian
	02/18	TH		1723296.2

7 AD	New Moon (UT Julian)	Week day	Jerusalem (UT+2)	Julian
	2/6 10:13	SU	12:13	1723650.9
			Jerusalem (@ +18)	Julian
			02/07 6:13	1723651.7
	Ideal Month Start	Week day		Julian
	02/08	TU		1723652.2

8 AD	New Moon (UT Julian)	Week day	Jerusalem (UT+2)	Julian
	2/25 11:18	SA	13:18	1724035.0
			Jerusalem (@ +18)	Julian
			02/26 7:18	1724035.7
	Ideal Month Start	Week day		Julian
	02/27	M		1724036.2

Month B

5 AD	New Moon (UT Julian)	Week day	Jerusalem (UT+2)	Julian
	3/28 14:24	SA	16:24	1722971.1
			Jerusalem (@ +18)	Julian
			03/29 10:24	1722971.9
	Ideal Month Start	Week day		Julian
	03/30	M		1722972.2

6 AD	New Moon (UT Julian)	Week day	Jerusalem (UT+2)	Julian
	3/18 3:13	TH	05:13	1723325.6
			Jerusalem (@ +18)	Julian
			03/18 23:13	1723326.4
	Ideal Month Start	Week day		Julian
	03/19	F		1723326.2

7 AD	New Moon (UT Julian)	Week day	Jerusalem (UT+2)	Julian
	3/7 19:44	M	21:44	1723680.3
			Jerusalem (@ +18)	Julian
			03/08 15:44	1723681.1
	Ideal Month Start	Week day		Julian
	03/09	W		1723681.2

8 AD	New Moon (UT Julian)	Week day	Jerusalem (UT+2)	Julian
	3/25 20:42	SU	22:42	1724064.4
			Jerusalem (@ +18)	Julian
			03/26 16:42	1724065.1
	Ideal Month Start	Week day		Julian
	03/27	TU		1724065.2

Month C

5 AD	New Moon (UT Julian)	Week day	Jerusalem (UT+2)	Julian
	4/27 2:44	M	04:44	1723000.6
			Jerusalem (@ +18)	Julian
			04/27 22:44	1723001.4
	Ideal Month Start	Week day		Julian
	04/29	W		1723002.2

6 AD	New Moon (UT Julian)	Week day	Jerusalem (UT+2)	Julian
	4/16 12:28	F	14:28	1723355.0
			Jerusalem (@ +18)	Julian
			04/17 8:28	1723355.8
	Ideal Month Start	Week day		Julian
	04/18	SU		1723356.2

7 AD	New Moon (UT Julian)	Week day	Jerusalem (UT+2)	Julian
	4/6 3:52	W	05:52	1723709.7
			Jerusalem (@ +18)	Julian
			04/06 23:52	1723710.4
	Ideal Month Start	Week day		Julian
	04/08	F		1723711.2

8 AD	New Moon (UT Julian)	Week day	Jerusalem (UT+2)	Julian
	4/24 4:09	TU	06:09	1724093.7
			Jerusalem (@ +18)	Julian
			04/25 0:09	1724094.4
	Ideal Month Start	Week day		Julian
	04/26	TH		1724095.2

50 Hidden Rhythms in Prophecy

	Month A				Month B				Month C			
	New Moon				**New Moon**				**New Moon**			
	(UT Julian)	Week day	Jerusalem (UT+2)	Julian	(UT Julian)	Week day	Jerusalem (UT+2)	Julian	(UT Julian)	Week day	Jerusalem (UT+2)	Julian
9 AD	02/13 21:28	W	12/30 23:28	1724389.4	3/15 10:21	F	12:21	1724418.9	4/13 20:11	SA	22:11	1724448.3
			Jerusalem (@ +18)	Julian			Jerusalem (@ +18)	Julian			Jerusalem (@ +18)	Julian
			02/14 17:28	1724390.1			03/16 6:21	1724419.7			04/14 16:11	1724449.1
	Ideal Month Start	Week day		Julian	Ideal Month Start	Week day		Julian	Ideal Month Start	Week day		Julian
	02/15	F		1724390.2	03/17	SU		1724420.2	04/15	M		1724449.2
	New Moon				**New Moon**				**New Moon**			
	(UT Julian)	Week day	Jerusalem (UT+2)	Julian	(UT Julian)	Week day	Jerusalem (UT+2)	Julian	(UT Julian)	Week day	Jerusalem (UT+2)	Julian
10 AD	2/3 0:15	M	02:15	1724743.5	3/4 17:08	TU	19:08	1724773.2	4/3 7:02	TH	09:02	1724802.8
			Jerusalem (@ +18)	Julian			Jerusalem (@ +18)	Julian			Jerusalem (@ +18)	Julian
			02/03 20:15	1724744.3			03/05 13:08	1724774.0			04/04 3:02	1724803.5
	Ideal Month Start	Week day		Julian	Ideal Month Start	Week day		Julian	Ideal Month Start	Week day		Julian
	02/04	TU		1724744.2	03/06	TH		1724774.2	04/05	SA		1724804.2
	New Moon				**New Moon**				**New Moon**			
	(UT Julian)	Week day	Jerusalem (UT+2)	Julian	(UT Julian)	Week day	Jerusalem (UT+2)	Julian	(UT Julian)	Week day	Jerusalem (UT+2)	Julian
11 AD	2/21 17:44	SA	19:44	1725127.2	3/23 10:37	M	12:37	1725156.9	4/22 1:41	W	03:41	1725186.6
			Jerusalem (@ +18)	Julian			Jerusalem (@ +18)	Julian			Jerusalem (@ +18)	Julian
			02/22 13:44	1725128.0			03/24 6:37	1725157.7			04/22 21:41	1725187.3
	Ideal Month Start	Week day		Julian	Ideal Month Start	Week day		Julian	Ideal Month Start	Week day		Julian
	02/23	M		1725128.2	03/25	W		1725158.2	04/23	TH		1725187.2
	New Moon				**New Moon**				**New Moon**			
	(UT Julian)	Week day	Jerusalem (UT+2)	Julian	(UT Julian)	Week day	Jerusalem (UT+2)	Julian	(UT Julian)	Week day	Jerusalem (UT+2)	Julian
12 AD	2/10 18:42	W	20:42	1725481.3	3/11 10:44	F	12:44	1725510.9	4/10 3:00	SU	05:00	1725540.6
			Jerusalem (@ +18)	Julian			Jerusalem (@ +18)	Julian			Jerusalem (@ +18)	Julian
			02/11 14:42	1725482.0			03/12 6:44	1725511.7			04/10 23:00	1725541.4
	Ideal Month Start	Week day		Julian	Ideal Month Start	Week day		Julian	Ideal Month Start	Week day		Julian
	02/12	F		1725482.2	03/13	SU		1725512.2	04/12	TU		1725542.2

Reconstructing the Original Calendar 51

13 AD

	Month A				Month B				Month C			
	New Moon (UT Julian)	Week day	Jerusalem (UT+2)	Julian	New Moon (UT Julian)	Week day	Jerusalem (UT+2)	Julian	New Moon (UT Julian)	Week day	Jerusalem (UT+2)	Julian
	02/28 14:44	TU	12/30 16:44	1725865.1	3/30 4:33	TH	06:33	1725894.7	4/28 19:25	F	21:25	1725924.3
			Jerusalem (@ +18)	Julian			Jerusalem (@ +18)	Julian			Jerusalem (@ +18)	Julian
			03/01 10:44	1725865.9			03/31 0:33	1725895.4			04/29 15:25	1725925.1
	Ideal Month Start	Week day		Julian	Ideal Month Start	Week day		Julian	Ideal Month Start	Week day		Julian
	03/02	TH		1725866.2	04/01	SA		1725895.2	04/30	SU		1725925.2

14 AD

	New Moon (UT Julian)	Week day	Jerusalem (UT+2)	Julian	New Moon (UT Julian)	Week day	Jerusalem (UT+2)	Julian	New Moon (UT Julian)	Week day	Jerusalem (UT+2)	Julian
	2/18 1:48	SU	03:48	1726219.6	3/19 12:26	M	14:26	1726249.0	4/17 23:58	TU	01:58	1726278.5
			Jerusalem (@ +18)	Julian			Jerusalem (@ +18)	Julian			Jerusalem (@ +18)	Julian
			02/18 21:48	1726220.3			03/20 8:26	1726249.8			04/18 19:58	1726279.2
	Ideal Month Start	Week day		Julian	Ideal Month Start	Week day		Julian	Ideal Month Start	Week day		Julian
	02/19	TU		1726220.2	03/21	W		1726250.2	04/19	TH		1726279.2

15 AD

	New Moon (UT Julian)	Week day	Jerusalem (UT+2)	Julian	New Moon (UT Julian)	Week day	Jerusalem (UT+2)	Julian	New Moon (UT Julian)	Week day	Jerusalem (UT+2)	Julian
	2/7 17:25	TH	19:25	1726574.2	3/9 2:40	SA	04:40	1726603.6	4/7 11:38	SU	13:38	1726633.0
			Jerusalem (@ +18)	Julian			Jerusalem (@ +18)	Julian			Jerusalem (@ +18)	Julian
			02/08 13:25	1726575.0			03/09 22:40	1726604.4			04/08 7:38	1726633.7
	Ideal Month Start	Week day		Julian	Ideal Month Start	Week day		Julian	Ideal Month Start	Week day		Julian
	02/09	SA		1726575.2	03/11	M		1726605.2	04/09	TU		1726634.2

16 AD

	New Moon (UT Julian)	Week day	Jerusalem (UT+2)	Julian	New Moon (UT Julian)	Week day	Jerusalem (UT+2)	Julian	New Moon (UT Julian)	Week day	Jerusalem (UT+2)	Julian
	2/26 19:19	W	21:19	1726958.3	3/27 3:55	F	05:55	1726987.7	4/25 11:26	SA	13:26	1727017.0
			Jerusalem (@ +18)	Julian			Jerusalem (@ +18)	Julian			Jerusalem (@ +18)	Julian
			02/27 15:19	1726959.1			03/27 23:55	1726988.5			04/26 7:26	1727017.7
	Ideal Month Start	Week day		Julian	Ideal Month Start	Week day		Julian	Ideal Month Start	Week day		Julian
	02/28	F		1726959.2	03/29	SU		1726989.2	04/27	M		1727018.2

52 Hidden Rhythms in Prophecy

Month A

17 AD	New Moon (UT Julian)	Week day	Jerusalem (UT+2)	Julian
	02/15 9:42	M	12/30 11:42	1727312.9
			Jerusalem (@ +18)	Julian
			02/16 5:42	1727313.7
	Ideal Month Start	Week day		Julian
	02/17	W		1727314.2

18 AD	New Moon (UT Julian)	Week day	Jerusalem (UT+2)	Julian
	2/4 17:41	F	19:41	1727667.2
			Jerusalem (@ +18)	Julian
			02/05 13:41	1727668.0
	Ideal Month Start	Week day		Julian
	02/06	SU		1727668.2

19 AD	New Moon (UT Julian)	Week day	Jerusalem (UT+2)	Julian
	2/23 12:47	TH	14:47	1728051.0
			Jerusalem (@ +18)	Julian
			02/24 8:47	1728051.8
	Ideal Month Start	Week day		Julian
	02/25	SA		1728052.2

20 AD	New Moon (UT Julian)	Week day	Jerusalem (UT+2)	Julian
	2/12 12:35	M	14:35	1728405.0
			Jerusalem (@ +18)	Julian
			02/13 8:35	1728405.8
	Ideal Month Start	Week day		Julian
	02/14	W		1728406.2

Month B

New Moon (UT Julian)	Week day	Jerusalem (UT+2)	Julian
3/16 20:17	TU	22:17	1727342.3
		Jerusalem (@ +18)	Julian
		03/17 16:17	1727343.1
Ideal Month Start	Week day		Julian
03/18	TH		1727343.2

New Moon (UT Julian)	Week day	Jerusalem (UT+2)	Julian
3/6 8:12	SU	10:12	1727696.9
		Jerusalem (@ +18)	Julian
		03/07 4:12	1727697.7
Ideal Month Start	Week day		Julian
03/08	TU		1727698.2

New Moon (UT Julian)	Week day	Jerusalem (UT+2)	Julian
3/25 4:06	SA	06:06	1728080.8
		Jerusalem (@ +18)	Julian
		03/26 0:06	1728081.5
Ideal Month Start	Week day		Julian
03/27	M		1728082.2

New Moon (UT Julian)	Week day	Jerusalem (UT+2)	Julian
3/13 5:55	W	07:55	1728434.7
		Jerusalem (@ +18)	Julian
		03/14 1:55	1728435.5
Ideal Month Start	Week day		Julian
03/15	F		1728436.2

Month C

New Moon (UT Julian)	Week day	Jerusalem (UT+2)	Julian
4/15 4:28	TH	06:28	1727371.7
		Jerusalem (@ +18)	Julian
		04/16 0:28	1727372.4
Ideal Month Start	Week day		Julian
04/17	SA		1727373.2

New Moon (UT Julian)	Week day	Jerusalem (UT+2)	Julian
4/4 19:23	M	21:23	1727726.3
		Jerusalem (@ +18)	Julian
		04/05 15:23	1727727.1
Ideal Month Start	Week day		Julian
04/06	W		1727727.2

New Moon (UT Julian)	Week day	Jerusalem (UT+2)	Julian
4/23 16:30	SU	18:30	1728110.2
		Jerusalem (@ +18)	Julian
		04/24 12:30	1728110.9
Ideal Month Start	Week day		Julian
04/25	TU		1728111.2

New Moon (UT Julian)	Week day	Jerusalem (UT+2)	Julian
4/11 21:49	TH	23:49	1728464.4
		Jerusalem (@ +18)	Julian
		04/12 17:49	1728465.2
Ideal Month Start	Week day		Julian
04/13	SA		1728465.2

Reconstructing the Original Calendar 53

	Month A				Month B				Month C			
	New Moon				New Moon				New Moon			
	(UT Julian)	Week day	Jerusalem (UT+2)	Julian	(UT Julian)	Week day	Jerusalem (UT+2)	Julian	(UT Julian)	Week day	Jerusalem (UT+2)	Julian
21 AD	01/31 14:57	F	12/30 16:57	1728759.2	3/2 6:20	SU	08:20	1728768.8	3/31 22:18	M	00:18	1728818.4
			Jerusalem (@ +18)	Julian			Jerusalem (@ +18)	Julian			Jerusalem (@ +18)	Julian
			02/01 10:57	1728760.0			03/03 2:20	1728769.6			04/01 18:18	1728819.2
	Ideal Month Start	Week day		Julian	Ideal Month Start	Week day		Julian	Ideal Month Start	Week day		Julian
	02/02	SU		1728406.2	03/04	TU		1728790.2	04/02	W		1728819.2
	New Moon				New Moon				New Moon			
	(UT Julian)	Week day	Jerusalem (UT+2)	Julian	(UT Julian)	Week day	Jerusalem (UT+2)	Julian	(UT Julian)	Week day	Jerusalem (UT+2)	Julian
22 AD	2/19 12:14	TH	14:14	1729143.0	3/21 1:09	SA	03:09	1729172.5	4/19 15:16	SU	17:16	1729202.1
			Jerusalem (@ +18)	Julian			Jerusalem (@ +18)	Julian			Jerusalem (@ +18)	Julian
			02/20 8:14	1729143.8			03/21 21:09	1729173.3			04/20 11:16	1729202.9
	Ideal Month Start	Week day		Julian	Ideal Month Start	Week day		Julian	Ideal Month Start	Week day		Julian
	02/21	SA		1729144.2	03/22	SU		1729173.2	04/21	TU		1729203.2
	New Moon				New Moon				New Moon			
	(UT Julian)	Week day	Jerusalem (UT+2)	Julian	(UT Julian)	Week day	Jerusalem (UT+2)	Julian	(UT Julian)	Week day	Jerusalem (UT+2)	Julian
23 AD	2/9 0:53	TU	02:53	1729497.5	3/10 10:58	W	12:58	1729527.0	4/8 21:44	TH	23:44	1729556.4
			Jerusalem (@ +18)	Julian			Jerusalem (@ +18)	Julian			Jerusalem (@ +18)	Julian
			02/09 20:53	1729498.3			03/11 6:58	1729527.7			04/09 17:44	1729557.2
	Ideal Month Start	Week day		Julian	Ideal Month Start	Week day		Julian	Ideal Month Start	Week day		Julian
	02/10	W		1729498.2	03/12	F		1729528.2	04/10	SA		1729557.2
	New Moon				New Moon				New Moon			
	(UT Julian)	Week day	Jerusalem (UT+2)	Julian	(UT Julian)	Week day	Jerusalem (UT+2)	Julian	(UT Julian)	Week day	Jerusalem (UT+2)	Julian
24 AD	2/28 2:14	M	04:14	1729881.6	3/28 11:03	TU	13:03	1729911.0	4/26 19:50	W	21:50	1729940.3
			Jerusalem (@ +18)	Julian			Jerusalem (@ +18)	Julian			Jerusalem (@ +18)	Julian
			02/28 22:14	1729882.3			03/29 7:03	1729911.7			04/27 15:50	1729941.1
	Ideal Month Start	Week day		Julian	Ideal Month Start	Week day		Julian	Ideal Month Start	Week day		Julian
	03/01	TU		1729883.2	03/30	TH		1729912.2	04/28	F		1729941.2

54 Hidden Rhythms in Prophecy

	Month A				**Month B**				**Month C**				
	New Moon				New Moon				New Moon				
	(UT	Week	Jerusalem		(UT	Week	Jerusalem		(UT	Week	Jerusalem		
25 AD	Julian)	day	(UT+2)	Julian	Julian)	day	(UT+2)	Julian	Julian)	day	(UT+2)	Julian	
	02/16 18:36	F	12/30 20:36	1730236.3	3/18 3:47	SU	05:47	1730265.7	4/16 11:35	M	13:35	1730267.2	
			Jerusalem				Jerusalem				Jerusalem		
			(@ +18)	Julian			(@ +18)	Julian			(@ +18)	Julian	
			02/17 14:36	1730237.0			03/18 23:47	1730266.5			04/17 7:35	1730267.9	
	Ideal				Ideal				Ideal				
	Month	Week			Month	Week			Month	Week			
	Start	day		Julian	Start	day		Julian	Start	day		Julian	
	02/18	SU		1730237.2	03/20	TU		1730267.2	04/18	W		1730296.2	

	New Moon				New Moon				New Moon				
	(UT	Week	Jerusalem		(UT	Week	Jerusalem		(UT	Week	Jerusalem		
26 AD	Julian)	day	(UT+2)	Julian	Julian)	day	(UT+2)	Julian	Julian)	day	(UT+2)	Julian	
	2/6 7:25	W	09:25	1730590.8	3/7 19:19	TH	21:19	1730620.4	4/6 4:29	SA	06:29	1730649.7	
			Jerusalem				Jerusalem				Jerusalem		
			(@ +18)	Julian			(@ +18)	Julian			(@ +18)	Julian	
			02/07 3:25	1730591.6			03/08 15:19	1730621.1			04/07 0:29	1730650.4	
	Ideal				Ideal				Ideal				
	Month	Week			Month	Week			Month	Week			
	Start	day		Julian	Start	day		Julian	Start	day		Julian	
	02/08	F		1730592.2	03/09	SA		1730621.2	04/08	M		1730651.2	

	New Moon				New Moon				New Moon				
	(UT	Week	Jerusalem		(UT	Week	Jerusalem		(UT	Week	Jerusalem		
27 AD	Julian)	day	(UT+2)	Julian	Julian)	day	(UT+2)	Julian	Julian)	day	(UT+2)	Julian	
	2/25 5:14	TU	07:14	1730974.7	3/26 17:57	W	19:57	1731004.2	4/25 3:40	F	05:40	1731033.7	
			Jerusalem				Jerusalem				Jerusalem		
			(@ +18)	Julian			(@ +18)	Julian			(@ +18)	Julian	
			02/26 1:14	1730975.5			03/27 13:57	1731005.0			04/25 23:40	1731034.4	
	Ideal				Ideal				Ideal				
	Month	Week			Month	Week			Month	Week			
	Start	day		Julian	Start	day		Julian	Start	day		Julian	
	02/27	TH		1730976.2	03/28	F		1731005.2	04/27	SU		1731035.2	

	New Moon				New Moon				New Moon				
	(UT	Week	Jerusalem		(UT	Week	Jerusalem		(UT	Week	Jerusalem		
28 AD	Julian)	day	(UT+2)	Julian	Julian)	day	(UT+2)	Julian	Julian)	day	(UT+2)	Julian	
	2/14 7:49	SA	09:49	1731328.8	3/15 0:27	M	02:27	1731358.5	4/13 14:11	TU	16:11	1731388.1	
			Jerusalem				Jerusalem				Jerusalem		
			(@ +18)	Julian			(@ +18)	Julian			(@ +18)	Julian	
			02/15 3:49	1731329.6			03/15 20:27	1731359.3			04/14 10:11	1731388.8	
	Ideal				Ideal				Ideal				
	Month	Week			Month	Week			Month	Week			
	Start	day		Julian	Start	day		Julian	Start	day		Julian	
	02/16	M		1731330.2	03/16			1731359.2	04/15	TH		1731389.2	

Reconstructing the Original Calendar 55

29 AD

	Month A				Month B				Month C			
	New Moon (UT Julian)	Week day	Jerusalem (UT+2)	Julian	New Moon (UT Julian)	Week day	Jerusalem (UT+2)	Julian	New Moon (UT Julian)	Week day	Jerusalem (UT+2)	Julian
	02/02 7:29	W	12/30 9:29	1731682.8	3/4 0:59	F	02:59	1731712.5	4/2 17:30	SA	19:30	1731742.2
			Jerusalem (@ +18)	Julian			Jerusalem (@ +18)	Julian			Jerusalem (@ +18)	Julian
			02/03 3:29	1731683.6			03/04 20:59	1731713.3			04/03 13:30	1731743.0
	Ideal Month Start	Week day		Julian	Ideal Month Start	Week day		Julian	Ideal Month Start	Week day		Julian
	02/04	F		1731684.2	03/05	SA		1731713.2	04/04	M		1731743.2

30 AD

	New Moon (UT Julian)	Week day	Jerusalem (UT+2)	Julian	New Moon (UT Julian)	Week day	Jerusalem (UT+2)	Julian	New Moon (UT Julian)	Week day	Jerusalem (UT+2)	Julian
	2/21 2:21	TU	04:21	1732066.6	3/22 17:47	W	19:47	1732096.2	4/21 9:37	F	11:37	1732125.9
			Jerusalem (@ +18)	Julian			Jerusalem (@ +18)	Julian			Jerusalem (@ +18)	Julian
			02/21 22:21	1732067.3			03/23 13:47	1732097.0			04/22 5:37	1732126.7
	Ideal Month Start	Week day		Julian	Ideal Month Start	Week day		Julian	Ideal Month Start	Week day		Julian
	02/23	TH		1732068.2	03/24	F		1732097.2	04/23	SU		1732127.2

31 AD

	New Moon (UT Julian)	Week day	Jerusalem (UT+2)	Julian	New Moon (UT Julian)	Week day	Jerusalem (UT+2)	Julian	New Moon (UT Julian)	Week day	Jerusalem (UT+2)	Julian
	2/10 10:15	SA	12:15	1732420.9	3/11 22:20	SU	00:20	1732450.4	4/10 11:33	TU	13:33	1732480.0
			Jerusalem (@ +18)	Julian			Jerusalem (@ +18)	Julian			Jerusalem (@ +18)	Julian
			02/11 6:15	1732421.7			03/12 18:20	1732451.2			04/11 7:33	1732480.7
	Ideal Month Start	Week day		Julian	Ideal Month Start	Week day		Julian	Ideal Month Start	Week day		Julian
	02/12	M		1732422.2	03/13	TU		1732451.2	04/12	TH		1732481.2

32 AD

	New Moon (UT Julian)	Week day	Jerusalem (UT+2)	Julian	New Moon (UT Julian)	Week day	Jerusalem (UT+2)	Julian	New Moon (UT Julian)	Week day	Jerusalem (UT+2)	Julian
	1/31 0:13	TH	02:13	1732775.5	2/29 9:56	F	22:01	1732804.9	3/29 20:01	SA	22:01	1732834.3
			Jerusalem (@ +18)	Julian			Jerusalem (@ +18)	Julian			Jerusalem (@ +18)	Julian
			01/31 20:13	1732776.3			03/01 5:56	1732805.7			03/30 16:01	1732835.1
	Ideal Month Start	Week day		Julian	Ideal Month Start	Week day		Julian	Ideal Month Start	Week day		Julian
	02/01	F		1732776.2	03/02	SU		1732806.2	03/31	M		1732835.2

	Month A				Month B				Month C			
	New Moon				New Moon				New Moon			
	(UT	Week	Jerusalem		(UT	Week	Jerusalem		(UT	Week	Jerusalem	
33 AD	Julian)	day	(UT+2)	Julian	Julian)	day	(UT+2)	Julian	Julian)	day	(UT+2)	Julian
	02/18 1:49	W	12/30 3:49	1733159.6	3/19 10:39	TH	12:39	1733188.9	4/17 19:10	F	21:10	1733218.3
			Jerusalem				Jerusalem				Jerusalem	
			(@ +18)	Julian			(@ +18)	Julian			(@ +18)	Julian
			02/18 21:49	1733160.3			03/20 6:39	1733189.7			04/18 15:10	1733219.0
	Ideal				Ideal				Ideal			
	Month	Week			Month	Week			Month	Week		
	Start	day		Julian	Start	day		Julian	Start	day		Julian
	02/19	TH		1733160.2	03/21	SA		1733190.2	04/19	SU		1733219.2
	New Moon				New Moon				New Moon			
	(UT	Week	Jerusalem		(UT	Week	Jerusalem		(UT	Week	Jerusalem	
34 AD	Julian)	day	(UT+2)	Julian	Julian)	day	(UT+2)	Julian	Julian)	day	(UT+2)	Julian
	2/7 17:31	SU	19:31	1733514.2	3/9 3:27	TU	05:27	1733543.6	4/7 11:43	W	13:43	1733573.0
			Jerusalem				Jerusalem				Jerusalem	
			(@ +18)	Julian			(@ +18)	Julian			(@ +18)	Julian
			02/08 13:31	1733515.0			03/09 23:27	1733544.4			04/08 7:43	1733573.7
	Ideal				Ideal				Ideal			
	Month	Week			Month	Week			Month	Week		
	Start	day		Julian	Start	day		Julian	Start	day		Julian
	02/09	TU		1733515.2	03/11	TH		1733545.2	04/09	F		1733574.2
	New Moon				New Moon				New Moon			
	(UT	Week	Jerusalem		(UT	Week	Jerusalem		(UT	Week	Jerusalem	
35 AD	Julian)	day	(UT+2)	Julian	Julian)	day	(UT+2)	Julian	Julian)	day	(UT+2)	Julian
	2/26 17:44	SA	19:44	1733898.2	3/28 4:06	M	06:06	1733927.7	4/26 12:06	TU	14:06	1733957.0
			Jerusalem				Jerusalem				Jerusalem	
			(@ +18)	Julian			(@ +18)	Julian			(@ +18)	Julian
			02/27 13:44	1733899.0			03/29 0:06	1733928.4			04/27 8:06	1733957.8
	Ideal				Ideal				Ideal			
	Month	Week			Month	Week			Month	Week		
	Start	day		Julian	Start	day		Julian	Start	day		Julian
	02/28	M		1733899.2	03/30	W		1733929.2	04/28	TH		1733958.2

Table 2 Range of years between 8 BC and 35 AD showing the ideal first day of each month for three months surrounding the Vernal equinox

Table 2 presents the start date for three months in each year for the range of years. This is the ideal start of the month based on the new moon observation rules. The table can seem like an overwhelming series of numbers. But let's go through an example of how this information was determined.

Each year consists of three sections; one for each month. As we've seen, there are several methods of intercalation that could have been used for a given year. It is not immediately obvious as to which of the three possible months would have actually been the start of the first month for that year. Solving for the start of three months allows us to compare each method of intercalation in a later section.

	Month A New Moon (UT Julian)	Week day	Jerusalem (UT+2)	Julian
8 BC	02/10 10:19	M	02/10 12:19	1718541.9
			Jerusalem (@ +18)	Julian
			02/11 6:19	1718542.7
	Ideal Month Start	Week day		Julian
	02/12	W		1718543.2

Let's consider Month A for 8 BC.

The first four columns of the first row contain information dealing with the time of the New Moon phase conjunction. This occurred on February 10 using the Julian calendar. The time was 10:19 am UT. UT is Universal Time and is equivalent to Greenwich Mean Time. The day of the week was Monday. This works out to 1718541.9 Julian days.

A Julian day differs from a Julian year. A Julian day is a system of calendar standardization which allows for easier conversion between different calendar systems. It is based on a fixed point in time that is considered well ancient of known historical records. A Julian day starts at noon. Converting to

Julian days allows easy calendar arithmetic and shows which months would have had twenty-nine days and which would have been thirty days in length. This provides a way of verification of the calculations.

The third column lists the time at Jerusalem (UT +2) since this is the location where observation of the first sliver after the new moon would have been witnessed.

The second row shows the addition of eighteen hours from the time of conjunction. The actual conjunction is not directly visible but only becomes visible after a further eighteen hours minimum – and also depending on weather conditions at the time. For this particular month, the time at Jerusalem was Tuesday, February 11 at 6:19 am.

Using this information, we can work out the ideal start of this month (shown on the third row). Even though minutes are listed, we are really only concerned with the hour. In this case, the first moon sliver had the possibility of being visible after early morning. Taking into account that the moon's position in the sky sets soon after sunset at this time of the month, this would give a lot of opportunity for it to have been seen. There is a very good chance that the next day would have been the start of the new month; that new month starting with the start of the day at sunset of that evening. This would be Tuesday evening into Wednesday, February 12. The Julian day equivalent is listed with the day starting at 6 pm.

	Month B New Moon (UT Julian)	Week day	Jerusalem (UT+2)	Julian
8 BC	3/12 3:35	W	05:35	1718571.6
			Jerusalem (@ +18)	Julian
			03/12 23:35	1718572.4
	Ideal Month Start	Week day		Julian
	03/14	F		1718573.2

The following month would begin either twenty-nine or thirty days later. This depended on when the next New Moon would be visible after conjunction on Wednesday, March 12, at 5:35 am Jerusalem time. Remember that the first sliver of the moon is not visible until after another eighteen hours on average. This would be around 11:35 pm allowing for some leeway. The question is if the moon would have been observable at this time. The moon sets slightly after sunset around this time of the month so there is only a very small window for it to be seen as the darkness grows. The moon would have already slipped beneath the horizon before witnesses could have observed the small crescent. With that being the twenty-ninth day of that month, there would have been no witnesses at the Beth Yaazek calendar court the next day. Therefore, the following day would automatically be considered the start of the next month; Thursday evening/Friday, March 14.

	Month C New Moon (UT Julian)	Week day	Jerusalem (UT+2)	Julian
8 BC	4/10 18:50	TH	20:50	1718601.3
			Jerusalem (@ +18)	Julian
			04/11 14:50	1718602.0
	Ideal Month Start	Week day		Julian
	04/12	SA		1718602.2

In the third example, the New Moon conjunction took place on Thursday, April 10, around 8:50 pm Jerusalem time. Roughly 18 hours later in the afternoon of Friday, the first sliver of the moon could start to be noticed until the moon set after sunset that day. This was the twenty-ninth day of the month. Witnesses could have given testimony on the following day which would then have been considered the start of the next month; previous Friday evening/current Saturday, April 12.

Each month can be considered in this fashion for as many years as need to be investigated. Again, it must be stated that this is only under ideal conditions. Environmental factors could have gotten in the way of observation. But the end result still provides a series of dates based on possible observations which can be compared with the various methods of fixed intercalation.

Various Intercalation Results

Using the previous table of theoretical month start dates, another table can be constructed which lists when each year would have started and on which day of the week (refer to Table 3). The various methods of intercalation that have been presented allow this to be done quite easily.

Reconstructing the Original Calendar 61

Year (BC/AD)	AM (Tishri as start)	Modern (Hillel II)	Nisan 1		Babylonian Chronology	Nisan 1		First Ordinc Albiruni (minus 0)	Nisan 1		Vernal Equinox Rule (by Nisan 16)	Nisan 1		Abib Barley Rule	Nisan 1		AM (Tishri as start)	Year (BC/AD)
8	3753		Mar 13	TH		Apr 13	SU	•	Apr 12	SA		Mar 14	F	•	Apr 12	SA	3753	8
7	3754	•	Mar 31	TU		Apr 02	TH		Apr 01	W	•	Apr 01	W		Apr 01	W	3754	7
6	3755		Mar 20	SA	•A	Apr 20	TU		Mar 21	SU		Mar 21	SU		Mar 21	SU	3755	6
5	3756		Mar 09	TH		Apr 08	SA	•	Apr 08	SA		Mar 10	F	•	Apr 08	SA	3756	5
4	3757	•	Mar 29	TH		Mar 29	TH		Mar 29	TH	•	Mar 29	TH		Mar 29	TH	3757	4
3	3758		Mar 17	SU	•A	Apr 17	W		Mar 18	M		Mar 18	M		Mar 18	M	3758	3
2	3759		Mar 06	TH		Apr 07	M		Apr 06	SU		Mar 08	SA	•	Apr 06	SU	3759	2
1	3760	•	Mar 25	TH		Mar 26	F		Mar 26	F	•	Mar 26	F		Mar 26	F	3760	1
1	3761		Mar 15	TU	•A	Apr 14	TH	•	Apr 14	TH		Mar 15	TU	•	Apr 14	TH	3761	1
2	3762	•	Apr 02	SU		Apr 03	M		Apr 03	M	•	Apr 03	M		Apr 03	M	3762	2
3	3763		Mar 22	TH	•A	Apr 22	SU		Mar 23	F		Mar 23	F		Mar 23	F	3763	3
4	3764		Mar 11	TU		Apr 10	TH	•	Apr 10	TH		Mar 11	TU	•	Apr 10	TH	3764	4
5	3765	•	Mar 31	TU		Mar 30	M		Mar 30	M	•	Mar 30	M		Mar 30	M	3765	5
6	3766		Mar 20	SA	•A	Apr 18	SU		Mar 19	F		Mar 19	F		Mar 19	F	3766	6
7	3767		Mar 08	TU		Apr 08	F		Apr 08	F		Mar 09	W	•	Apr 08	F	3767	7
8	3768	•	Mar 27	TU		Mar 28	W		Mar 27	TU		Mar 27	TU		Mar 27	TU	3768	8
9	3769		Mar 16	SA	•A	Apr 16	TU		Apr 15	M		Mar 17	SU	•	Apr 15	M	3769	9
10	3770		Apr 03	TH		Apr 05	SA		Apr 05	SA	•	Apr 05	SA		Apr 05	SA	3770	10
11	3771		Mar 24	TU	•U	Mar 25	W		Mar 25	W		Mar 25	W		Mar 25	W	3771	11
12	3772		Mar 12	SA		Apr 12	TU		Apr 12	TU		Mar 13	SU	•	Apr 12	TU	3772	12
13	3773	•	Apr 01	SA		Apr 01	SA		Apr 01	SA	•	Apr 01	SA		Apr 01	SA	3773	13
14	3774		Mar 20	TU	•A	Apr 20	F		Mar 21	W		Mar 21	W		Mar 21	W	3774	14
15	3775		Mar 09	SA		Apr 09	TU	•	Apr 09	TU		Mar 11	M	•	Apr 09	TU	3775	15
16	3776	•	Mar 28	SA		Mar 29	SU		Mar 29	SU	•	Mar 29	SU		Mar 29	SU	3776	16
17	3777		Mar 18	TH	•A	Apr 17	TH		Mar 18	TH		Mar 18	TH		Mar 18	TH	3777	17
18	3778		Mar 06	SU		Apr 06	W	•	Apr 06	W		Mar 08	TU	•	Apr 06	W	3778	18
19	3779		Mar 25	SA		Mar 27	M		Mar 27	M	•	Mar 27	M		Mar 27	M	3779	19
20	3780		Mar 14	TH	•A	Apr 14	SU	•	Apr 13	SA		Mar 15	F	•	Apr 13	SA	3780	20
21	3781	•	Apr 01	TU		Apr 03	TH		Apr 02	W	•	Apr 02	W		Apr 02	W	3781	21
22	3782		Mar 22	SU	•A	Apr 21	TU		Mar 22	SU		Mar 22	SU		Mar 22	SU	3782	22
23	3783		Mar 11	TH		Apr 11	SU	•	Apr 10	SA		Mar 12	F	•	Apr 10	SA	3783	23
24	3784	•	Mar 30	TH		Mar 30	TH		Mar 30	TH	•	Mar 30	TH		Mar 30	TH	3784	24
25	3785		Mar 20	TU	•A	Apr 18	W		Mar 20	TU		Mar 20	TU		Mar 20	TU	3785	25
26	3786		Mar 09	SA		Apr 08	M		Apr 08	M		Mar 09	SA	•	Apr 08	M	3786	26
27	3787	•	Mar 27	TH		Mar 28	F		Mar 28	F	•	Mar 28	F		Mar 28	F	3787	27
28	3788		Mar 16	TU	•A	Apr 15	TH		Mar 15	TH		Mar 16	TU	•	Apr 15	TH	3788	28
29	3789	•	Apr 03	SU		Apr 05	TU		Apr 04	M	•	Apr 04	M		Apr 04	M	3789	29
30	3790		Mar 23	TH	•U	Mar 25	SA		Mar 24	F		Mar 24	F		Mar 24	F	3790	30
31	3791		Mar 13	TU		Apr 12	TH	•	Apr 12	TH		Mar 13	TU	•	Apr 12	TH	3791	31
32	3792	•	Apr 01	TU		Apr 01	TU		Mar 31	M	•	Mar 31	M		Mar 31	M	3792	32
33	3793		Mar 21	SA	•A	Apr 19	SU		Mar 21	SA		Mar 21	SA		Mar 21	SA	3793	33
34	3794		Mar 09	TU		Apr 09	F	•	Apr 09	F		Mar 11	TH	•	Apr 09	F	3794	34
35	3795	•	Mar 29	TU		Mar 30	W		Mar 30	W	•	Mar 30	W		Mar 30	W	3795	35

Table 3: Range of years between 8 BC-35 AD showing ideal start of year based on various intercalation methods

The first column makes use of the modern Jewish calendar method (Hillel II rules) even though this method did not come into use until well after the first century AD. However, this is the current method usually relied on by scholars when trying to work out chronology for this period of time.

The next column uses dates listed in the "Babylonian Chronology." It is useful to show how a nearby culture with similar calendar rules decided to calculate their year. These dates are also valid to consider since the Jewish calendar of the period had adopted features of the Babylonian calendar a few hundred years prior during their time of exile.

The third intercalation method is that described by Al-Biruni as the First Ordine which he claims was used in the Syrian area of that era – this was the region where the Jewish people lived.

The fourth column makes use of the vernal equinox rule: if the vernal equinox (March 20/21 Gregorian calendar) has not occurred before what would be Nisan 16, then add a leap month.

The final column allows for the observation of the abib state of barley. If what would be Nisan 1 occurs before mid March (i.e. it would occur before abib barley could be observable in ideal conditions), then add a leap month.

As the results of each calendar method are reviewed, some interesting observations can be made. The modern Jewish calendar shows that the postponement rules are in place. Nisan 1 can only begin on a Sunday, Tuesday, Thursday or Saturday. Using this method, the majority of occurrences of Nisan 1 begin in March and sometimes they begin very early in March. One can surmise that this truly is not the accurate calendar since it contradicts with the biblical instructions for the abib barley. This places in question any chronology that bases its dating using this calendar method.

Reviewing the dates from the "Babylonian Chronology" shows that Nisan 1 could begin on any day of the week. Nisan 1 often occurred in April, even up to April 21.

The dates based on Al-Biruni's First Ordine have no postponement rules included, although there could have been. The dates in the table are based solely on the times of the New Moon and the metonic cycle of years for this method. Nisan 1 is kept between the vernal equinox and the middle of April.

The next calendar method lists the results of the Vernal Equinox rule. It is significant to notice that the results are identical to the modern Jewish calendar. The weekdays occur usually one day later since the modern calendar is tied to the lunar conjunction itself and does not depend on observation. It can be surmised that the modern calendar rules were originally based on having the Vernal Equinox occur by Nisan 16.

The final calendar method is based on using the abib barley rule; that is, assuming the flowering occurred in early March and the state of abib was after mid March. Again, there are no weekday postponement rules included. The results are entirely dependent on the times of the observable New Moon phases. The results show that Nisan 1 is kept between the Vernal Equinox and mid-April – allowing for the winter barley to reach a harvestable state by the Feast Days. Notice also that the resulting metonic cycle is identical to Al-Biruni's First Ordine cycle – a cycle that he states originated from the Syrian region. This is credible evidence that this particular fixed cycle order was most likely the method of intercalation during this time period. Applying this hypothesis will lead to some surprising "coincidences" as we continue.

Summary

There has been a lot of technical ground covered in this section. Important concepts were introduced that are essential when comparing various calendars and methods of chronology. God laid out certain calendar instructions for the Hebrews that, when followed, would allow the Feasts of the Lord to be celebrated at their appropriate time.

Several possible methods of ancient calendar construction were explored. The calendars based on fixed intercalation methods, by definition, are tied only to astronomical cycles and not to observable environmental conditions. At the time when the fixed rules were instituted though, they did match current conditions. However, as the centuries passed, they began to drift.

Only the calendar method which relies on observation accurately takes into account the instructions given to the Hebrews. Observing the barley ties the calendar to a fixed and limited time period based on the astronomical cycles, yet still allows for variation due to local environmental conditions. The previous section is key for understanding what follows.

Part 2

Gabriel's 70 Weeks Recorded by Daniel

Overview

In the Introduction I began by describing how I had come across a translation of the 70 Weeks Prophecy with which I was not familiar. The discussion to this point has laid the groundwork for the Hebrew calendar, and now this prophecy can be thoroughly explored. It is mainly concerned with time – that is one of its intriguing mysteries and perennial attractions. There is a timeline associated with the prophecy. But only with a solid foundation for the construction of the Hebrew calendar can we develop an accurate understanding of the prophecy.

There have been so many interpretations through the years about what the prophecy might mean and entire books have been written explaining all the variations. I will only concentrate on one of the most well known interpretations however. Let's begin with a brief historical background of when the prophecy was given.

After a civil war, the kingdom of Israel split into two with Israel to the north and Judah to the south. Around 600 BC, only the kingdom of Judah remained as the homeland of the Jewish people. Roughly one hundred years prior, the northern kingdom of Israel had been conquered and taken into exile by the Assyrians, the ruling empire of the time. However, the Babylonian nation was on the rise and broke the Assyrian influence over the region in 609 BC and became the new ruling power. Over a period of years and after several sieges, Jerusalem was destroyed and the majority of the population was deported into exile as well. In 539 BC, the Medo-Persians defeated Babylon and took their place as the new dominant empire of the region.

Daniel had been taken into captivity after the first attacks by the Babylonians against Judah. During his lifetime in Babylon, he rose to very high prominence in the political circles. This was not of his doing though. Over the years, he had received several prophetic visions and had trusted in God for their proper interpretation. Nebuchadnezzar, the king of Babylon, recognized the power of the God that Daniel trusted in and rewarded Daniel because of this.

Years went by and when the Babylonian empire was defeated, Daniel began to take another look at the prophecies of Jeremiah. From his studies, he concluded that the time of the Jewish exile was at an end. It was during a prayer of intercession on behalf of his people that the archangel Gabriel appeared to Daniel and outlined a prophecy concerning the future of the Jewish people in answer to his prayer.

The prophecy consists of an overall period of 70 weeks. There are several reasons given for what will be accomplished during this period of time. It is further defined as consisting of an ordered series of three time periods: 7 weeks, 62 weeks and 1 week. There are descriptions of what would take place within and between these time periods.

Those are the essential facts of the prophecy. With any more embellishment, it enters into the realm of interpretation based on how the prophecy spoken by Gabriel is read. This prophecy is found in Chapter 9 of Daniel.

Chapter 8

The Interpretations by Anderson and Hoehner

As mentioned, there have been many possible interpretations given through the centuries. I have a lot of respect for the explanation proposed by Sir Robert Anderson in the late nineteenth century and then later revised by Harold Hoehner in the mid 1970's. They brought an order to a seemingly unsolvable prophecy. Theirs is one of the few interpretations that treat the text in a literal fashion and not allegorically – a main reason for its popularity and widespread acceptance. The faith of many people has been strengthened because of how they demonstrated the intricate accuracy of the Scriptures. It is important to note that they both used the King James translation in order to develop their interpretation of the prophecy.

> "Know therefore and understand, [that] from the going forth of the commandment to restore and to build Jerusalem unto the Messiah the Prince [shall be] seven weeks, and threescore and two weeks: the street shall be built again, and the wall, even in troublous times. And after threescore and two weeks shall Messiah be

cut off, but not for himself: and the people of the prince that shall come shall destroy the city and the sanctuary; and the end thereof [shall be] with a flood, and unto the end of the war desolations are determined." (Daniel 9:25-26) [KJV]

Let's examine what they have proposed and hold the previous study of the Hebrew calendar as a standard to what some say is an airtight interpretation.

ANDERSON'S INTERPRETATION

The "weeks" spoken of are treated as weeks of years; that is, they are groupings of seven years. Anderson begins by grouping the first 7 Weeks with the next 62 Weeks and treats them as one unit of sixty-nine weeks of years (i.e. 483 years). He goes on to determine the starting point (he refers to this by the Latin phrase "terminus a quo") and when the sixty-nine weeks end ("terminus ad quem").

He considers three possible starting points. These are three historical decrees given by Persian kings which deal with the Jewish exiles and the return to their homeland. He determines that there was only one decree containing the permission to rebuild Jerusalem's walls and this was given by Artaxerxes when Nehemiah petitioned him with this request. It is the only Persian decree that allowed the rebuilding of the city itself and not just of the temple. Anderson calculated that the date was March 14, 445 BC, Nisan 1 in the Jewish calendar.

From this date and going forward 483 years, the resulting date of 37/38 AD is considered too late for anything prophetically significant; specifically matching the "cutting off" of an anointed one – attributed to Jesus of Nazareth.

Anderson posits that the Bible contains an additional definition of what constitutes a year – a prophetic year. This is not 365.25 days but 360 days in length. This "shortened" year allows the terminus of the sixty-nine weeks to fall within the accepted time period of when Jesus Christ was sacrificed. Actually, it is much more accurate than that – to the very day.

He describes that by taking the total number of days in 483 prophetic years, converting that back into solar years, the terminus ad quem falls on April 6, 32 AD. This date was Nisan 10 which is the date of the Messiah's triumphal entry into Jerusalem. A few days later, Jesus was "cut off" as the prophecy says.[24]

HOEHNER'S INTERPRETATION

Hoehner reexamined Anderson's calculations and based on new evidence, sought to improve on them. He explained that Anderson erred in the following areas. First, Anderson assumed the starting point for the sixty-nine weeks began in 445 BC. Hoehner determined that the date of the decree which the Bible specifies was in twentieth year of Artaxerxes should actually be dated one year later based on how the ascension years for Persian kings were determined. He replaced the date with Nisan 1, March 5, 444 BC.

Second, Hoehner said Anderson erred by placing the crucifixion in 32 AD. The Bible states that the crucifixion occurred on Passover, a feast which always falls on Nisan 14. Using the Jewish calendar[25], he said that in 32 AD, Nisan 1 was actually on Tuesday, April 1. Counting forward fourteen days

---

24 [Anderson]
25 The modern Jewish calendar method

lands on Monday, April 14. This is not the Friday that Anderson thought it was.[26]

Third, Hoehner said Anderson mixed Julian and Gregorian year lengths inconsistently which led to calculation errors. Hoehner proposed improvements which solved the noted deficiencies. He placed Artaxerxes' decree in 444 BC and still considered the start of the sixty-nine weeks as Nisan 1. However, he recognized that there is no specific date given by Nehemiah so the date could be anytime in that month – but no earlier.

Instead of 32 AD, Hoehner placed the Friday crucifixion on April 3, 33 AD. As a result, when counting sixty-nine weeks of years using 360-day prophetic years and converting using the Gregorian calendar, he arrived at March 30, 33 AD as the date of Nisan 10 – the triumphal entry.[27] This interpretation is what is considered the "airtight case" and has not been improved on since 1975.

CRITIQUES BASED ON THE JEWISH CALENDAR

There are, however, some critiques that can be made about Hoehner's calculations that, unfortunately, make his solution unworkable as well. His start and end dates use the Julian calendar dating method. His calculations, though, make use of the more accurate Gregorian calendar system including the more accurate year length. As a result, the start of the sixty-nine weeks at March 5, 444 BC and end at March 30, 33 AD would not be the accurate dates according the Gregorian calendar. He doesn't make this distinction.

---

26 This can be confirmed by referring back to Table 2
27 [Hoehner]

The date he determines as Nisan 1, March 5, 444 BC using the Julian calendar is converted to February 28, 444 using the Gregorian system. As previously discussed, this date in February is much too early for Nisan 1 to actually have occurred in the Hebrew/Babylonian calendar. Nisan 1 should actually start one month later. This can be confirmed in the "Babylonian Chronology" as a source which contains the ancient records of when Nisan 1 occurred for that year across the empire. It lists Nisan 1 to have occurred on April 3.[28] If this date was just a few days different from Hoehner's proposal it could possibly be reconciled within the margin of error of ancient dates. However, this is a difference of an entire month and as result, the exact number of days that Hoehner's system requires, no longer fit.

In addition, Hoehner rightly recognizes that Daniel was considering the original 70 years "of captivity" as literal years and that they should not be considered symbolically as some other interpretations have done. Daniel considered the time period according to the common cultural understanding of the calendar system of his day. Yet, Hoehner (and Anderson) do treat the years given in the prophecy differently. They are treated not as literal years but convert them into shortened "prophetic" years; something for which the biblical text does not give clear evidence.

---

28 [Parker] p. 30

Chapter 9

Changing a Comma into a Period Changed Everything

There is an alternate interpretation of the 70 Weeks prophecy which both treats the text literally and also makes use of the usual understanding of a year (i.e. not shortened "prophetic" years). Some word studies are needed for this. Although Hoehner goes into much detail when explaining the word usage of "weeks" to point out that it is referring to weeks of years and not weeks of days,[29] he does not do the same for other key words in the passage such as "command" or "decree."

THE STRUCTURE OF THE PASSAGE

First, let's look at several translations of the prophetic passage and try to get a sense of why certain interpretations have resulted.

"Know therefore and understand, [that] from the going forth of the commandment to restore and to build

---

29 [Hoehner] p. 57

Jerusalem unto the Messiah the Prince [shall be] seven weeks, and threescore and two weeks: the street shall be built again, and the wall, even in troublous times. And after threescore and two weeks shall Messiah be cut off, but not for himself: and the people of the prince that shall come shall destroy the city and the sanctuary; and the end thereof [shall be] with a flood, and unto the end of the war desolations are determined." [KJV]

"Know and understand this: From the time the word goes out to restore and rebuild Jerusalem until the Anointed One, the ruler, comes, there will be seven 'sevens,' and sixty-two 'sevens.' It will be rebuilt with streets and a trench, but in times of trouble. After the sixty-two 'sevens,' the Anointed One will be put to death and will have nothing. The people of the ruler who will come will destroy the city and the sanctuary. The end will come like a flood: War will continue until the end, and desolations have been decreed." [NIV]

"So you are to know and discern that from the issuing of a decree to restore and rebuild Jerusalem until Messiah the Prince there will be seven weeks and sixty-two weeks; it will be built again, with plaza and moat, even in times of distress. Then after the sixty-two weeks the Messiah will be cut off and have nothing, and the people of the prince who is to come will destroy the city and the sanctuary. And its end will come with a flood; even to the end there will be war; desolations are determined." [NASB]

"Know therefore and discern, that from the going forth of the commandment to restore and to build Jerusalem unto the anointed one, the prince, shall be seven weeks, and threescore and two weeks: it shall be built again, with street and moat, even in troublous times. And after the threescore and two weeks shall the anointed one be cut off, and shall have nothing: and the people of the prince that shall come shall destroy the city and the sanctuary; and the end thereof shall be with a flood, and even unto the end shall be war; desolations are determined." [ASV]

Notice that all four of these translations combine the first 7 Weeks and the next 62 Weeks together into one time period with the combination making use of a comma. It would seem that this is the reason English language readers have most often treated the two sets of Weeks as one unit – especially since the release of the KJV.

Now let's consider three other translations.

"Know therefore and understand that from the going forth of the word to restore and build Jerusalem to the coming of an anointed one, a prince, there shall be seven weeks. Then for sixty-two weeks it shall be built again with squares and moat, but in a troubled time. And after the sixty-two weeks, an anointed one shall be cut off, and shall have nothing; and the people of the prince who is to come shall destroy the city and the sanctuary. Its end shall come with a flood, and to the end there shall be war; desolations are decreed." [RSV]

"Know therefore and understand that from the going out of the word to restore and build Jerusalem to the coming of an anointed one, a prince, there shall be seven weeks. Then for sixty-two weeks it shall be built again with squares and moat, but in a troubled time. And after the sixty-two weeks, an anointed one shall be cut off and shall have nothing. And the people of the prince who is to come shall destroy the city and the sanctuary. Its end shall come with a flood, and to the end there shall be war. Desolations are decreed." (ESV)

"Know therefore and discern, that from the going forth of the word to restore and to build Jerusalem unto one anointed, a prince, shall be seven weeks; and for threescore and two weeks, it shall be built again, with broad place and moat, but in troublous times. And after the threescore and two weeks shall an anointed one be cut off, and be no more; and the people of a prince that shall come shall destroy the city and the sanctuary; but his end shall be with a flood; and unto the end of the war desolations are determined." [TNK]

These translations make a definite break between the 7 Weeks and the 62 Weeks. Each time period is given a distinct purpose. A period (punctuation) is added in the text in the first two translations. The last translation is the 1917 English Tanakh, a version from a Jewish perspective. It too makes a distinct separation by using a semi-colon.

HISTORY OF THE TEXT

It would seem that the translators had a difficult time trying to make sense of a passage dealing with very precise timing and wording. The obvious must be pointed out – the various English versions are translating from a text in a different language – that of Hebrew. In order to gain a richer understanding, investigating the history of the original text is in order. We enter the field of "textual criticism," an immense area of scholarship. Starting down this road quickly gets very technical, very contentious and very emotionally charged. But it is an essential area which must be investigated since many other proposed interpretations base their entire understanding of the passage on a single English translation's grammar and word usage.

Masoretic Text

The first English language translations date to the beginning of the Reformation period. The Old Testament was translated from Hebrew manuscripts scribed by the Masoretes. These were a Jewish sect who were active between the 8th and 10th centuries AD and were located at Tiberias on Lake Gennesaret. Their name is derived from the Hebrew word "masora" meaning "tradition." The Masoretes developed a written system of vowel points because until that time, Hebrew manuscripts contained only consonants with the proper pronunciation passed down by oral tradition. Their goal was to preserve in their manuscripts the proper Hebrew pronunciation due to the extreme difficulties the Jewish population had and continued to face after the Diaspora of the first century.[30]

Just as there are textual variants in the Greek New Testament manuscripts, there were also Hebrew variant manuscripts over the centuries until the Masoretes attempted to standardize the text. The oldest complete Hebrew manuscript discovered is Codex B19A which contains a scribal note with a date of 1008 AD and stating it was written in Cairo.[31] The manuscript is located in Saint Petersburg and, originally known as *Codex Leningradensis,* it is now known as *Codex Petropolitanus.*

Qumran Scrolls

Around 1950, the commonly referred to Dead Sea scrolls were discovered around Qumran. These consist of many scrolls and thousands of fragments

---

30 [Levin]
31 [Levin]

dating from the second and first centuries BC with some dating as far back as the third century BC.[32] The Old Testament text is represented in various forms but what was discovered of extreme importance was that the Masoretic text matches text found at Qumran dating ten centuries earlier.

It's unfortunate that the fragments of the book of Daniel found in Caves 1 and 6 were very few in number. But according to scholar Hasel:

> "Based on the overwhelming conformity of these Qumran Daniel manuscripts with each other and with the MT[Masoretic Text], despite the few insignificant variants that agree with the Septuagint, it is evident that the MT is the well-preserved key text for the book of Daniel."[33]

SEPTUAGINT

A translation of the Hebrew Old Testament exists which is just as ancient as the oldest scrolls found at Qumran – this is the Greek Septuagint written circa 250 BC. The Greek language had become the scholarly language throughout the middle-east as the Greek empire expanded its influence over the centuries. The translation originated from the desire of the famous library in Alexandria to include the holy writings of the Jewish people. The Septuagint is named after the seventy translators (abbreviated as LXX.).

However, there were problems with the original Greek translation of Daniel as is described in the preface of the 1851 Bronton edition of the Septuagint:

---

32 [Levin]
33 [Hasel]

"The real Septuagint text of the book of Daniel was, at a very early period, neglected by the church, and the version of Theodotion was substituted in its place. Hence the book of Daniel contained in almost all manuscripts and printed editions of the Septuagint belongs properly to Theodotion, and not to that version."

"Indeed, for many centuries, the real Septuagint of Daniel was supposed to be lost: it was, however, discovered in a manuscript in the palace of Prince Chigi, at Rome. Bianchini transcribed it from this manuscript (known by the name of Codex Chisianus), and from his copy it was published by Simon de Magistris, in 1772. This edition and other separate reprints were, however, not very accurate. The manuscript itself was recollated for Holmes; and in his edition the real Septuagint of Daniel is given, as well as that of Theodotion."[34]

One main problem with the translation by the original seventy is that they modified the text of Daniel (including Chapter 9) so that it gave the appearance that all the prophecies had been completely fulfilled during the time of Antiochus Epiphanes. Even Theodotion's translation which became the accepted one after the second century AD contains much paraphrasing and differs significantly in places from the Masoretic Hebrew.

---

34 [Brenton]

Aramaic Peshitta and Targum

Another ancient translation of the Old Testament is written in the Aramaic language and dates from the early centuries AD. Aramaic is a very ancient language of the region and dates to as far back as the time of Abraham. There are actually four passages in the Hebrew Old Testament written in Aramaic:

> Genesis 31:47
> Jeremiah 10:11
> Ezra 4:8-6:18, 7:12-26
> Daniel 2:4-7:28

The Aramaic scholar Greenspahn describes the linguistic environment of the early centuries in this way:

> "Although Greek became increasingly important in Judea at this time, Aramaic continued to play a prominent role in Jewish life and culture until it was displaced by Arabic many centuries later. The language of this period, which extends from the second century B.C.E. to the second century CE, is designated Middle Aramaic. This is the form of Aramaic found in the Dead Sea Scrolls and the New Testament. Some scholars also trace the earliest layers of the targumim to the Pentateuch (Onqelos) and the Prophets (Jonathan) to this time."[35]

The "targumim" he refers to are the Aramaic translations/paraphrases of the Hebrew scriptures that were used since the time of the Babylonian exile when Aramaic replaced Hebrew in common speech. In order for the worship in the synagogues to be understandable, these Aramaic texts were used.[36]

---

35 [Greenspahn] p. 95
36 [Levin]

An Aramaic translation of Scripture has been used by the various church denominations in the middle-east – the Peshitta (in Syriac meaning "the simple"). A very important point is that this translation dates from before the fifth century AD when, during that time, differences in theology split the church and each formed their own religious traditions. However, each resulting sect kept the Peshitta as their scriptures.

There are no surviving records as to who were the original translators of the Peshitta. Compare this with the fact that the translators of the Septuagint and of the Latin Vulgate are known. A biblical scholar writing in 1915 states:

> "Exactly how old the Peshitto is, no one can now tell. We trace it back to the fourth century, where we find it quoted by Ephrem; but beyond that we can only conjecture. But it has been the current and common version of the Syrians, from that time till the present; and our extant manuscripts go back as early as A.D. 464"[37]

> "This version, as appears from internal evidence, was made directly from the Hebrew, and before the Massoretic points came into use. It is quoted and commented upon by Ephrem Syrus, in the fourth century; and has enjoyed the same reception among the Aramean Christians, of whatever sect, as the Peshitto New Testament."[38]

> "It is universally pronounced to be a judicious and faithful translation; and has been regarded as a sure guide to the true state of the Hebrew text probably as early as the second century."[39]

---

37 [Murdock] p. 490
38 [Murdock] p. 504
39 [Murdock] p. 504

In the Masoretic text, portions of Daniel are written in Hebrew and portions in Aramaic. Scholars even as late as 2002 have no clear understanding of why this is:

> "The mixture of languages in the other cases is peculiar. Some have speculated that the books of Ezra and Daniel were written entirely in Hebrew and that the Aramaic sections are a translation that was substituted for the original. Others have proposed that these books were first written in Aramaic, in which case the Hebrew sections are a replacement. Alternatively, the shift may have been intentional, whether as a result of combining passages that were originally written in different languages or for some particular stylistic effect."[40]

Therefore, comparing the Masoretic text with the Aramaic Peshitta Old Testament is beneficial. Both texts are based on manuscripts of similar ancient age and both texts match each other quite closely. Comparison allows more clear insight into problematic Hebrew words and meanings by investigating how the Aramaic has chosen to translate these words. In addition, it could very well be that the Aramaic is much closer to the original if, in fact, the entire book of Daniel was written in that language – which no one has been able to definitively determine.

HEBREW AND ARAMAIC INTERLINEAR

Based on the previous historical information, it is obvious that the Hebrew as found in the Masoretic manuscripts is extremely important to investigate. The following table is an interlinear rendering of Daniel 9:24-27. It must be remembered that Hebrew (and Aramaic) do not

---

40 [Greenspahn] p. 99

contain capital letters or punctuation. Both languages are read from right to left but the table is presented vertically for ease of understanding.

The Hebrew is from the Westminster Leningrad Codex with English based on Strong's Concordance along with Brown-Driver-Briggs as provided by www.biblehub.com.

The Aramaic is based on the text in the Ambrosianus manuscript dating from the sixth or seventh century AD with English based on "A Compendious Syriac Dictionary" by J. Payne-Smith published in 1902 as provided at cal1.cn.huc.edu.

S#	Translit	Hebrew	English	Morph	Aramaic	English
Verse 24						
7620	šā-ḇu-'îm	שָׁבֻעִים	weeks	Noun	ܫܒܥܝܢ	seventy
7657	šiḇ-'îm	שִׁבְעִים	seventy	Noun	ܫܒܘܥܝܢ	weeks
2852	neḥ-taḵ	נֶחְתַּךְ	are decreed	Verb	ܢܬܬܣܝܡܘܢ	are placed/ imposed upon
5921	'al-	עַל־	on	Prep	ܥܠ	on
5971	'am-mə-ḵā	עַמְּךָ ׀	your people	Noun	ܥܡܟ	people/nation
5921	wə-'al-	וְעַל־	and on	Prep	ܘܥܠ	and on
5892	'îr	עִיר	city	Noun	ܡܕܝܢܬܐ	capital city
6944	qāḏ-še-ḵā	קָדְשֶׁךָ	your holy	Noun	ܕܩܘܕܫܟ	of holiness
3607	lə-ḵal-lê	לְכַלֵּא	to finish	Verb	ܠܡܫܠܡ	and to complete
6588	hap-pe-ša'	הַפֶּשַׁע	the trans-gression	Noun	ܚܘܒܐ	debt/sin
2856	ū-lə-hā-ṯêm	וּלְהָתֵם	to make an end	Verb	ܘܠܡܚܪܒܘ	and to destroy
2403	ḥaṭ-ṭāṯ	חַטָּאת	of sin	Noun	ܚܛܝܬܐ	sin
	q	ק	-			
3722	ū-lə-ḵap-pêr	וּלְכַפֵּר	and to forgive	Verb	ܠܡܚܣܝܘ	to forgive
5771	'ā-wōn,	עָוֹן	iniquity	Noun	ܥܘܠܐ	crime/injustice
935	ū-lə-hā-ḇî	וּלְהָבִיא	and to bring in	Verb	ܘܠܡܝܬܝܘ	and to bring
6664	ṣe-ḏeq	צֶדֶק	righteousness	Noun	ܙܕܩܐ	that which is proper or right
					ܕܡܢ	which is from
5769	'ō-lā-mîm;	עֹלָמִים	everlasting	Noun	ܥܠܡ	eternity
2856	wə-laḥ-tōm	וְלַחְתֹּם	and to seal	Verb	ܘܠܡܫܠܡ	and to fulfill
2377	ḥā-zō-wn	חָזוֹן	the vision	Noun	ܚܙܘܐ	the prophetic vi-sion
5030	wə-nā-ḇî,	וְנָבִיא	and prophecy	Noun	ܘܢܒܝܐ:	and the Prophets
4886	wə-lim-šō-aḥ	וְלִמְשֹׁחַ	and to anoint	Verb	ܘܠܡܫܝܚܐ	and anointed one
6944	qō-ḏeš	קֹדֶשׁ	the most	Noun	ܩܘܕܫ	holy
6944	qā-ḏā-šîm.	קָדָשִׁים	Holy place	Noun	ܩܘܕܫܝܢ.	holies(ie. most holy)
Verse 25						
3045	wə-ṯê-ḏa'	וְתֵדַע	and know	Verb	a ܘܬܕܥ	and know
7919	wə-ṯaś-kêl	וְתַשְׂכֵּל	and under-stand	Verb	ܘܬܣܬܟܠ	also understand
4480	min-	מִן־	from	Prep	ܡܢ	from
4161	mō-ṣā	מֹצָא	the going forth	Noun	ܡܦܩܢܗ	the going out/exiting

Changing a Comma into a Period Changed Everything

S#	Translit	Hebrew	English	Morph	Aramaic	English
1697	dā-ḇār,	דְּבַר	of the word	Noun	ܡܠܬܐ	the word/promise
7725	lə-hā-šîḇ	לְהָשִׁיב	to restore	Verb	ܠܡܗܦܟ	to return
1129	wə-liḇ-nō-wṯ	וְלִבְנוֹת	and to build	Verb	ܘܠܡܒܢܐ	and to build/rebuild
3389	yə-rū-šā-lim	יְרוּשָׁלִַ֗ם	Jerusalem	Noun	ܠܐܘܪܫܠܡ	Jerusalem
5704	'aḏ-	עַד	to	Prep	ܥܕܡܐ	until the coming/reach the time of
4899	mā-šî-aḥ	מָשִׁיחַ	anointed one	Noun	ܡܫܝܚܐ	anointed one
5057	nā-ḡîḏ,	נָגִיד	prince	Noun	ܡܠܟܐ	king/ruler/emperor/caliph
7620	šā-ḇu-'îm	שָׁבֻעִים	[shall be] weeks	Noun	ܫܒܘܥܐ	weeks
7651	šiḇ-'āh;	שִׁבְעָה	seven	Noun	ܫܒܥܐ	seven
7620	wə-šā-ḇu-'îm	וְשָׁבֻעִים	and weeks	Noun	ܘܫܒܘܥܐ	and weeks
8346	šiš-šîm	שִׁשִּׁים	sixty	Noun	ܫܬܝܢ	sixty
8147	ū-šə-na-yim,	וּשְׁנַיִם	and two	Noun	ܘܬܪܝܢ	and two
7725	tā-šūḇ	תָּשׁוּב	return	Verb	ܢܗܦܘܟ	returned
1129	wə-niḇ-nə-ṯāh	וְנִבְנְתָה	and shall be build	Verb	ܘܢܬܒܢܐ	and rebuilt
					ܠܐܘܪܫܠܡ	for Jerusalem
7339	rə-ḥō-wḇ	רְחוֹב	the street	Noun	ܫܘܩܐ	street/market/public square
2742	wə-ḥā-rūṣ,	וְחָרוּץ	and the wall	Adj	ܦܠܛܝܬܐ	also open place/plaza
6695	ū-ḇə-ṣō-wq	וּבְצוֹק	in troublous/anguish	Noun	ܠܥܠܡ	to the end of a season
6256	hā-'it-tîm.	הָעִתִּים	times	Noun	ܙܒܢܐ	stretch of time
Verse 26						
310	wə-'a-ḥă-rê	וְאַחֲרֵי	and after	Adv	ܘܒܬܪ	and after
7620	haš-šā-ḇu-'îm	הַשָּׁבֻעִים	weeks	Noun	ܫܒܘܥܐ	weeks
8346	šiš-šîm	שִׁשִּׁים	sixty	Noun	ܫܬܝܢ	sixty
8147	ū-šə-na-yim,	וּשְׁנַיִם	and two	Noun	ܘܬܪܝܢ	and two
3772	yik-kā-rêṯ	יִכָּרֵת	shall be cut off	Verb	ܢܬܩܛܠ	will be executed/slaughtered
4899	mā-šî-aḥ,	מָשִׁיחַ	anointed one	Noun	ܡܫܝܚܐ	anointed one
369	wə-'ên	וְאֵין	but not	Prt	ܘܠܐ	and then not existing

S#	Translit	Hebrew	English	Morph	Aramaic	English
	lōw;	לֽוֹ	to	Prep	ܠܗ	for
5892	wə-hā-'îr	וְהָעִיר	and the city	Noun	ܘܡܕܝܢܬܐ	also the city
6944	Wə-haq-qō-ḏeš	וְהַקֹּדֶשׁ	and the sanctuary	Noun	ܕܩܘܕܫܐ	of holiness
7843	yaš-ḥîṯ	יַשְׁחִית	shall destroy	Verb	ܢܬܚܒܠ	will perish/be destroyed
5971	'am	עַם	people	Noun	ܥܡ	at the time of those who belong to
5057	nā-ḡîḏ	נָגִיד	of prince	Noun	ܡܠܟܐ	king/ruler/emperor/caliph
935	hab-bā	הַבָּא	that shall come	Verb	ܕܐܬܐ	who is to come/inflict upon
7093	wə-qiṣ-ṣōw	וְקִצּוֹ	and the end	Noun	ܘܫܘܠܡܗ	also the end
7858	ḇaš-še-ṭep̄,	בַשֶּׁטֶף	[shall be] thereof with a flood	Noun	ܒܫܘܛܦܢܐ	along with a flood
5704	wə-'aḏ	וְעַד	and to	Prep	ܘܥܕܡܐ	and until
7093	qêṣ	קֵץ	the end	Noun	ܠܫܘܠܡܐ	to the end
4421	mil-ḥā-māh,	מִלְחָמָה	of the war	Noun	ܕܩܪܒܐ	of war/battles
2782	ne-ḥĕ-re-ṣeṯ	נֶחֱרֶצֶת	are determined	Verb	ܕܦܣܝܩܬܐ	decreed/time of judgement
8074	šō-mê-mō-wṯ.	שֹׁמֵמוֹת׃	desolations	Verb	ܕܚܒܠܐ	damage/ruination
Verse 27						
1396	wə-hiḡ-bîr	וְהִגְבִּיר	and cause to confirm/prevail	Verb d	ܘܢܥܫܢ	and to be made strong/to fortify
1285	bə-rîṯ	בְּרִית	the covenant	Noun	ܕܩܝܡܐ	treaty/covenant
7227	lā-rab-bîm	לָרַבִּים	with many	Adj	ܠܣܓܝܐܐ	for many
7620	šā-ḇū-a'	שָׁבוּעַ	for week	Noun	ܫܒܘܥܐ	for week
259	'e-ḥā ;	אֶחָד	one	Adj	ܚܕ	one
2677	wa-ḥă-ṣî	וַחֲצִי	and half	Noun	ܘܦܠܓܗ	and half
7620	haš-šā-ḇū-a'	הַשָּׁבוּעַ	of the week	Noun	ܫܒܘܥܐ	week
7673	yaš-bîṯ	יַשְׁבִּית ׀	cause to cease	Verb	ܘܢܒܛܠ	and to stop/cease
2077	ze-ḇaḥ	זֶבַח	the sacrifice	Noun	ܕܒܚܬܐ	sacrifice
4503	ū-min-ḥāh,	וּמִנְחָה	and the offering	Noun	ܘܩܘܪܒܢܐ	and offerings

S#	Translit	Hebrew	English	Morph	Aramaic	English
5921	wə-'al	וְעַל	and upon	Prep	ܘܥܠ	and on/above
3671	kə-nap̄	כְּנַף	the wing/ extremity	Noun	ܓܘܕܢܗ	pinnacle/wing/ bosom
8251	šiq-qū-ṣîm	שִׁקּוּצִים	of abominations	Noun	ܕܓܠܘܬܐ	of abomination/ impurity
8074	mə-šō-mêm,	מְשֹׁמֵם	that makes desolate	Verb	ܡܚܒܠ	which destroys/corrupts
5704	wə-'aḏ-	וְעַד־	and even until	Prep	ܥܕܡܐ	until
3617	kā-lāh	כָּלָה	the destruction/completion	Noun	ܓܡܝܪܘܬܐ	the completion
2782	wə-ne-ḥĕ-rā-ṣāh,	וְנֶחֱרָצָה	that determined/ decreed	Verb	ܕܦܬܓܡܐ	of the judgements
5413	tit-taḵ	תִּתַּךְ	shall be poured/rained	Verb	ܐܬܬܣܝܡ	imposed/placed down on
5921	'al-	עַל־	on/over	Prep	ܥܠ	over/above
8074	šō-mêm.	שֹׁמֵם׃	made desolate	Verb	ܡܚܒܠ	that which destroys/corrupts
	p̄	פ	-			

Table 4: Daniel 9:24-27 Hebrew and Aramaic with English equivalent [BibleHub] [CAL]

When these two texts are compared, the following observations can be made. First, the grammar and word order are almost identical. This makes sense since both languages are very closely related.

Verse 24 lists several reasons for what the 70 weeks of years are said to accomplish. The Hebrew and Aramaic use identical concepts until the final one. At that point, the Hebrew uses two verbs: 1. to seal up the vision and the prophecy and 2. to anoint the most holy place. "Sealing up" is commonly understood by commentators as to mean "fulfill." However, this word as used elsewhere in Daniel means to shut up and conceal (i.e. Daniel 12:4 and 12:9). However, the Aramaic words that are used definitely mean "to fulfill; complete."

The Hebrew word which has been translated here as "prophecy" when it is used elsewhere in the Old Testament refers to the individual(s) as the source and not the words that are grouped together as "the prophecy." The Aramaic term that is used is the plural "prophets" and refers to the whole of the inspired Prophetic literature. The connotation of the two texts is quite different since the Hebrew is referring only to the single prophecy currently being given but the Aramaic refers to the entirety of the prophetic literature which will see fulfillment by the termination of the 70 Weeks.

In addition, the Hebrew makes use of the verb form of "to anoint" but the Aramaic uses a noun as "the anointed." This is the third noun in the list of that which will be fulfilled: the vision, the prophetic literature and the most holy anointed one. Again, this leads to a very different meaning between the two texts. The Aramaic is a more comprehensive statement of what is ultimately accomplished at the completion of the period of time.

The Hebrew text uses the term "decreed" three times through the passage:

1. verse 24 - 70 weeks are "decreed" (S# 2852) which is from a root word meaning "cut, cut off, divide"
2. verse 26 - to the end of the war desolations are "decreed" (S#2782) which is from a root word meaning "to cut, sharpen, to wound"
3. verse 27 - until the completion of "that which is decreed" (S#2782) also from "to cut, sharpen, to wound"

This can be considered a very violent prophecy with the choice of the words used. Even in verse 26 the anointed is said he will be "cut off." The Aramaic also makes use of "decreed" which originates from words meaning "to cut, to divide." However, a different word is used in verse 24. There a word meaning "to impose; place down upon" is used. This same word occurs in verse 27 where the Hebrew uses "rain down upon." The prophetic statement in Aramaic begins and ends in the same manner: judgement is laid down from above.

One of the most significant things to notice is the arrangement of the time cues within the prophecy. To illustrate this, the previous table makes use of four shaded columns labled: 'a', 'b', 'c', 'd'. Section 'a' describes a period of seven weeks and contains two nouns: "anointed one" and "prince." A lot of English translations capitalize these nouns forcing a certain interpretation. However, the original text has no such capitalization. There is no punctuation in Hebrew (or Aramaic) and immediately the following 62 Weeks is stated. This is section 'b' and contains the statement regarding rebuilding the city of Jerusalem. Then there is the preposition "and after" which starts section 'c' and refers to the single noun "anointed one" and a future personality using the single noun "prince." The final section 'd' contains the final one week and describes actions of the future "prince."

Even though the first two sections have usually been combined together in many English translations, the passage in Hebrew can be viewed as four separate and distinct sections. There are no punctuation marks in Hebrew that force any sections to be combined together. Notice that in verse 27, the time periods of "week one" and "half week" occur immediately adjacent without any break. This is exactly the same as in verse 25 where Week 7 and Week 62 are stated. Many English language translators choose to combine the weeks together as found in verse 25 but aren't consistent with verse 27 and separate out "week one" from the "half week." They properly realize that Gabriel has spoken of seventy weeks total and therefore, the last week and the half week cannot be added together as a single unit – this would add up to more than seventy weeks. Lastly, the preposition "after" in verse 26 specifically refers back to the sixty-two week period and is an important indication that it is to be understood as a separate time period from the first seven weeks.

In verse 23, Gabriel instructs Daniel, "Therefore consider the word and understand the vision." The word "vision" is the Hebrew "mareh" (S#4758). In Numbers 8:4b, "mareh" is translated as "pattern"; this pattern being used when making the lampstands. It was like a blueprint.

> "From its base to its flowers, it was hammered work; according to the **pattern** that the Lord had shown Moses, so he made the lampstand." (Numbers 8:4b) [emphasis added]

Earlier in Daniel, "vision" is translated twice – each from a different Hebrew word:

> "The vision of the evenings and the mornings that has been told is true, but seal up the vision, for it refers to many days from now." (Daniel 8:26)

The first instance makes use of "mareh" and refers to the number of evening-morning units first mentioned back in Daniel 8:14. The second word is translated from "chazon" (S# 2377) meaning "dream, oracle, vision." This verse demonstrates a distinction when talking about a pattern of numbers as opposed to a sequence of visible events.

I propose that Gabriel did not give Daniel a vision like a movie playback but instead, a visual pattern or blueprint of separate time periods. Exploring what this pattern could be is the focus of the next chapter.

Chapter 10

How Many Are There?

Let's now take a closer look at the individuals described in the three sections where they occur. Each of the sections make use of either one or both of two Hebrew words: "mashiach" and/or "nagiyd"

mashiach (S#4899)
- anointed, anointed one
- of the Messiah, Messianic prince
- of the king of Israel
- of the high priest of Israel
- of Cyrus
- of the patriarchs as anointed kings

nagiyd (S#5057)
- leader, ruler, captain, prince
- ruler, prince
- prince-overseer
- ruler (in other capacities)
- princely things

The individual described in the first section of Weeks uses both words together; "anointed one, prince." The second individual described after the second section uses just the one word "anointed one." And the individual in the last section is described using just the one word "prince."

Traditionally, when the 7 and the 62 weeks are considered as a unit and combined together, the two individuals described are also combined and the entire section is considered to be referring to the Jewish Messiah with both words "mashiach" and "nagiyd." However, could the word "nagiyd" or "prince" be used to describe the Messiah? This word occurs forty-four times in the Old Testament but none of the other usages refer to the Jewish Messiah. But, there is one well known passage where the Messiah is referred to as a "prince" – as "Prince of Peace." This is found in Isaiah 9:6; however, the word for Prince used there is the Hebrew word "sar" (S#8269) which is defined as "chieftain, chief, ruler, official, captain, prince." "Sar" occurs 421 times in the Old Testament and includes uses when speaking of angelic and religious positions of authority. For example, Daniel uses the word "sar" to describe the "Prince of princes."

> "...and he [referring to the prince to come] shall even rise up against the **Prince of princes**, and he shall be broken—but by no human hand." (Daniel 8:25) [emphasis added]

The word is also used in Daniel 8:11 for the "prince of the host" of heaven. The instances where "nagiyd" is used, however, only describe earthly authority. It would seem that Daniel would have used the word "sar" when writing the 70 Weeks passage if he wanted to specify the Jewish Messiah in the first 7 Weeks. So who then is this "anointed one" that is being referred to?

There is one other ruler that is called "anointed one" in the Bible: Cyrus, the Persian king. This is found in Isaiah 45:1.

> "Thus says the Lord **to his anointed, to Cyrus**, whose right hand I have grasped, to subdue nations before him and to loose the belts of kings, ... I have stirred him up in righteousness, and I will make all his ways level; he shall build my city and set my exiles free, not for price or reward," says the Lord of hosts." (Isaiah 45:1, 13) [emphasis added]

In the previous chapter of Isaiah, Cyrus is again tied to the rebuilding of Jerusalem and the temple.

> "[God] who says of Cyrus, 'He is my shepherd, and he shall fulfill all my purpose'; saying of Jerusalem, 'She shall be built,' and of the temple, 'Your foundation shall be laid.'" (Isaiah 44:28)

Therefore, based on the use of "nagiyd" and Isaiah's prophecies about an "anointed one", the individual described in Daniel 9:25 is most likely referring to an earthly king – Cyrus.

Then the individual described after the second section (62 Weeks) using only the one word "mashiach" would refer to the expected Jewish Messiah. This is the commonly understood interpretation of this section since it describes the complete destruction of Jerusalem and the anointed one having been cut off before that event happens.

The final individual, referred to only as "nagiyd", would be a third personality. This would indeed allow the three sections to be considered as separate periods of time; each section describing a different and unique individual.

Chapter 11

Who Gave the Command?

The action which kicks off the whole series of Weeks has to do with what the KJV translates as a "commandment" and the NASB translates as a "decree." Usually this starts a discussion of which Persian king issued a decree, the purpose of which was the rebuilding of the city of Jerusalem. There are three possible decrees of kings which are mentioned in Scripture and the debate continues as to which one is the correct one. However, the Bible states that there are actually four decrees:

> "And the elders of the Jews built and prospered through the prophesying of Haggai the prophet and Zechariah the son of Iddo. They finished their building by decree of the **God of Israel** and by decree of **Cyrus** and **Darius** and **Artaxerxes** king of Persia..." (Ezra 6:14) [emphasis added]

Let's look at the meaning of the word used in Daniel 9:25 that starts the action: "from the going out of the word...". It is the Hebrew word "dabar" (S#1697) defined as "speech, word." It is used 1,441 times in the Old Testament. Elsewhere, the same word "dabar" is used along with an additional adjective as a "royal order" of King Ahasuerus in the Book of Esther, events which occurred a few decades after Daniel's era:

> "If it please the king, let a **royal order** go out from him, and let it be written among the laws of the Persians and the Medes so that it may not be repealed..." (Esther 1:19a) [emphasis added]

Notice that the king spoke the royal order and then as a separate action it was written down. In the other passages, the word is not used of a king's written decree but only of the act of speaking.

There are two words used in Daniel for when a king is communicating. The book of Daniel is partially written in Hebrew and partially in Aramaic. In the Aramaic portion, the word "millah" (S#4406) is used twenty-four times and is defined as "a word, command, discourse, or subject -- commandment, matter, thing. Word." This word only occurs in the book of Daniel. In the Aramaic Peshitta version of Daniel, this same word is used throughout including where the word "dabar" is used in Hebrew (for example Daniel 9:25). None of the uses of these terms refers to a king's decree.

The second word is "dath" (S# 1882) defined as "a royal edict or statute -- commandment, commission, decree, law, manner." This is used thirty-five times and occurs in the books of Ezra, Esther and Daniel. The word is used for edicts of the Persian kings and of the Law of God. It occurs in Daniel 6:5, 8, 12, 15 describing the communication of Darius the Mede. This same Darius was the ruler at the time when Daniel recorded the 70 Weeks prophecy (Daniel 9:1). If the utterance regarding the rebuilding of Jerusalem would refer to a king's decree, it would seem that this other word which implies a royal order would have been used instead.

The word "dabar" is used in another very common way throughout the Old Testament. Whenever prophets speak on behalf of God, according to the "Word of the LORD", the word used is "dabar." The word actually occurs several other times in Daniel 9:

> "He made me understand, speaking with me and saying, "O Daniel, I have now come out to give you insight and understanding. At the beginning of your pleas for mercy a **word** went out, and I have come to tell it to you, for you are greatly loved. Therefore consider the **word** and understand the vision."" (Daniel 9:22-23) [emphasis added]

Both times the "word" is "dabar" and is referring to the words spoken by God. However, there is an even bigger clue as to what the "word" is referring to which is found at the very beginning of the passage:

> "In the first year of Darius the son of Ahasuerus, by descent a Mede, who was made king over the realm of the Chaldeans – in the first year of his reign, I, Daniel, perceived in the books the number of years that, according to the **word** of the Lord to Jeremiah the prophet, must pass before the end of the desolations of Jerusalem, namely, seventy years." (Daniel 9:1-2) [emphasis added]

The initial action which culminated in the 70 Weeks prophecy started when Daniel read and comprehended the "word of the Lord" that Jeremiah had written down. He dealt with the number of years that it would take for Jerusalem's time of desolation to be complete. This is found in a letter of prophecy he wrote from Judah to the exiles (Jeremiah 29) who had been taken to Babylon – this included Daniel.

> "For thus says the Lord: When seventy years are completed for Babylon, I will visit you, and I will fulfill to

you my **promise** and bring you back to this place. For I know the plans I have for you, declares the Lord, plans for welfare and not for evil, to give you a future and a hope. Then you will call upon me and come and pray to me, and I will hear you. You will seek me and find me, when you seek me with all your heart. I will be found by you, declares the Lord, and I will restore your fortunes and gather you from all the nations and all the places where I have driven you, declares the Lord, and I will bring you back to the place from which I sent you into exile." (Jeremiah 29: 10-14) [emphasis added]

Again "dabar" is used and is translated as "promise" in verse 10. Jeremiah's letter speaks of the seventy years that Daniel was pondering – and finally understood. Notice that the seventy years are specifically connected with Babylon – not Jerusalem and not with the time of the exile. This is where I believe a great misunderstanding has occurred. It is traditionally assumed that the Jewish people were in Babylonian exile for a total of seventy years. It is commonly stated that the first group of exiles were taken in 605 BC by Nebuchadnezzar. After Babylon was conquered in 539 BC, the Persian king Cyrus issued a decree during his first regnal year in 538 BC which allowed the return to Jerusalem. This is not a period of seventy years, however. This is a discrepancy which many have tried to resolve.

Although it is true that 605 BC marks the first of several deportations of the population, Daniel 1:3-4a states that first deportation only consisted of "some of the people of Israel, both of the royal family and of the nobility, youths without blemish." The biblical account in II Kings 24 describes the next large deportation after Nebuchadnezzar captured Judah and forced them to become a vassal state, a situation King Jehoiakim endured for only three years until he rebelled. Then, when Nebuchadnezzar returned and captured the city:

> "...he carried away all Jerusalem and all the officials and all the mighty men of valor, 10,000 captives, and all the craftsmen and the smiths. None remained, except the poorest people of the land." (2 Kings 24:14)

The final deportation occurred when Jerusalem was completely destroyed:

> "And he burned the house of the Lord and the king's house and all the houses of Jerusalem; every great house he burned down. And all the army of the Chaldeans, who were with the captain of the guard, broke down the walls around Jerusalem. And the rest of the people who were left in the city and the deserters who had deserted to the king of Babylon, together with the rest of the multitude, Nebuzaradan the captain of the guard carried into exile." (2 Kings 25:9-11)

Therefore, supposing the seventy years of exile started in 605 BC does not include the majority of the Jewish population. It is certainly problematic to associate a time period of seventy years with any of these three deportations. But where has this common assumption come from?

THE SEVENTY YEARS

There are five biblical passages where a period of seventy years are mentioned. Two of the references seem to tie the seventy years to the exile but a closer examination will show that this is not the case.

The first mention of seventy years occurs earlier in Jeremiah's book, where he prophesies during 605 BC, King Nebuchadnezzar's first year as king:

"Therefore thus says the Lord of hosts: Because you have not obeyed my words, behold, I will send for all the tribes of the north, declares the Lord, and for Nebuchadnezzar the king of Babylon, my servant, and I will bring them against this land and its inhabitants, and against all these surrounding nations. I will devote them to destruction, and make them a horror, a hissing, and an everlasting desolation. Moreover, I will banish from them the voice of mirth and the voice of gladness, the voice of the bridegroom and the voice of the bride, the grinding of the millstones and the light of the lamp. This whole land shall become a ruin and a waste, and **these nations shall serve the king of Babylon seventy years**. Then **after seventy years are completed, I will punish the king of Babylon and that nation**, the land of the Chaldeans, for their iniquity, declares the Lord, making the land an everlasting waste." (Jeremiah 25: 8-12) [emphasis added]

Notice that the period of God's judgement is not just for Judah but includes all the surrounding nations as well. The rest of Chapter 25 of Jeremiah describes how he visited the surrounding nations' kings and announced God's judgement on them. They would be under Babylon's thumb for a period of seventy years and then after the completion of that period, God would place Babylon under judgement.

The second reference occurs in the narrative of 2 Chronicles:

"...to **fulfill the word of the Lord by the mouth of Jeremiah**, until the land had enjoyed its Sabbaths. All the days that it lay desolate it kept Sabbath, **to fulfill seventy years**." (2 Chronicles 36: 21) [emphasis added]

This passage links the completion (fulfillment) of the seventy years with prophecy found in Jeremiah, who did not even address the subject of missed Sabbaths. The Jewish homeland was able to make up for its missed Sabbath years but this was a byproduct of the period of the seventy year judgement on the entire region by the Babylonians. It does not say that the number of missed Sabbaths were seventy in total. Leviticus states a prophecy of a future time of exile:

> "Then the land shall enjoy its Sabbaths as long as it lies desolate, while you are in your enemies' land; then the land shall rest, and enjoy its Sabbaths. As long as it lies desolate it shall have rest, the rest that it did not have on your Sabbaths when you were dwelling in it." (Leviticus 26:34-35)

The passage states that the land will make up for missed Sabbaths *while* it is desolate and "you are in your enemies' land." The full desolation and the clearing out of the population did not happen until the time of Jerusalem's destruction in 586 BC. Again, the period from 586 BC to 539 BC is not a period of seventy years.

Josephus, usually considered an accurate historian, has been relied upon for confirmation for the period of exile lasting seventy years in total. He references the previous passages when he states:

> "In the first year of the reign of Cyrus which was the seventieth from the day that our people were removed out of their own land into Babylon, God commiserated the captivity and calamity of these poor people, according as he had foretold to them by Jeremiah the prophet, before the destruction of the city, that after they had served Nebuchadnezzar and his posterity, and after they had undergone that servitude seventy years, he would restore them again to the land of their fathers, and they

should build their temple, and enjoy their ancient prosperity."[41]

However, in another work, he contradicts this information when he states:

> "These accounts agree with the true histories in our books; for in them it is written that Nebuchadnezzar, in the eighteenth year of his reign, laid our temple desolate, and so it lay in that state of obscurity for fifty years; but that in the second year of the reign of Cyrus its foundations were laid, and it was finished again in the second year of Darius."[42]

This account does match accurate historical dates. Unfortunately, he is among the first not to recognize the distinctions being made within the biblical passages and many others have followed suit.

The third mention of seventy years is found in Zechariah 1:12:

> "Then the angel of the Lord said, 'O Lord of hosts, how long will you have no mercy on Jerusalem and the cities of Judah, against which you have been angry these seventy years?'" (Zechariah 1:12)

Verse 7 of the chapter mentions the exact day that he gave this prophecy: "On the twenty-fourth day of the eleventh month, which is the month of Shebat, in the second year of Darius" – this was in 521 BC. Seventy years before, God had removed His Shekinah Glory from the temple in Jerusalem as described in Ezekiel 8-11.

The fourth mention of seventy years is in Zechariah 7:5:

> "In the fourth year of King Darius, the word of the Lord came to Zechariah on the fourth day of the ninth month,

---

41 [Josephus] Antiquities XI, 1, 1
42 [Josephus] Against Apion I, 154

> which is Chislev. ..."Say to all the people of the land and the priests, When you fasted and mourned in the fifth month and in the seventh, for these seventy years, was it for me that you fasted?"" (Zechariah 7:1, 5)

It had been seventy years since the final siege of Jerusalem and its eventual destruction in the fifth month of 586 BC.

The last passage specifically mentioning seventy years occurs in Isaiah 23 where he records an oracle warning the coastal city of Tyre, located north of Israel. He recorded prophecies during the eighth century BC at the height of the Assyrian empire and before the exile of the northern kingdom of Israel. The oracle begins by describing the world-renowned success Tyre and its sister city of Sidon have had as a sea faring merchant culture. They distributed the grain of Egypt throughout the Mediterranean (v 2-3). Ezekiel 27:12-25 lists the many other surrounding nations and the goods that were traded through this central hub. This led to incredible pride and God was planning to use them as an object lesson (v 5-12). However, verse 13 states: "Behold the land of the Chaldeans!" The surprise in this prophecy was that God intended to use the Babylonians as His agent of destruction. This seemed impossible since at this time the Assyrians had completely subjugated the Babylonians and "this is the people that was not; Assyria destined it for wild beasts" (v 13).

Nevertheless, just as in the prophecies of Jeremiah connecting the surrounding nations with a period of seventy years, "Tyre will be forgotten for seventy years" (v 15). At the end of that period, Tyre would be rebuilt and her merchant empire would be restored. This time, the profits would not be for their selfish gain "but her merchandise will supply abundant food and fine clothing for those who dwell before the Lord" (v 18).

Ezekiel records the prophesied destruction:

"Nebuchadnezzar king of Babylon made his army labor hard against Tyre. Every head was made bald, and every shoulder was rubbed bare, yet neither he nor his army got anything from Tyre to pay for the labor that he had performed against her. Therefore thus says the Lord God: Behold, I will give the land of Egypt to Nebuchadnezzar king of Babylon; and he shall carry off its wealth and despoil it and plunder it; and it shall be the wages for his army. I have given him the land of Egypt as his payment for which he labored, because they worked for me, declares the Lord God." (Ezekiel 29:18-20)

Ezra and Nehemiah record the prophesied restoration of the merchant economy:

"But the foundation of the temple of the Lord was not yet laid. So they gave money to the masons and the carpenters, and food, drink, and oil to the Sidonians and the Tyrians to bring cedar trees from Lebanon to the sea, to Joppa, according to the grant that they had from Cyrus king of Persia." (Ezra 3:6b-7)

"And I said to the king, "If it pleases the king, let letters be given me to the governors of the province Beyond the River, that they may let me pass through until I come to Judah, and a letter to Asaph, the keeper of the king's forest, that he may give me timber to make beams for the gates of the fortress of the temple, and for the wall of the city, and for the house that I shall occupy." And the king granted me what I asked, for the good hand of my God was upon me." (Nehemiah 2:7-8)

Upon examination, none of these statements about seventy years can be tied to the actual number of years of Jewish exile. So what was Daniel considering and finally understood at the start of Daniel 9? If the end of the empire of Babylon occurred in 539 BC, seventy years prior would be in 609 BC. That time period saw battles between the waning empire of the Assyrians who were allied with Egypt against the rising power of Babylon and her allies. A major battle occurred in 609 BC where the power of the Assyrians was broken and the era of Babylon began.

During that same battle, the Egyptian Pharaoh Necho killed King Josiah of Judah. Josiah had been a faithful reformer and reintroduced God's laws to the Jewish people. God promised him the following:

> "Behold, I will gather you to your fathers, and you shall be gathered to your grave in peace, and your eyes shall not see all the disaster that I will bring upon this place and its inhabitants." (2 Chronicles 34:28)

From Josiah's death in 609 BC onwards, Judah and the other surrounding nations were under threat from Babylon – for the next seventy years, until 539 BC.

Then, in the first year of Darius (539-538 BC), Daniel states that he had understood what Jeremiah had written in his letter (Jeremiah 29) and that the allotted time for Babylon was now over. The letter urged the exiles to call upon God, pray and seek Him with all their heart. This is the reason for Daniel's intercessory prayer in verses 3 through 19. In fact, his prayer is of such significance that many do not realize why God chose to speak the 70 Week prophecy in response. In verse 11, Daniel references "the curse and oath that are written in the Law of Moses." Forty years after the Exodus from Egypt, Moses gave his last instructions to Israel which included prophecy of both blessings and curses:

> "...all the nations will say, 'Why has the Lord done thus to this land? What caused the heat of this great anger?'

Then people will say, 'It is because they abandoned the covenant of the Lord, the God of their fathers, which he made with them when he brought them out of the land of Egypt, and went and served other gods and worshiped them, gods whom they had not known and whom he had not allotted to them. Therefore the anger of the Lord was kindled against this land, bringing upon it all the curses written in this book, and the Lord uprooted them from their land in anger and fury and great wrath, and cast them into another land, as they are this day'...

And when all these things come upon you, the blessing and the curse, which I have set before you, and you call them to mind among all the nations where the Lord your God has driven you, and return to the Lord your God, you and your children, and obey his voice in all that I command you today, with all your heart and with all your soul, then the Lord your God will restore your fortunes [captives] and have mercy on you, and he will gather you again from all the peoples where the Lord your God has scattered you." (Deuteronomy 29:24-28, 30:1-3)

During the dedication of the first temple four hundred and fifty years later, Solomon's prayer was also prophetic:

"If they sin against you—for there is no one who does not sin—and you are angry with them and give them to an enemy, so that they are carried away captive to the land of the enemy, far off or near, yet if they turn their heart in the land to which they have been carried captive, and repent and plead with you in the land of their captors, saying, 'We have sinned and have acted perversely and wickedly,' if they repent with all their mind and with all their heart in the land of their enemies, who carried them captive, and pray to you toward their land, which you gave to their fathers, the city that you have chosen, and the house that I have built for your name, then hear in heaven your dwelling place their prayer and their plea, and maintain their cause and forgive your people who have sinned against you, and all their transgressions that they have committed against you, and grant them compassion in the sight of those who carried them captive, that they may have compassion on them (for they are your people, and your heritage, which you brought out of Egypt, from the midst of the iron furnace)." (I Kings 8:46-51)

Four hundred and thirty years later, Daniel uses the very phrases from both of these passages within his prayer. He recognized that this was a prophetic pivot point and was convinced that the time of Jerusalem's judgement was over and was petitioning God to fulfill what He had promised. The time was up. "O Lord, pay attention and act. Delay not." (Daniel 9:19)

Chapter 12

The 7 Weeks

Gabriel instructs Daniel in Chapter 9:25 to both "know" and "understand" what he is about to say as he lays out the 70 Weeks prophecy. This implies that it was possible for Daniel to make sense of what was to follow.

The first time period, of 7 Weeks, starts from the issuing of a statement ("dabar") concerning two aspects about Jerusalem. The first is the Hebrew word "shub" (S#7725) and is defined as "to turn back, return." English translations always translate this word as "restore" in this passage. When used elsewhere, it is translated as "return." For example, the same word is used twice in the passage describing the captivity and eventual return of Egypt in the same era. The first instance in the following passage is translated "restore" and the second is translated as "bring them back."

> "For thus says the Lord God: At the end of forty years I will gather the Egyptians from the peoples among whom they were scattered, and I will **restore** the fortunes of Egypt and **bring them back** to the land of Pathros, the land of their origin, and there they shall be a lowly kingdom." (Ezekiel 29:13-14) [emphasis added]

The second aspect regarding Jerusalem is the Hebrew word "banah" (S# 1129) defined as "to build." Taken together then, the triggering statement is about the return to and the rebuilding of Jerusalem.

As we saw previously, the word "dabar" in this passage is also used when prophets speak on behalf of God. Before the angel's visit, Daniel had been studying what Jeremiah had to say on the subject of the completion of seventy years and the subsequent return to his homeland. Gabriel points Daniel to another prophecy found in Jeremiah which he states is the start of an additional new period of seventy; not seventy years but seventy weeks of years. Daniel would have been able to search this out and understand its connection to the 70 Weeks while he was still alive. If, as it is usually assumed, the start of the first 7 Weeks is Artaxerxes' decree in 444 BC (about one hundred years later), Daniel would have been long dead and could not have seen the start of the answer to his intercessory prayer which God had rewarded.

The "word of the Lord" which Gabriel referenced is found in Jeremiah 32. This event occurred during the 18th year of Nebuchadnezzar, during the last siege of Jerusalem and the year of its destruction in 587 BC. God informs Jeremiah to expect his cousin to approach him and want to sell him some property. This Jeremiah does and has the deed signed, witnessed and sealed. He is then instructed to place this binding transaction along with an open deed inside a jar so that they both will be preserved through the prophesied city's destruction. The reason given is:

> "For thus says the Lord of hosts, the God of Israel: 'Houses and fields and vineyards shall again be bought in this land.'" (Jeremiah 32: 15)

During a siege no one could enter or leave and the future of the people of Judah indeed looked grim. Even Jeremiah couldn't understand how it would be possible that the property he had just purchased would do him any good. He asked for understanding from God. God's response is in verses 26-44 and confirms that Jerusalem will be captured and completely demolished "so that I will remove it from my sight" (verse 31b). But verse 37 and verses 42-44 offer future hope:

> "Behold, I will gather them from all the countries to which I drove them in my anger and my wrath and in great indignation. I will **bring them back** to this place, and I will make them dwell in safety." (Jeremiah 32:37) [emphasis added]

> "For thus says the Lord: Just as I have brought all this great disaster upon this people, so I will bring upon them all the good that I promise them. Fields shall be bought in this land of which you are saying, 'It is a desolation, without man or beast; it is given into the hand of the Chaldeans.' Fields shall be bought for money, and deeds shall be signed and sealed and witnessed, in the land of Benjamin, in the places about Jerusalem, and in the cities of Judah, in the cities of the hill country, in the cities of the Shephelah, and in the cities of the Negeb; for I will **restore their fortunes**, declares the Lord." (Jeremiah 32:42-44) [emphasis added]

Verse 37 contains the same word "shub" or "bring them back" as found in the 7 Week description. Verses 42-44 describe the restoration of the land and of Jerusalem. "Restore their fortunes" in verse 44 is the same phrase seen previously in Ezekiel 29:13 and can also be translated as "return the captives." This passage in Jeremiah contains both aspects that Gabriel says should signal the start of the 7 Weeks and uses the identical words found in Daniel 9.

Nebuchadnezzar was coronated in 605 BC. His 18th year was in 587 BC – the year Jeremiah received this prophecy. Starting the 7 Weeks of years (49 years) from that point would end in 538 BC. This is the year that Cyrus proclaimed that the Jewish exiles could return to Jerusalem and resettle their land.

$$587 \text{ BC} + 49 \text{ years} = 538 \text{ BC}$$

"Now in the first year of Cyrus king of Persia, that the word of the Lord by the mouth of Jeremiah might be fulfilled, the Lord stirred up the spirit of Cyrus king of Persia, so that he made a proclamation throughout all his kingdom and also put it in writing: "Thus says Cyrus king of Persia, 'The Lord, the God of heaven, has given me all the kingdoms of the earth, and he has charged me to build him a house at Jerusalem, which is in Judah. Whoever is among you of all his people, may the Lord his God be with him. Let him go up.'" (2 Chronicles 36:22-23)

This decree of Cyrus is also repeated in Ezra 1:1-4. Notice that this was in fulfillment of the prophecy of Jeremiah and not necessarily the prophecy in Isaiah where Cyrus is specifically mentioned by name.

Therefore, the 7 Weeks refers to the forty-nine year period between God's promise that the exiles would return to resettle Jerusalem, and the decree of Cyrus who granted permission for it to take place. Daniel saw the fulfillment of the first 7 Weeks within his lifetime and it was proof of God's answered prayer and of the trustworthy completion of the still future Weeks of years.

Chapter 13

The 62 Weeks

Depending on which English translation is read, after a starting point has been decided on for the 7 Weeks, the common assumption is then to immediately combine the following 62 weeks into the same period of time. This would mean:

(7 weeks x 7) + (62 weeks x 7) = 483 years total

Taking 538 BC (Cyrus' decree) and adding 483 years, the end result is 55 BC. This date does not fit the description of the next mentioned anointed one. How should this group of Weeks be considered?

We have to jump to the last 1 Week described at the end of the prophecy for a clue. Anderson, Hoehner and other Scripture literalists recognize that the events described in the final 1 Week do not match with any historical events up until the present. They interpret the passage as a still future time period of seven years. This is especially evident when considering the stated purposes of the entire prophecy.

> "...to finish the transgression, to put an end to sin, and to atone for iniquity, to bring in everlasting righteousness..." (Daniel 9:24b)

The final fulfillment of these purposes has not been accomplished yet. It is recognized that there exists a gap of unspecified years between the end of the 62 Weeks and the start of the final 1 Week.

I have already conjectured that Gabriel was outlining a pattern in time; explicitly laying out three distinct and separate periods of years. If so, there would not just be a gap between the last two sets of Weeks but also a gap between the first and second sets of Weeks; again, an unspecified amount of time. Examining the description of what occurs in the 62 Weeks will specify exactly when that group of weeks should start.

The subject of the 62 Weeks is the rebuilding of the city of Jerusalem itself and that it will be a time of distress and anguish. Anderson's and Hoehner's recognition that the decree of Artaxerxes as the starting point for this period can be considered accurate. However, since they combine the first 7 Weeks together with the 62 Weeks, they have difficulty explaining what the purpose of those first 7 Weeks is during this period. Another scholar who agrees with this approach has suggested that it took forty-nine years to completely rebuild the city:

> "The best explanation seems to be that beginning with Nehemiah's decree and the building of the wall, it took a whole generation to clear out all the debris in Jerusalem and restore it as a thriving city. This might well be the fulfillment of the forty-nine years. The specific reference to streets again addresses our attention to Nehemiah's situation where the streets were covered with debris and needed to be rebuilt. That this was accomplished in troublesome times is fully documented by the book of Nehemiah itself."[43]

In their system of interpretation, these two time periods merge and it remains unclear as to why Gabriel separated them in the first place. They are only able to speculate. There is no evidence given for the proposal that the ultimate restoration of

---

43 [Walvoord] p. 227

Jerusalem took forty-nine years (seven weeks). According to the prophetic passage the *entire* 62 Week period is described as a "troubled time."

Laying that aside for the moment, if after some unspecified gap of years, the 62 Week countdown is started with Artaxerxes' decree in 444 BC to rebuild Jerusalem, going forward a period of 434 years (62 x 7) would terminate in 10 BC. This is roughly close to the accepted time period of the birth of Jesus Christ. However, God is not just *close* but *exact.*

REBUILDING JERUSALEM

The events described at the beginning of the book of Nehemiah are the connection for the start of the 62 Weeks. Nehemiah was cupbearer to the Persian king Artaxerxes and received a report about the current state of Jerusalem:

> "The remnant there in the province who had survived the exile is in great trouble and shame. The wall of Jerusalem is broken down, and its gates are destroyed by fire." (Nehemiah 1:3)

Later, even after the point when the city walls had just been rebuilt, Nehemiah states that the city inside was still in ruin:

> "The city was wide and large, but the people within it were few, and no houses had been rebuilt." (Nehemiah 7:4)

Jerusalem needed a lot of work. A few months after receiving the troubling report, sometime during the month of Nisan which was in Artaxerxes' twentieth year, Nehemiah asked for and received permission to return to Jerusalem and rebuild the walls and the city. Artaxerxes gave him letters allowing passage through the empire and for gathering resources needed for the construction of the gates and wall. Nothing is mentioned about his actual journey to Jerusalem and an unspecified time gap occurs between verses 8 and 9 in chapter 1.

Although a year is mentioned, there is no date of the month given when this request occurred. In other biblical narratives, if the writer thought the specific date was important, then it was included. In this case, are we to assume that the exact day of the decree is not important? Some further investigation is needed to determine when the rebuilding of Jerusalem began since this is the stated purpose of the 62 Weeks.

Following his request of Artaxerxes, Nehemiah's next mentioned date is of the completion of the wall of Jerusalem:

> "So the wall was finished on the twenty-fifth day of the month Elul, in fifty-two days." (Nehemiah 6:15)

Elul is the 6th month of the Jewish calendar; roughly the end of September. Counting back fifty-two days from that point, the construction of the wall began on the 3rd day of Av. Nehemiah 2:9 states that he arrived in Jerusalem at least three days before the start of construction; the 29th of Tammuz (roughly mid August).

Examining the calendar dates of 444 BC recorded in the "Babylonian Chronology", the month of Nisan occurred in early to mid April.[44][45] Is it likely that Nehemiah could have procured the needed building resources, prepared a new group of Jewish settlers, journeyed with a large caravan several hundred miles west and met with the governors of the surrounding region all within the time period of at most three and a half months?

---

44 [Parker] p. 30
45 This date also matches the abib barley calendar method described previously.

There is another similar journey of returning exiles during that period which is described in the Bible – in Ezra 7:

> "And there went up also to Jerusalem, in the seventh year of Artaxerxes the king, some of the people of Israel, and some of the priests and Levites, the singers and gatekeepers, and the temple servants. And Ezra came to Jerusalem in the fifth month, which was in the seventh year of the king. For on the first day of the first month he began to go up from Babylonia, and on the first day of the fifth month he came to Jerusalem, for the good hand of his God was on him." (Ezra 7:7-9)

Ezra describes his journey starting in Babylon on Nisan 1 and arriving in Jerusalem on Av 1. Just the journey itself took four months and he implies that they made very good time. Nehemiah, on the other hand, had to begin his journey in Susa, the capital of the Persian empire and not from Babylon.

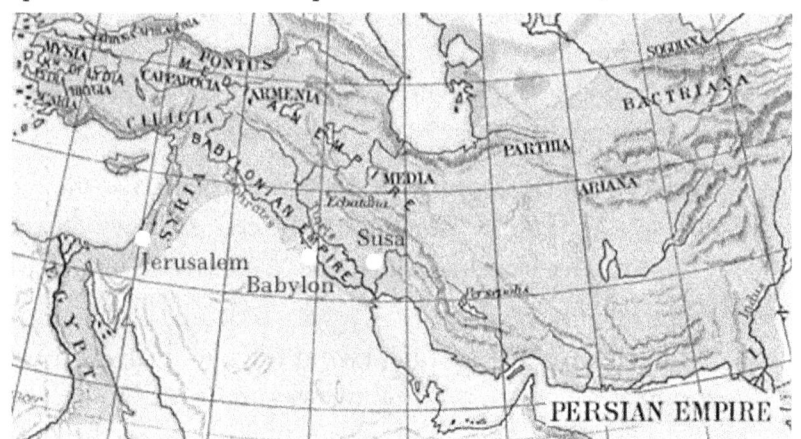

Illustration 1: Map of Susa, Babylon and Jerusalem [Grove]

This would be a further two hundred miles away to the east. It is therefore doubtful that the rebuilding could have occurred in the same year as Artaxerxes' decree. There is another account describing Nehemiah's time written by the historian Josephus who wrote in the first century AD:

"Now when he was come to Babylon, and had taken with him many of his countrymen, who voluntarily followed him, he came to Jerusalem in the twenty and fifth year of the reign of Xerxes."[46]

Biblical scholar John Bright considers this account by Josephus reputable:

"The Bible gives the impression that Nehemiah set out at once, accompanied by a military escort (Neh. 2:9). But Josephus (Ant. XI, 5, 7) who follows the Septuagint text, the first part of which is preserved in I Esdras, places his arrival only in 440. Though assurance is impossible, this may be correct. If Nehemiah first went to Babylon and collected Jews to accompany him (as Josephus has it), and then, having presented his credentials to the satrap of Abar-nahara, attended to the procurement of building materials before proceeding to Jerusalem (as he possibly did, since work was begun soon after his arrival), the date is not unreasonable. In any event, by 440 at the very latest he was in Jerusalem and had taken charge of affairs there."[47]

However, in Josephus' next passage he states that the walls took two years and four months to complete which contradicts Nehemiah's statement that the walls were finished in just fifty-two days:

"And this trouble he underwent for two years and four months: for in so long a time was the wall built, in the twenty-eighth year of the reign of Xerxes, in the ninth month."[48]

---

46 [Josephus] Antiquities XI, 5, 7
47 [Bright] p. 381
48 [Josephus] Antiquities XI, 5, 8

It is possible that the basic walls and gates were complete in fifty-two days and that it took the remaining time to fully shore up the wall's towers and fortifications.

Taking into account what Josephus records, there occurred a gap of four years between the issuing of the decree and the time when Jerusalem began to be rebuilt. 440 BC should be considered the start of the 62 Weeks.

$$440 \text{ BC} + 62 \text{ Weeks} = 6 \text{ BC}$$
$$(434 \text{ years})$$

6 BC is a very likely date for the birth of Jesus the Anointed One. We'll consider this more fully in a later chapter. Assuming this date for now, we can determine the proposed gap between the first two sets of Weeks.

$$538 \text{ BC} - 440 \text{ BC} = 98 \text{ years}$$
$$(14 \text{ Weeks of years})$$

Interestingly, notice that the unspoken gap of ninety-eight years also consists of Weeks of years. There is indeed a pattern emerging.

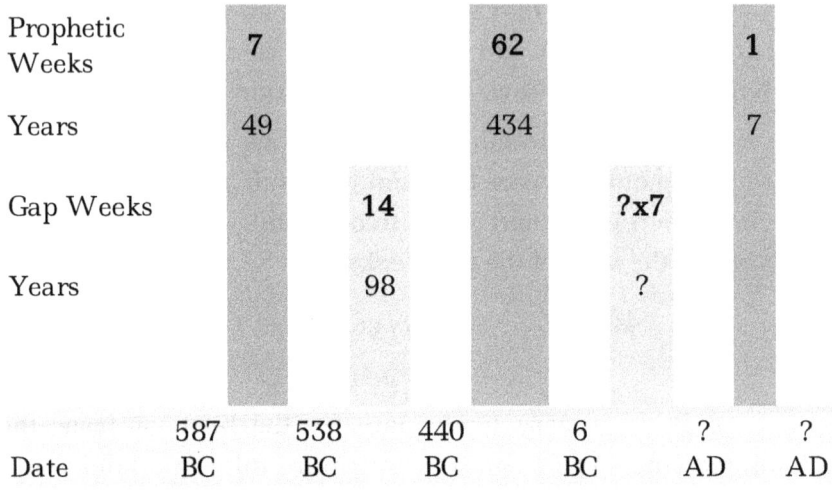

Table 5: Proposed pattern of weeks of years showing specified weeks and unspecified gaps

TIME OF DISTRESS AND ANGUISH

The period of reconstruction during Nehemiah's time wasn't the only time the walls were rebuilt and the temple restored, however. Most scholars who try to combine the first 7 Weeks with the following 62 Weeks and apply it to this time period do not recognize this. Over the following centuries, through the entire period of the 62 Weeks, Jerusalem faced multiple periods of destruction; it was truly a time of hardship. This period included the conquest by Antiochus Epiphanes and the Maccabean revolt. Josephus chronicled this period. Here are some passages relating how Jerusalem fared during this period with emphasis added.

> "And when he [Antiochus] had pillaged the whole city[Jerusalem], some of the inhabitants he slew, and some he carried captive, together with their wives and children, so that the multitude of those captives that

were taken alive amounted to about ten thousand. He also burnt down the finest buildings; and when he had **overthrown the city walls**, he built a citadel in the lower part of the city, for the place was high and overlooked the temple, on which account he fortified it with high walls, and towers, and put into it a garrison of Macedonians."[49]

There were threats of annihilation against the people.

"When King Antiochus heard of these things, he was very angry at what had happened: ...and that he should conquer Judea, and take its inhabitants for slaves, and **utterly destroy Jerusalem**, and abolish the whole nation."[50]

"Judas also **rebuilt the walls round about the city**; and reared towers of great height against the incursions of enemies, and set guards therein."[51]

"...they went out of the temple. But when Antiochus came into it, and saw how strong the place was, he broke his oaths, and **ordered his army that was there to pluck down the walls to the ground**; and when he had so done, he returned to Antioch."[52]

"I [Alexander, the son of Antiochus Epiphanes] also **give you leave to repair and rebuild your temple**, and that all be done at my expences. I also allow you to **build the walls of your city, and to erect high towers,**

---

49 [Josephus] Antiquities XII, 5, 4
50 [Josephus] Antiquities XII, 7, 2
51 [Josephus] Antiquities XII, 7, 7
52 [Josephus] Antiquities XII, 9, 7

and that they be erected at my charge. And if there be any fortified town that would be convenient for the Jewish country to have very strong, let it be so built at my expences."[53]

"When Simon and Jonathan had finished these affairs, they returned to Jerusalem, where Jonathan gathered all the people together, and took counsel to **restore the walls of Jerusalem**, and to **rebuild the wall that encompassed the temple**, which had been thrown down, and to make the places adjoining stronger by very high towers; and besides that, to build another wall in the midst of the city, in order to exclude the market-place from the garrison which was in the citadel, and by that means to hinder them from any plenty of provisions; and moreover, to make the fortresses that were in the country much stronger, and more defensible, than they were before."[54]

"Some time after this, when Alexander, the son of Aristobulus, made an incursion into Judea, Gabinius came from Rome into Syria, as commander of the Roman forces. He did many considerable actions: and particularly made war with Alexander, since Hyrcanus was not yet able to oppose his power, but was **already attempting to rebuild the wall of Jerusalem, which Pompey had overthrown** although the Romans, which were there, restrained him from that his design."[55]

---

53 [Josephus] Antiquities XIII, 2, 3
54 [Josephus] Antiquities XIII, 5, 11
55 [Josephus] Antiquities XIV, 5, 2

"And now **Herod**, in the eighteenth year of his reign, and after the acts already mentioned, undertook a very great work, that is, **to build of himself the temple of God, and make it larger in compass, and to raise it to a most magnificent altitude**, as esteeming it to be the most glorious of all his actions, as it really was, to bring it to perfection."[56]

---

56 [Josephus] Antiquities XV, 11, 1

Chapter 14

The 1 Week

Let's consider the final 1 Week before investigating the activities between the 62 Weeks and the 1 Week. The Week begins with a covenant or treaty. Halfway through the Week, sacrifice and offerings are stopped and the abomination of desolation occurs. The first half of verse 27 reads: "And he shall make a strong covenant with many for one week." This is a very pivotal verse since this marks for many people the start of the yet future portion of the prophecy. There are those who consider this entire section already having seen fulfillment at the time of the destruction of Jerusalem in the first century. This will be addressed but for many, on this one phrase they hang an entire prophetic system. Here again we must critically examine traditional understandings and compare them with how the Hebrew words are used elsewhere. The Hebrew passage starts with three significant words and we'll examine each one in turn.

THE VERB

The first word that begins the sentence is the Hebrew "gabar" (S# 1396) which is defined to mean "exceed, confirm, be great, be mighty, prevail, strengthen, be stronger." Most English translations add the pronoun "he" as the subject of all the verbs in this section. For example the ESV has: "he shall make a strong covenant", "he shall put an end to sacrifice" and "shall come one who makes desolate." There are no pronouns used in the Hebrew (or Aramaic). They are added as a result of the particular form of the Hebrew verbs; they specify masculine singular. Translators associate these verbs with the last stated antecedent found in the previous verse – the "prince to come." Translations such as these result in the common interpretation that the start of the final 70th Week begins when the prince to come actively strengthens or confirms a treaty with many. The treaty is assumed to be a peace treaty allowing the temple sacrifices to commence. This is assumed since at the mid-point of the Week, the then ongoing sacrifices and offerings are suddenly forced to stop.

However, examining the verb forms more closely reveals that they are in the "hiphal" state or, in other words, the subject does not actively do the action but is instead the cause of the action. A Hebrew grammar states: "the grammatical subject of a given Hifil verb is an entity (E1) which causes another entity (E2) to do something or become something whereby E1 might execute the action himself or charge some other entity (E3) with the task. It could involve compulsion(9), but not necessarily."[57] The subject, although responsible, is secondary to the action on the object. Almost all English translations are quite clear in making the subject directly active by either stating "he shall make" or "he shall confirm" instead of more accurately rendering the subject as the cause of the action to occur. The act of strengthening or making firm is a causal result of his other intentional actions.

---

57 [Jouon] p. 151

It is always helpful to compare other similar usages of the terms. Of direct relevance, earlier in Daniel 9, most translations also make use of the word "confirm." "He has confirmed his words, which he spoke against us..." (Daniel 9:12). Daniel is stating that God has caused His word that He spoke earlier to be raised, to stand up and be fulfilled. The Hebrew verb is from the root "qum" (S# 6965) and is also in the hiphal state. Here, God, as the subject, does not directly raise His words, but by His subsequent actions, His initial words are caused to stand. Here are two different words used in the Hebrew but the translators have chosen to make use of the same English concept. This shows how vital it is to investigate the details in the ancient text itself.

Daniel 9:27 is the only place where that particular singular verb form of "gabar" occurs in the Hebrew Scriptures. There is one instance where the plural form occurs: "With our tongue we will prevail" (Psalm 12:4). The usage here suggests more than just strengthening but has the sense of overcoming and being victorious – which is a notable added intensity in meaning.

Since the Hebrew hardly provides any other places in which to compare the usage, it is helpful to examine the Aramaic translation as well. Then the Hebrew equivalent word can be examined to see if that gives any further insights. There are three relevant passages where the same Aramaic verb form as Daniel 9:27 occurs. First, in Exodus 4:21 where it states "I will harden his heart." The Hebrew equivalent makes use of "chazaq" (S# 2388) or "to be or grow firm, strong, strengthen." The meanings of the two words are indeed very similar.

The second passage is in Daniel 11:1 where "I [Gabriel]...stood to strengthen and protect [the archangel Michael]." Here two verbs are used that work together to express the concept. The first word makes use of the same "chazaq." The second is from the root "maoz" (S# 4581) meaning "a protection."

The third is found in Deuteronomy 3:28: "But charge Joshua and encourage and strengthen him." The word translated as "encourage" is again "chazaq." The other is from the Hebrew "amets" (S# 553) meaning "to be stout, strong, bold, alert."

These various uses suggest a sense of resoluteness, or shoring up against adversity – both in a positive or negative manner. There is an adjustment in character involved not merely the nebulous idea of strength or firmness.

THE NOUN

The second word in Daniel 9:27 is the noun "berith" (S# 1285) and is commonly used of the covenant between God and Israel in the Old Testament (the vast majority of the 1,285 times it occurs). Actually, the word occurs earlier in the chapter within Daniel's initial prayer:

> "I prayed to the LORD my God and made confession, saying, "O Lord, the great and awesome God, who keeps covenant and steadfast love with those who love him and keep his commandments..."" (Daniel 9:4)

In Leviticus, God is the One confirming His covenant with His nation if they remain faithful to Him: "I will turn to you and make you fruitful and multiply you and will confirm my covenant with you" (Leviticus 26:9). The word translated as "confirm" (S#6965) means "to fulfill."

The word for covenant, "berith", was also used (though, less commonly) between Israel and her neighbors:

> "And he said, "I brought you up from Egypt and brought you into the land that I swore to give to your fathers. I said, 'I will never break my covenant with you, and you

shall make no covenant with the inhabitants of this land...'" (Judges 2:1b)

The word occurs seven times within Daniel 9 to 11. A particularly significant occurrence is in Chapter 11:

> "Armies shall be utterly swept away before him and broken, even the prince of the **covenant**. And from the time that an **alliance** is made with him he shall act deceitfully, and he shall become strong with a small people." (Daniel 11:22-23) [emphasis added]

In this passage, both "covenant" and "alliance" are used in a portion that has seen historical fulfillment. It describes the rise of Antiochus Epiphanes in 175 BC when he deposed the last of the hereditary line of Zadok, the High Priest. Onias III was removed in favor of an alliance with the Jews who supported the Hellenization of Judea. "Prince of the covenant" is used to signify the leader of those who followed the godly laws. The word translated as "alliance" is from "chabar" (S# 2266) meaning "to unite, be joined, to charm." Earlier in the chapter, the Hebrew "meshar" (S# 4339) is used meaning "agreement, equity, arrangement." Every time the word for "covenant" is used in Daniel, it is used of the relationship between God and His faithful Jewish people which leads to a specific assumption of its use in Daniel 9:27. An entirely different Hebrew word for alliance or agreement is used when talking about the future evil rulers and their machinations.

There is a significant usage of "covenant" in Isaiah 42 where God describes His chosen servant:

> "Behold my servant, whom I uphold,
>   my chosen, in whom my soul delights;
> I have put my Spirit upon him;
>   he will bring forth justice to the nations.
> He will not cry aloud or lift up his voice,
>   or make it heard in the street;

> a bruised reed he will not break,
>> and a faintly burning wick he will not quench;
>> he will faithfully bring forth justice.
> He will not grow faint or be discouraged
>> till he has established justice in the earth;
>> and the coastlands wait for his law.
>
> Thus says God, the Lord,
>> who created the heavens and stretched them out,
>> who spread out the earth and what comes from it,
>> who gives breath to the people on it
>> and spirit to those who walk in it:
> "I am the Lord; I have called you in righteousness;
>> **I will take you by the hand and keep you;**
> **I will give you as a covenant for the people,**
>> **a light for the nations,**
>> to open the eyes that are blind,
> to bring out the prisoners from the dungeon,
>> from the prison those who sit in darkness.
> I am the Lord; that is my name;
>> my glory I give to no other,
>> nor my praise to carved idols.
> Behold, the former things have come to pass,
>> and **new things** I now declare;
> **before they spring forth**
>> I tell you of them." (Isaiah 42:1-9) [emphasis added]

In verse 1, God describes this individual as His chosen and has anointed him with His Spirit making him God's anointed one. Later, in verse 6, God announces that He will give the anointed one "as a covenant for the people." "The people" is the Hebrew word "am" (S#5971) and is commonly used for the Jewish nation. This is as opposed to the word used in the next phrase of "gowyim" (S#1471) which is commonly used to refer to the Gentile nations. Here is a direct reference of something coming that is new; that God will give the anointed one as a covenant and he will belong to the many.

The phrase "take you by the hand and keep you" is also very relevant to Daniel 9:27 although it is not immediately obvious in the English translation. The word translated as "will take you by" is "chazaq" (S#2388) or "make strong, strengthen" which we have seen before. The word for "your hand" is "bəyādekā" (S#3027) and is figuratively used of someone's power, control and possessions. The word translated as "keep you" is "wə'es·sā·rə·kā" (S#5341) meaning "watch over, guard, preserve." Here is a statement that God will increase the strength of this anointed's possessive power and will watch over the people with whom the covenant is made.

THE ADJECTIVE

The third word in Daniel 9:27 is the adjective which describes the covenant and is from the Hebrew root "rabbim" (S# 7227) meaning "many, much." In addition it is prefixed by the preposition "to/for." Most translations render the phrase "covenant *with* many" however, it occurs elsewhere in Daniel 11:33 and most translations include "to" so the preposition is not treated consistently in English. The preposition as found in the Aramaic is also "to/for" and signifies relationship, possession and marks the definite direct object; it is the "covenant *belonging to* the many."

Although this exact phrase does not occur elsewhere in the Hebrew Old Testament, this idea of a covenant for many is stated in the Aramaic Peshitta New Testament. This phrase is found in two of the accounts of the last supper of Jesus:

"And he took a cup, and when he had given thanks he gave it to them, saying, "Drink of it, all of you, for this is my blood of the [new] **covenant**, which is poured out **for many** for the forgiveness of sins.""" (Matthew 26:27,28) [emphasis added]

"And he said to them, "This is my blood of the [new] **covenant**, which is poured out **for many**."" (Mark 14:24) [emphasis added]

Both English translations insert the clause "which is poured out" between "covenant" and the adjective "for many." This word order matches the Greek passage of Mark. However, the Greek passage of Matthew reads "covenant for many." Both passages in Aramaic place the verb clause at the end of the phrase so that the two adjectives are directly after the noun that they describe: literally "covenant new for many."[58] This is a direct reference to the passage in Isaiah 42 that we examined earlier.

Each vision that Daniel experienced portrayed the same future history by using different concepts and different terms. It is always about a future ruler who causes a remnant of the godly people to be challenged, refined, perfected and strengthened until the final fulfillment. The last summary statement about this group occurs in Daniel 12: "Many shall purify themselves and make themselves white and be refined, but the wicked shall act wickedly. And none of the wicked shall understand, but those who are wise shall understand." (Daniel 12: 10).

Throughout Daniel 7, these faithful are described as saints or "qaddish" (S# 6922) or holy ones. Daniel 8:24 refers to them as "mighty" or "atsum" (S# 6099) which can also have the sense of being "numerous." However, in the Aramaic, the

---

58 [Dukhrana] Matt. 26:27, 28; Mark 14:24

word specifically means "strong, firm, fortified." This passage describes the faithful as already being mighty and strong in character. Daniel 9:27 shows them when the process begins at the start of the final Week. The people of the covenant will be caused to be strong and stand firm. Throughout Daniel 11:29-35, the many are linked to the covenant and a time of being "refined, purified, and made white." Daniel 12:3 specifies the ultimate reward for those who have instructed the many in the ways of righteousness. All of these passages describe the many and how their character will undergo a strengthening through the hardships brought about by the final ruler.

Therefore, instead of a very tenuous reference to the "prince to come" who makes a peace treaty, the words as they occur in Isaiah and later in Daniel would seem to point to a very different understanding of the first phrase of Daniel 9:27. When these concepts are applied, there seems to be a contrast being made between verse 26 and verse 27. In verse 26, the result of the anointed one being cut off is that he "is not" or, in other words, the covenant between he and the specific people this prophecy is targeting will not exist or be in place. And to further underscore this, even the visible objects of the covenant – that of Jerusalem and the temple – are destroyed at that point. However, in verse 27, the covenant these people possess will be caused to be fortified or strengthened so that it will again exist throughout the final 1 Week because the visible signs of worship, that of daily offering and sacrifice, are again taking place – at least until the middle of the final Week. And to be clear, this does not support the idea of Replacement Theology or that the Church assumes the position of Israel in this covenant relationship. Daniel 9 is addressed to the Jewish people and its subject matter is entirely concerned with God's work with His chosen nation.

MIDDLE OF THE WEEK

Even though the future ruler mentioned in verse 26 might not be actively doing the action of the first phrase of verse 27, the next actions mentioned do have a direct connection with him. Verses 24-27 are an overview of history from the Jewish people's perspective. The chapters 10-12 which follow give a much more detailed description of future events starting from Daniel's time until the end of the 70 Weeks. Scholars can determine historical fulfillment of events described in Daniel 10 up through Daniel 11:28. From Daniel 11:36 and onwards most scholars consider referring to a yet future time – sometime within the last 1 Week. This is evident from the Bible interpreting itself which is found at the end of the prophecy where 3 ½ years are specified as the latter half of 1 Week:

> "And I heard the man clothed in linen, who was above the waters of the stream; he raised his right hand and his left hand toward heaven and swore by him who lives forever that it would be for a **time, times, and half a time,** and that when the shattering of the power of the holy people comes to an end **all these things would be finished.**" (Daniel 12:7) [emphasis added]

It is verses 29-35 that are not as clearly defined where history morphs into yet future events:

> "At the time appointed he shall return and come into the south, but it shall not be this time as it was before. For ships of Kittim shall come against him, and he shall be afraid and withdraw, and shall turn back and be enraged and take action against the holy covenant. He shall turn back and pay attention to those who forsake the holy covenant. Forces from him shall appear and profane the temple and fortress, and shall take away the regular burnt offering. And they shall set up the abomi-

nation that makes desolate. He shall seduce with flattery those who violate the covenant, but the people who know their God shall stand firm and take action. And the wise among the people shall make many understand, though for some days they shall stumble by sword and flame, by captivity and plunder. When they stumble, they shall receive a little help. And many shall join themselves to them with flattery, and some of the wise shall stumble, so that they may be refined, purified, and made white, until the time of the end, for it still awaits the appointed time." (Daniel 11:29-35)

There are those who seek to interpret this entire passage as having been fulfilled at the time of Antiochus Epiphanes – who did place an idol in the temple of Jerusalem and stop the Jewish system of offerings. This would make sense except for two major issues. First, verse 35 specifically gives the time cue "the time of the end." And secondly, Jesus points to a yet future tragedy when the "abomination of desolation spoken of by the prophet Daniel" takes place (Matthew 24:15). Jesus was answering the disciples' question of when will be "the end of the age" (Matthew 24:3b).

However, there are those who accept that Jesus was speaking of a time yet future from His statement but seek to find total fulfillment when Titus destroyed Jerusalem and the temple in 70 AD. They point to the account by the historian Josephus as proof of the "abomination of desolation":

"And now the Romans, upon the flight of the seditious into the city, and upon the burning of the holy house itself, and of all the buildings round about it, brought their ensigns to the temple and set them over against its eastern gate; and there did they offer sacrifices to them, and there did they make Titus imperator with the greatest acclamations of joy."[59]

However, Josephus describes how the temple was burnt before Titus even had a chance to enter it and this was not according to his orders. He only entered once the whole complex was already engulfed and did not do anything to desecrate the holy sanctuary. The Roman sacrifices that were made afterwards, occurred outside the temple complex proper and were set up against the wall since no buildings remained standing. It is very problematic to associate these actions with fulfillment of Daniel 11 or the final 70th Week.

Returning to Daniel 11:29-35, notice the parallels with Daniel 9:27. Both passages mention that the daily offerings are caused to cease and the abomination of desolation is set up. Daniel 11:31 states that the ruler's army is responsible for this which also matches the verb tense in Daniel 9:27 where these events are caused to happen by the ruler. But only two of the events of Daniel 9:27 match – a supposed peace treaty by the final ruler is not mentioned at all. However, Daniel 11 does include the word "covenant" several times in the passage; along with the adjective "holy." The passage describes two groups of people. First are those who are followers of the holy covenant whom the future ruler takes hostile action against (verse 30), who instruct many about the covenant and are killed by the sword and fire and made captive and plundered (verse 33). The second group are those who reject the covenant and who the ruler takes advantage of with flattery (verse 32). The holy covenant plays a very prominent role in the passage. Verse 32 also states that "the people who know their God shall stand firm". The word translated as "stand firm" is the same root word "chazaq" (S#2388) that has been used continually through the passages that have been examined. The final statement

---

[59] [Josephus] Wars 6, 316

about the covenant for many is in the recorded interpretation in Daniel 12:

> "Many shall purify themselves and make themselves white and be refined, but the wicked shall act wickedly. And none of the wicked shall understand, but those who are wise shall understand." (Daniel 12:10)

ABOMINATION OF DESOLATION

The "abomination of desolation" is a phrase that has intrigued many through the ages. As mentioned, Antiochus Epiphanes desecrated the temple in 167 BC and stopped the sacrifices. Jesus said that this would happen again at a future time. Daniel 9:27 contains a word describing the abomination – "kanaph" (S#3671) – which is translated all sorts of ways in various English translations: edge, wing, flap, overspreading. There is no consensus as to the meaning. In addition, the preposition "al" meaning "on, upon, above" is used which most translations do not accurately represent. This is unfortunate since considering these details in the text show that Daniel 9 is not referring to Antiochus at all.

Examining the Aramaic Peshitta, a text of similar ancient origin as the Masoretic Hebrew, there is more insight as to the proper meaning. The same Aramaic word found in Daniel 9:27 is found in Matthew 4 and Luke 4:9 of the second temptation of Jesus:

> "Then the devil took him to the holy city and set him **on the pinnacle** of the temple and said to him, "If you are the Son of God, throw yourself down, for it is written, 'He will command his angels concerning you,'"" (Matthew 4:5,6) [emphasis added]

The word found in both passages is "k'enp,a" meaning "battlement, highest point of a structure, pinnacle"[60]. The preposition used is also "on, above." Applying this back to Daniel 9, the abomination is placed on or above some high place of the future temple structure. Although there probably will also be some action taken inside the sanctuary itself, Daniel is specifically including this detail as the sign to watch out for.

It is also interesting to compare how the two terms "abomination" and "of desolation" are used since the terms are used by Jesus and directly tied to Daniel. The terms occur twice together: Matthew 24:15 and Mark 13:14. For "abomination" the Greek word "bdelygma" (S#946) is used and is defined as "an accursed thing." The same passage in Aramaic uses the word "Tanp,t,a" and is defined as "defiled, unclean, impure, filthy"[61]. Although the Greek term is only found two other times in the Gospels, the Aramaic word occurs eighteen other times in the Gospels and is always used to describe the evil/unclean demons.

Two different Aramaic words translated as "desolation" are used in the Old Testament and New Testament. In Daniel, the word "ḥabbāl" defined as "to damage, destroy, corrupt"[62] is used. It occurs 40 times in the Aramaic scriptures including the following notable usages: Genesis 5:13 – destruction of the pre-flood world, Genesis 13:10 – destruction of Sodom and Gomorrah, Exodus 12:23 – the destroying angel of the Passover, Matthew 6:19 – where moth and rust corrupt. The Aramaic word used instead in the New Testament is "Huwrb'a" defined as "wilderness, plain, desolation"[63]. Jesus also uses the word in

---

60 [Dukhrana] Matthew 4:5,6
61 [Dukhrana] Matthew 24:15, Mark 13:14
62 [CAL] Daniel 9:27
63 [Dukhrana] Matthew 24:15

Luke 21:20 in his warning sign of when the desolation of Jerusalem is near. The word occurs 24 times in the Gospels and is used of the wilderness/desolate area that was the home of John the Baptizer and of the places Jesus withdrew to to get away from the crowds of people.

Even though the word used in Daniel "ḥabbāl" is not used in the same phrase in the New Testament, a similar word is found earlier in Jesus' discussions of the abomination recorded in Matthew 24 and Mark 13. This occurs in Matthew 24:8 and Mark 13:8 describing "only the beginning of birth pains" and is the word "Heb,le" defined as "sorrows, travail, pangs, throes."[64] The two words are related in that they both contain the same root consonants and only the vowel pronunciation is different.

NOTE OF INTEREST

There is another phrase of interest when comparing the Aramaic version's choice of words. Gabriel informs Daniel:

> "But you, Daniel, shut up the words and seal the book, until the time of the end. Many **shall run to and fro**, and knowledge shall increase." (Daniel 12:4) [emphasis added]

The Hebrew root word is "shuwt" (S#7751) and is defined as "go eagerly, quickly, to and fro".[65] The Aramaic uses a different word which is defined as "to seek, to beg, to inquire, to investigate."[66] This same word is used twelve other times in the Aramaic portion of the Hebrew version of Daniel. It really has

---

64 [Dukhrana] Mathew 24:8, Mark 13:8
65 [BibleHub] Daniel 12:4
66 [CAL] Daniel 12:4

nothing to do with transportation getting faster as technology improves as some would interpret this passage. The proper sense is that as the time of the final end approaches, many will seek and petition God for understanding and answers will be revealed for the prophecies sealed since the time of Daniel.

Summary

We have investigated various aspects of the 70 Weeks prophecy Gabriel gave to Daniel. Anderson's very popular interpretation, although attempting to interpret the prophecy literally, when compared with the details of the Hebrew calendar, cannot be considered accurate.

An alternative interpretation was developed which is based on examining the prophetic text in the Hebrew and Aramaic languages. Although a unique view, it still treats the passage in a literal fashion. A pattern of time emerged where the three distinct groups of Weeks are separated by an unspoken and unspecified number of years which also consist of Weeks of years. In a few chapters, an additional layer of calendar investigation will be added which will give additional credibility for this pattern of time.

The three separate groups of Weeks were investigated. The first, ending with King Cyrus, is especially important since Gabriel specifically points to prophecies in Jeremiah as the starting point for the 70 Weeks. This first group of Weeks was fulfilled during Daniel's lifetime and was a direct answer to his prayer which was the reason for Gabriel's visit in the first place.

The return to and rebuilding of Jerusalem was the main consideration of the 62 Weeks. Determining an accurate timeline of Nehemiah's activities is an important key in revealing how the blueprint of the unspoken gaps between the Weeks have been laid out. This results in the year of 6 BC as a very significant year.

The final 1 Week contained three concepts that have intrigued many through the ages. Instead of the covenant for many being linked directly with the prince to come, evidence was developed that the connection is with the anointed one as something new that God was doing for His people. Similar phrases used in Isaiah, Daniel 10-11 and the Aramaic language Gospels tied these concepts together. Comparisons of word usage for how "abomination" and "of desolation" are used within the Old and New Testaments rounded out the discussion.

The next part will investigate the activities described immediately after the 62 Weeks; namely of an Anointed One.

Part 3

The Birth and Sacrifice of Jesus Christ

Overview

We have investigated the three sets of Weeks of years. I propose that the end of the 62 Weeks occurred in 6 BC. The passage in Daniel then continues and states that after the 62 Weeks is complete, an anointed one would be killed and the city of Jerusalem and the temple would be destroyed. Jerusalem was destroyed and the population dispersed in 70 AD. It is commonly viewed that the anointed one spoken of is Christ Jesus, whose lifetime was indeed before the destruction of Jerusalem. Can the investigation into the Hebrew calendar shed light on the birth and death and resurrection of this Anointed One?

Chapter 15

The Year of Christ's Birth

Many people have tried to pin down exactly when the birth of Jesus occurred. I propose that 6 BC is the actual year and would like to focus on a few of the major details in the Gospel narratives that point to this general time: the reign of King Herod, the census of Augustus, the governorship of Quirinius and the quest of the Magi. In presenting the various topics, only a summary of the evidences are discussed. Much more detail is given in the sources that are listed and in fact, entire books have been written about these topics themselves.

KING HEROD

Nowhere in Scripture is the exact numerical year or even the exact date given for the birth. It is surprising that even though the change in eras from BC to AD is based on the birth of Jesus Christ, there is still so much uncertainty about the chronology of the period. The year numbering for BC/AD of the Julian/Gregorian calendar was determined by a monk named Dionysius around 525 AD.

Originally the years were numbered beginning with the founding of Rome or the first year of Emperor Diocletian. Dionysius did not want the years to rely on a pagan ruler but wanted to memorialize the "Incarnation of our Lord Jesus Christ." Since that time, however, scholars have realized he had determined the wrong date but they have not found any obvious reason for his error.[67]

In Matthew's gospel, King Herod plays an integral role in the narrative of the birth. Scholars have alternatively placed Herod's death in either 4 BC or 1 BC. The birth of Jesus is considered at least two years prior since Herod desired the death of all the male children in Bethlehem younger than two years old (Matthew 2:13). As a result, dates proposed for the Nativity are in 6 BC or 3 BC and some propose various years within this range.

Although the Bible does not contain any details which can be used to date the reign of Herod, the writings of the historian Josephus do. These various details, like puzzle pieces, can be used to reconstruct the dates for the start and end of his reign.

Herod was installed as ruler by order of Octavian, the Roman emperor. His subsequent mission was to attack and capture Jerusalem and depose Antigonus, the current ruler. Josephus records the siege of the city as taking place during summer and describes how the residents "persisted in this war to the very last; and this they did while a mighty army lay round about them, and while they were distressed by famine and the want of necessaries, for this happened to be a Sabbatic year."[68] Since, by definition, Sabbatic years occurred every seven years, it would seem to be a simple thing to determine which year this was. However, no official temple records have

---
67 [EWB]
68 [Josephus] Antiquities 14, 16, 2

been found which might state when these years occurred.[69] Josephus includes several other historical markers:

> "This destruction befell the city of Jerusalem when Marcus Agrippa and Caninius Gallus were consuls of Rome on the hundred eighty and fifth olympiad, on the third month, on the solemnity of the fast."[70]

Investigating the details in the reverse order, the mentioned Jewish fast is probably the Day of Atonement, a fast that always occurs on the tenth day of Tishri. This fast is known as the most solemn day: "It is a Sabbath of solemn rest to you" (Deuteronomy 16:31). Josephus states this was in the third month as related to the start of the Olympiad. The Olympiad started on the day of the first full moon after the summer solstice which confirms that the third month contained the Day of Atonement in the calendar. This was in the 185th Olympiad; each a group of four years. The first Olympiad occurred in 776 BC with the 185th range of years between 40 and 37 BC. Agrippa and Gallus were made consuls of Rome in 37 BC.

Josephus continues and describes the death of Herod:

> "Now it happened, that during the time of the high priesthood of this Matthias, there was another person made high priest for a single day, **that very day which the Jews observed as a fast**. The occasion was this: This Matthias the high priest, on the night before that day when the fast was to be celebrated, seemed, in a dream, to have conversation with his wife; and because he could not officiate himself on that account, Joseph, the son of Ellemus, his kinsman, assisted him in that sacred

---

69 A chronology of the Bible which accurately takes into account all dates mentioned in Scripture would verify the Sabbatical year cycle. However, that is not the focus of this work and this evidence can not be developed here.

70 [Josephus] Antiquities 14, 16, 4

office. But Herod deprived this Matthias of the high priesthood, and burnt the other Matthias, who had raised the sedition, with his companions, alive. And **that very night there was an eclipse of the moon.**"[71] [emphasis added]

"When he [Herod] had done these things, he died, the fifth day after he had caused Antipater to be slain; having reigned, since he had procured Antigonus to be slain, thirty-four years; but since he had been declared king by the Romans, thirty-seven."[72]

Shortly after a legislated period of mourning, a group formed committed to violence in order to avenge the death of Matthias and others that Herod had put to death. Their demise occurred "upon the approach of that feast of unleavened bread, which the law of their fathers had appointed for the Jews at this time, which feast is called the Passover."[73]

These details specify that Herod's death occurred shortly after a lunar eclipse during a fast and shortly before the following Passover which was thirty-four years from the time Antigonus had been executed. Since the Jewish calendar is tied to phases of the moon, a lunar eclipse can only occur at the middle of a month during the full moon phase. The only Jewish fast which occurs during the middle of the month is the Fast of Esther or Purim which takes place in February/March.

---

71 [Josephus] Antiquities 17, 6, 4
72 [Josephus] Antiquities 17, 8, 1
73 [Josephus] Antiquities 17, 9, 3

Date	Eclipse	Time	
Mar 13, 4 BC	partial	3:37 TD	During Purim
Sep 5, 4 BC	partial		Not visible in Judea
Jan 31, 3 BC	penumbral		Not visible in Judea
Mar 2, 3 BC	penumbral	4:02 TD	During Purim
Jul 27, 3 BC	penumbral		Not during fast
Aug 26, 3 BC	penumbral		Not during fast

Table 6: List of lunar eclipses around Herod's death

Although the 3 BC eclipse occurred during the appropriate time of the year, the particular type of eclipse would have been very difficult to observe. The partial eclipse during March of 4 BC is the most likely candidate. The Passover took place a month later with the death of Herod having occurred between those events. Starting at 37 BC and using inclusive reckoning, thirty-four years later also ends in 4 BC.

CAESAR AUGUSTUS

Caesar Augustus wrote of his accomplishments during his reign and listed the various times a census was taken: 28 BC, 8 BC and 14 AD.

> "When I was consul the fifth time (29 B.C.E.), I increased the number of patricians by order of the people and senate. I read the roll of the senate three times, and in my sixth consulate (28 B.C.E.) I made a census of the people with Marcus Agrippa as my colleague. I conducted a lustrum, after a forty-one year gap, in which lustrum were counted 4,063,000 heads of Roman citizens. Then again, with consular imperium I conducted a lustrum alone when Gaius Censorinus and Gaius Asinius were consuls (8 B.C.E.), in which lustrum were counted

4,233,000 heads of Roman citizens. And the third time, with consular imperium, I conducted a lustrum with my son Tiberius Caesar as colleague, when Sextus Pompeius and Sextus Appuleius were consuls (14 A.C.E.), in which lustrum were counted 4,937,000 of the heads of Roman citizens."[74]

Although the census of 14 AD is obviously too late to be the one referenced by Luke, there have been questions raised when trying to connect the 8 BC census of Augustus. It is said that the census was only of Roman citizens in Roman provinces – which Judea was not at that time. However, there are records that show other Roman client kingdoms were included in these types of census. The requirement that all family members, no matter their nationality, had to go personally to their place of ancestry instead of just to the local taxation centre has been shown as a Roman requirement in ancient papyri. The purpose wasn't to pay taxes at that point, but to register all family members for taxation in the future.[75]

Quirinius

Luke's narrative mentions Quirinius. In Luke 2:2, almost all popular English translations give him the title of governor of Syria. However, historical records show that Quirinius did not have the title and position of Governor until 6 AD and he oversaw a census of the region after that point. This is detailed in the writings of Josephus. This information gives rise to what some say is a contradiction since the time period of the 8 BC census can not be reconciled with the historical information pointing to after 6 AD.

---

74 [Augustus]
75 [Caesar]

Date	Name
23-13 BC	M. Agrippa
ca. 12-10 BC	M. Titius
9-6 BC	S. Sentius Saturninus
6-4 BC	P. Quinctilius Varus
4-1 BC	L. Calpurnius Piso (?)
1 BC – 4 AD	Gaius Caesar
4 – ca. 5 AD	L. Volusius Saturninus
6 – after 7 AD	P. Sulpicius Quirinius
13- 17 AD	Q. Caecilius Metellus Creticus Silanus

Table 7: Roman governors of Syria from 23 BC - 17 AD[76]

The word translated as "governor" as used in Luke's Greek gospel is not a noun but a verb – "was governing" (S#2230). This does not state an official governmental title but is pointing to the time when Quirinius was active in that provincial region of Syria. Records do exist that show he was active in the region's political structure over the decade previous to his official position of Governor; however, records don't exist as to the exact timing of his positions.[77] A possible translation of Luke 2:2 reads: "it was the first census in the period of time when Quirinius was governing in Syria." Therefore, Luke is making a definite distinction between Quirinius' later census and the earlier one he oversaw on behalf of Augustus.

Tertullian's writings in 211 AD make mention of the census that is recorded in Luke's narrative. However, instead of stating that the title of Governor belonged to Quirinius, he lists the historically accurate name of Sentius Saturninus. "At that time there were censuses that had been taken in Judea under Augustus by Sentius Saturninus, in which they may have

---

76 [Molnar] p.59
77 [Compton] p. 45-54

enquired about Jesus' ancestry."[78] The supposed textual contradiction does not even get mentioned in his discussion.

The second issue raised about Luke 2:2 is the Greek usage of the word "first." Many English translations treat it as an adjective for the census (i.e. "this first census"). However, the King James version treats it as an adverb: "this taxing was first made". Dr. Wallace, a New Testament Greek scholar, says "this issue cannot be resolved with certainty,"[79] and especially does not like the option of treating it as an adjective of the census since he claims there is difficulty in finding multiple censuses. But he does not offer a theory of how to reconcile the two censuses which have historical evidence of occurring a decade apart.

When comparing the passage in Greek with the Aramaic, the order matches word for word. Although the Greek grammatical rules are imprecise, the grammatical rules of Aramaic are similar to Hebrew in that adjectives are placed after the nouns that they modify. In this passage it is clearly meant as "the first census."[80]

THE MAGI

The Magi are mysterious characters who appear without introduction during the nativity narrative and just as suddenly disappear without another mention. Various fanciful Christmas legends have been created to fill in the unknown details. However, these are the things that are known with certainty. They arrive from the east of Judea (Matthew 1:1) sometime after they had witnessed some astro-

---

78 [Tertullian] p. 363
79 [Wallace]
80 [Dukhrana] Luke 2:2

nomical observations which intrigued them to such an extent that they sought answers from the rulers in Jerusalem (Matthew 1:2). Note that they observed the "star" rising in the eastern direction but Judea was to their west; the phenomenon did not specifically point them in a certain direction or lead them to Jerusalem. The astronomical observation had characteristics that the Magi deemed significant; but the rest of the population did not recognize this or even realize anything out of the ordinary had happened (Matthew 1:3).

Even though the New Testament gives hardly any details as to who these Magi were, there are some tantalizing clues in the Old Testament.

> "Then the king gave Daniel high honors and many great gifts, and made him ruler over the whole province of Babylon and chief prefect over all the wise men of Babylon." (Daniel 2:48)

The Hebrew word translated as "wise men" is 'chakkim' (S#2445). The same passage in the Aramaic Peshitta also uses the word 'hakkim' meaning "wise, a scholar, sage."[81] Daniel was made head over all the "wise men" which consisted of several classifications in Nebuchadnezzar's royal court and are listed in multiple passages: Daniel 2:10, 4:7, 5:7, 5:11, 5:15.

---

81 [CAL] Daniel 2:27

Words used in the Hebrew text:

English meaning	Translit	Hebrew	S#
wise men	chakkim	חַכָּמִין	2445
conjurer, enchanter	ashaph	אַשָּׁף	826
magician	chartom	חַרְטֹם	2749
diviners from root "to cut, determine"	gezar	גְזַר	1505
Chaldean	kasday	כַּשְׂדָּי	3779

Equivalent words used in the Aramaic text:

English meaning	Translit	Aramaic
wise	hakkim	ܚܟܝܡܐ
reciter of incantations, snake charmer	asop	ܐܫܘܦܐ
sorcerer	harras	ܚܪܫܐ
magus, Magian	mgus	ܡܓܘܫܐ
Chaldean; astrologer	kalday	ܘܟܠܕܝܐ

The similarity of the Hebrew and Aramaic languages is again evident with the use of a couple of almost identical words. The words used that are different maintain a similar meaning. Within the classes, there is a notable differentiation made between the native Chaldeans and the immigrant Magi. Although the Hebrew text does not make use of the term "magi", the equivalent term used of "gezar" would suggest that what is meant is a "diviner." The Magi were preoccupied with omens and looked to astronomic observations; however, not in the modern sense of personal astrology but as to how events in the heavens portended major cultural events.

Cultures often borrow terms from other languages and the meanings then shift as the years advance. This happened with the term "magi" when the Greeks adopted it. It began as a description of a people group but then began to be used only of their most famous caste of priests. Eventually it morphed into a derogatory term for the dark arts and for mysterious and unexplainable activities. This is very evident in the resulting English language terms of "magic" and "magician." This shift in meaning is evident in the work of Herodotus' "Histories."

It is also evident in the Greek New Testament. The English word "magi" is first used in Matthew 2:1 and is translated from the Greek "magoi" (S# 3097). The term is also found in Acts 13:16: "When they had gone through the whole island as far as Paphos, they came upon a certain magician, a Jewish false prophet named Bar-Jesus." This individual was not of the Magian people group; he was Jewish. The Aramaic Peshitta uses the word for sorcerer "harras" here instead.[82] Even though the meaning of the Greek word was already indistinct, the Aramaic use of "magi" in Matthew suggests the more traditional meaning of the term and not that of "sorcerer."

The Magi or Magians as a people group existed during the time of Daniel, through to the New Testament period and onwards. Descriptions of them are included in a work written circa 1000 AD by the moslem scholar Al-Biruni who described the calendar and the religions of the various peoples that lived around him. His writings describe the region before the rise of the Ottoman empire in the fourteenth century and well before the conquest of Constantinople in 1453 AD. He includes de-

---

82 [Dukhrana] Acts 13:16

scriptions of the various Jewish sects, Christians, moslems and Zoroastrians. He was in a unique position to record this knowledge since he was descended from the people of the area: Chorasmia, modern day Uzbekistan.

> "Now I shall mention the months of the Magians of Transoxiana, the people of Khwarizm and of Sughd."[83] Al-Biruni's geographical list places the origin of the Magian people in the area of modern Uzbekistan. This was the homeland of Zoroaster (circa 600 BC) who was a contemporary of Daniel.

> "But afterwards when Zoroaster appeared and introduced the religion of the Magi, when the **kings transferred their residence from Balkh to Persis and Babel** and occupied themselves with the affairs of their religion..."[84] [emphasis added]

The Magi were followers of Zoroaster and were originally centred in Balkh (Bactria in Greek), located in modern northern Afghanistan. They migrated to Persis, the homeland of the ancient Persians which is in modern southern Iran. They also made their home in Babel (Babylon). It was a long-lived religion throughout the area and up through the New Testament period during the Parthenian Empire which existed to the east of the Roman Empire:

> "We return now to our subject, and go on to state that the **Persians adhered to the Magian religion of Zaradusht**, that they had no schism or dissension in it till the time came when Jesus rose, and his pupils spread through all the world preaching the Gospel."[85] [emphasis added]

Al-Biruni describes the influence of the Magian religion after the earlier downfall of the Babylonian empire:

---
83 [Sachau] p. 56
84 [Sachau] p. 220
85 [Sachau] p. 189

"For the Sabians are the remnant of the Jewish tribes who remained in Babylonia, when the other tribes left it for Jerusalem in the days of Cyrus and Artaxerxes. Those remaining tribes felt themselves attracted to the rites of the Magians, and so they inclined (were inclined, i.e. Sabi) towards the religion of Nebukadnezzar, and **adopted a system mixed up of Magism and Judaism** like that of the Samaritans in Syria. The greatest number of them are settled at Wasit, in Sawad-al'irak, in the districts of Ja'far, Aljamida, and the two Nahr-alsila."[86] [emphasis added]

"As regards the Sabians, we have already explained that this name applies to the real Sabians, i.e. to the remnants of the captive Jews in Babylonia, whom Nebukadnezar had transferred from Jerusalem to that country. After having freely moved about in Babylonia, and having acclimatized themselves to the country, they found it inconvenient to return to Syria; therefore they preferred to stay in Babylonia. Their religion wanted a certain solid foundation, in consequence of which **they listened to the doctrines of the Magians**, and inclined towards some of them. So their religion became a mixture of Magian and Jewish elements like that of the so-called Samaritans who were transferred from Babylonia to Syria."[87] [emphasis added]

These fascinating details by Al-Biruni lead to speculation of just how much influence Daniel could have had as the head of the Magi during his lifetime. The further combination of Jewish prophetic concerns with the Zoroastrian focus on astronomy throughout the ensuing centuries would have been discussed by the scholarly elite. If, as has been previously discussed, Gabriel

---
86 [Sachau] p.188
87 [Sachau] p.314

allowed Daniel to understand the 70 Weeks prophecy by giving him "insight and understanding" (Daniel 9:22), at least the beginning of the timeline must have been tracked. As a result, the Magi could possibly have been waiting for the end of the next period of 62 Weeks and the arrival of a Jewish "anointed one" (Daniel 9:26) in Judea. They would have known exactly when the reconstruction of Jerusalem had started since they were much closer to the time when ancient scrolls containing these records still existed. Therefore, a "star" appearing in the heavens at an expected time of significance would have been extremely important confirmation and made them anxious to investigate further. This could answer the question of how they knew they were looking for "he who has been born king of the Jews" (Matthew 2:2).

Even into the time of the Parthian empire (to the east of and concurrent with the Roman empire), the Magi were not considered native people as the historian Strabo recorded:

> "...that the Council of the Parthians, according to Poseidonius, consists of two groups, one that of kinsmen, and the other that of wise men and Magi, from both of which groups the kings were appointed..."[88]

This longer section from Laertius gives much more detail about the Magi:

> "The Persians have had their Magi, the Babylonians or Assyrians their Chaldaeans, and the Indians their Gymnosophists; and among the Celts and Gauls there are the people called Druids or Holy Ones.
>
> Clitarchus...also says that the Chaldaeans apply themselves to astronomy and forecasting the future; while the Magi spend their time in the worship of the gods, in sacrifices and in prayers, implying that none but them-

---

88 [Strabo] Geography 11.9

selves have the ear of the gods. They propound their views concerning the being and origin of the gods, whom they hold to be fire, earth, and water; they condemn the use of images, and especially the error of attributing to the divinities difference of sex. They hold discourse of justice, and deem it impious to practise cremation; but they see no impiety in marriage with a mother or daughter, as Sotion relates in his twenty-third book. Further, they practise divination and forecast the future, declaring that the gods appear to them in visible form. Moreover, they say that the air is full of shapes which stream forth like vapour and enter the eyes of keen-sighted seers. They prohibit personal ornament and the wearing of gold. Their dress is white, they make their bed on the ground, and their food is vegetables, cheese, and coarse bread; their staff is a reed and their custom is, so we are told, to stick it into the cheese and take up with it the part they eat.

With the art of magic they were wholly unacquainted, according to Aristotle in his *Magicus* and Dinon in the fifth book of his *History* Dinon tells us that the name Zoroaster, literally interpreted, means "star-worshipper"; and Hermodorus agrees with him in this. Aristotle in the first book of his dialogue *On Philosophy* declares that the Magi are more ancient than the Egyptians; and further, that they believe in two principles, the good spirit and the evil spirit, the one called Zeus or Oromasdes, the other Hades or Arimanius. This is confirmed by Hermippus in his first book about the Magi, Eudoxus in his *Voyage round the World*, and Theopompus in the eighth book of his *Philippica*. The last-named author says that according to the Magi men will live in a future life and be immortal, and that the world will endure through their invocations. This is again confirmed by

Eudemus of Rhodes. But Hecataeus relates that according to them the gods are subject to birth. Clearchus of Soli in his tract *On Education* further makes the Gymnosophists to be descended from the Magi; and some trace the Jews also to the same origin. Furthermore, those who have written about the Magi criticize Herodotus. They urge that Xerxes would never have cast javelins at the sun nor have let down fetters into the sea, since in the creed of the Magi sun and sea are gods. But that statues of the gods should be destroyed by Xerxes was natural enough."[89]

The Magi had an important role in the vast Persian empire and its governmental centres were located throughout Asia Minor. The Parthians, as successors of the Persian empire had periodic violent dealings with the Romans and King Herod in particular. The influential Magi would have been a well known part of the political landscape of the time.

Matthew states that the Magi came from the east. What exactly did the term "east" mean? Certainly Babylon and the Parthian empire were located to the east of Judea. But the Bible refers to a specific area as "east." When Abraham lived in Canaan, he desired to focus on Isaac as the fulfillment of God's covenant promise and sent his other sons away to the "east country."

> "But to the sons of his concubines Abraham gave gifts, and while he was still living he sent them away from his son Isaac, eastward to the east country." (Genesis 25:6)

Some years later, Isaac desired Jacob to marry from within his own people group. "Then Jacob went on his journey and came to the land of the people of the east." (Genesis 29:1) This was the city of Haran, north-east of Canaan and in modern day southern Turkey.

---

89 [Hicks] Prologue

During the conquest of Canaan by the Israelites, there is a connection made between Kedar, the son of Ishmael, and Arabah to the east. Arabah is from the word "arab" (S# 6148) which means "mixed" and also "to trade, barter."

> "Now these are the kings of the land whom the people of Israel defeated and took possession of their land beyond the Jordan toward the sunrise, from the Valley of the Arnon to Mount Hermon, with all the Arabah eastward..." (Joshua 12:1)

1 Chronicles 1:29 identifies Kedar with Nebaioth (the Nabataeans). Later prophets continue to connect Kedar with the East. "Rise up, advance against Kedar! Destroy the people of the east! (Jeremiah 49:28). They are described as having camels, flocks and curtains (tents). Ezekiel 27:21 states: "Arabia and all the princes of Kedar." Isaiah 21:13-17 connects Kedar with Arabia, Dedan and Tema. One tribe of Israel "lived to the east as far as the entrance of the desert this side of the Euphrates, because their livestock had multiplied in the land of Gilead." (1 Chronicles 5:9)

These passages specify that the East consisted of the area outside the borders of Israel which included from northern Syria south to modern day Saudi Arabia. East ended before the Euphrates River so that Babylon and Persia were already part of the Far East. The whole area was described as Arabah/Arabia, the land of the Arabs. Jamieson's Bible Commentary says:

> "The Arabs divide their country into the north, called Sham, or "the left"; and the south, called Yemen, or "the right"; for they faced east; and so the west was on their left, and the south on their right. Arabia-Deserta was on the east, Arabia-Petræa on the west, and Arabia-Felix on the south."[90]

---

90 [Jamieson] p. 311

Arabia was a special place in the Scriptures. Moses' final blessing on Israel mentions several locations in Arabia:

> "The Lord came from Sinai
> and dawned from Seir upon us;
> he shone forth from Mount Paran" (Deuteronomy 33:1)

God gave the Law to Moses and the Israelites while in Arabia and it was there that they wandered for forty years. Sinai and Mount Horeb both describe the same location which is in Arabia as Paul specifically states in Galatians 4:25: "Now Hagar is Mount Sinai in Arabia." This also ties Hagar and the descendants of Ishmael to the area as well. Paul goes on to state that he spent time in Arabia after his conversion. "[B]ut I went away into Arabia, and returned again to Damascus." (Galatians 1:17) Since he was a Pharisee and well versed in the Law and history, he might very well have spent time at Sinai working through how Christ was the fulfillment of the Torah, his whole reason for existence until that point. He may have followed in the footsteps of Elijah who spent a period of renewal at Mount Horeb/Sinai:

> "And he arose and ate and drank, and went in the strength of that food forty days and forty nights to Horeb, the mount of God." (I Kings 19:8)

Isaiah 60 contains a prophecy of a future era of peace as the nations of the world come to Israel to worship God. The tribes of the East are listed:

> "A multitude of camels shall cover you,
> the young camels of Midian and Ephah;
> all those from Sheba shall come.
> They shall bring gold and frankincense,
> and shall bring good news, the praises of the Lord.
> All the flocks of Kedar shall be gathered to you;
> the rams of Nebaioth shall minister to you;

> they shall come up with acceptance on my altar,
> and I will beautify my beautiful house." (Isaiah 60:6-7)

These tribes are mentioned in 1 Chronicles 1:28-33 as sons of Jokshan, the son of Abraham's concubine Keturah and as the sons of Ishmael, also a son of Abraham. These were all sons that Abraham had sent away to the East country.

The previous quote from Deuteronomy mentions the place called "Seir" which is Mount Seir located near Petra in Jordan. This was the domain of the ancient Nabataeans who were named after Nebaioth, son of Joktan. One of their major gods was named "Dushara" which means "the god (dhu) of ash-Shara (Shara)."[91]

In the Hebrew language "Seir" is pronounced "say-eer" but by the Nabataeans it was "sha-ra." There are two Hebrew homonyms, sounding similar, which will become significant as we continue. The first is "sha-ar" (S# 8180) which means "a measure ie. hundred-fold." The second is "shaar" (S# 8176) which is "to think, calculate, or reckon."

Strabo describes the people of the area circa the first century:

> "The Nabataeans and Sabaeans, situated above Syria, are the first people who occupy Arabia Felix. They were frequently in the habit of overrunning this country before the Romans became masters of it, but at present both they and the Syrians are subject to the Romans...Beyond the enclosure the country is for the most part a desert, particularly towards Judaea. Through this is the shortest road to Jericho, a journey of three or four days, and five days to the Phoinicon (or palm plantation)...[T]he camel traders travel with ease and in safety from Petra, and back to Petra, with so

---

91 [Peterson] p. 12

large a body of men and camels as to differ in no respect from an army."[92]

The terms "Sabaeans" and "Sheba" have been mentioned several times through the quoted texts. The words are related with "Sheba" being the anglicized form. Who were these people? The most well known association is with the Queen of Sheba who left her country on a quest to investigate the unbelievable reports she'd been hearing about King Solomon. Modern scholars are still unsure as to exactly where this land of Sheba was due to issues with the conventional system of chronology. However, Jesus told us where Sheba was located as recorded in Matthew 12:42 and Luke 11:31. He refers to the "Queen of the South" coming "from the ends of the earth." The Greek word used for "south" is "notos" (S# 3558) and is similar to our understanding of the general southern direction. But the Aramaic Peshitta uses a much more specific word. The feminine form is used which specifies a geographic area as opposed to the masculine form which specifies a general direction. It is from the root word "ymn" or "to act with the right hand"[93].

Yemen is located at the "right hand" of Arabia or Arabia-Felix. "Felix" means "fertile" or "happy, blessed." Arabia is not commonly associated with being fertile, however, at one time the southern portion of Arabia was home to a very powerful and wealthy empire – the Sabeans. Strabo states:

> "The country of the Sabaei, a very populous nation, is contiguous [most of modern Yemen], and is the most fertile of all, producing myrrh, frankincense, and cinnamon...The people who live near each other receive, in continued succession, the loads of perfumes and deliver

---

92 [Strabo] Geography XVI.iv.21
93 [Dukhrana] Matthew 12:42

them to others, who convey them as far as Syria and Mesopotamia."⁹⁴

The area's fertility was a result of the construction of a massive dam near their capital city of Marib. It was one of the engineering marvels of the ancient world allowing a thriving culture. Their caravan trade routes went along the western side of Arabia, past the eastern side of the Jordan River and on towards Damascus. All along this route were colony settlements. However, the dam broke around the fifth century AD and caused widespread population migration. By the time of Al Biruni's writings circa the eleventh century, he recognized a large population of Sabeans living in the northern settlements, west of the Euphrates. He described the Sabeans as following a mixture of Jewish and Magian religious influences. Before the breach of the dam "their commerce brought the Sabaeans under Christian and Jewish influence; and, though the old gods were too closely connected with their life and trade to be readily abandoned, the great change in the trading policy... seems to have affected religion as well as the state. The inland gods lost importance with the failure of the overland trade, and Judaism and Christianity seem for a time to have contended for the mastery in South Arabia."⁹⁵

The name "Sheba" is mentioned several times through the Bible but does not refer to just one people group. There were multiple progenitors named "Sheba." Genesis 10:6 lists Seba and Raama as sons of Cush, son of Ham. Sheba and Dedan were Raama's sons. Cush was the progenitor of the Ethiopians and Egypt is commonly linked together with them.

Genesis 10:26 lists another Sheba, the son of Joktan and a descendant of Shem. At the time the geneology was written, this group had settled in the hill country of the east.

---

94 [Strabo] Geography XVI.iv.19
95 [Sabaeans]

1 Chronicles 1:28-33 lists another Sheba and Dedan but these were sons of Jokshan, the son of Abraham's concubine Keturah.

Job 1:15 mentions attacking Sabeans who were living in the same area as the Chaldeans near the Euphrates. A few chapters later, Job 6:18-19 talks about the caravans of Tema and Sheba and can be associated with the descendants of Ishmael.

References in the Bible sometimes connect the mentioned Sheba with Ham's line and other times Sheba is connected with Shems' line. Psalm 72:10b ties Sheba and Seba together. Isaiah 43:3 lists Egypt, Cush and Seba together. Ezekiel 27:22 and 38:13 says that Sheba and Raama were traders and merchants and descendant's of Ham. In 2 Chronicles 21:16 the descendants of Cush are described as living near the Arabians (as sons of Shem) during the time of King Jehoram in the divided kingdom era.

There is one other significant reference to Sheba which is found in Isaiah:

> "Thus says the LORD: "The wealth of Egypt and the merchandise of Cush, and the Sabeans, men of stature, shall come over to you and be yours; they shall follow you; they shall come over in chains and bow down to you. They will plead with you, saying: 'Surely God is in you, and there is no other, no god besides him.'"" (Isaiah 45:14)

At first glance, this prophecy as translated in the ESV does not seem to have anything to do with the nativity account. It is commonly recognized that Matthew's gospel focuses heavily on Jewish culture and prophetic concerns. Multiple times in Chapter 2, Matthew refers to Old Testament prophecies which were fulfilled at the time of Jesus' birth. Verses 5-6 refer to the prophecy of Bethlehem found in Micah 5:2. Verse 15 refers to God's son being called out Egypt which was originally found in Hosea 11:1. Verse 17 mentions the weeping of Ramah found in Jeremiah 31:15. Verse 23 states that Jesus would be called a Nazarene which suggests that the word is derived from "branch" and the prophecy found in Isaiah 11:1. Could it be that the Magi themselves were prophesied in the Old Testament, specifically in this prophecy of Isaiah, but have not been recognized as such?

Examining further, Isaiah 45:14 mentions three places. The first two: the "wealth of Egypt" and the "merchandise of Cush" are inanimate products. But the Sabaeans are described as a people group. Gold was mined in Egypt and Cush (Ethiopia) and is often tied to the prosperous kingdom of Sheba who were world-renowned spice traders with their frankincense and myrh (Jeremiah 6:20, Isaiah 60:6).

The translation describes the Sabaeans as "men of stature." The Hebrew word used is "middah" (S# 4060) and refers to measurement. Although other biblical uses of the word refer to tall people (Numbers 13:32, 1 Chronicles 11:23), the vast majority of the fifty-five instances where it is used, refer to the sense of measurement and this includes other contemporary prophets of Isaiah. The word used in the Aramaic Peshitta is "mušḥā" which means "measure; grade, rank, status; order, according to limits" and is from a base word meaning "to anoint" and "spread with oil."[96] The Sabaeans as well known merchant traders are known for measurement of spices, garments and other goods. But they are also men of rank or status as the term "magi" would suggest. It was pointed out previously that the Hebrew word for measurement "sha-ar" is a homonymn for "Sier." This was the major mountain associated

---

96 [CAL] Isaiah 45:14

with the Sabaean/Nabatean settlement located there along the well-traveled trade route to the east of Judea.

Continuing on in Isaiah, the first verb used is "abar" (S# 5674) which is "to cross over a border, pass through." The ESV translation has chosen to translate the next verbs as "they shall follow you; they shall come over in chains." However, the Hebrew words used would suggest something different.

The word translated as "chains" is "ziquah" (S# 2131). Although it can mean "chains", it can also mean the significantly different: "firebrand, missile, spark, shooting star, ray of light." Good exegesis considers how an author uses the same word elsewhere in his writings. Isaiah uses the word twice more very shortly later in his book:

> "Lo, all ye kindling a fire, girding on **sparks**, Walk ye in the light of your fire, And in the **sparks** ye have caused to burn, From my hand hath this been to you, In grief ye lie down!" (Isaiah 50:11) [YLT] [emphasis added]

Isaiah makes use of the verb "halak" (S# 1980) which has the sense of traveling or walking with purpose. Therefore, the literal meaning could very well be: "the Sabaeans quest after the sparks/ray of light." This gives quite a different spin on the passage and offers a significant possible tie to Matthew's narrative.

The next action in the passage includes the Hebrew words "shachah" (S# 7812) meaning "to fall down, bow down in worship" and "palal" (S# 6419) meaning "to pray." They recognize that there is only one God and that He is alive. Who are they addressing in the passage? "Truly, you are a God who hides himself, O God of Israel, the Savior" (Isaiah 45:15). The word used for "hides" is "sathar" (S# 5641) which includes the sense of hiding by covering oneself or concealing. The Aramaic equivalent includes the sense of clothing oneself.

As the passage continues, Isaiah contrasts with the makers of earthly idols who disgrace themselves because their creations are useless. The True God created the world to be filled with life and the only True God is the Saviour and will be worshiped as such.

Does this passage not accurately describe the mission of the Magi? Could this be an unrecognized fulfillment of Old Testament prophecy which Matthew records? The Sabaeans traveled in caravans which rivaled the size of armies and could have caused Herod and all of Jerusalem much worry when they arrived. They were termed "magi" due to the similarities of observing the heavens, searching for portents of impending cultural events. They were associated with wisdom and of high rank and with a play on words with "Seir", the major mountain located near their usual route of travel. In this case, they were familiar with the expected Jewish Messiah and after recognizing an important sign in the heavens, they went on a quest for the True God, the One who had clothed Himself in human form and who had shown the futility of the other gods that the surrounding cultures worshiped.

In the early centuries of the Church, Justin Martyr seems to have made the same connection:

> "Now this king Herod, at the time when the Magi came to him from Arabia, and said they knew from a star which appeared in the heavens that a King had been born in your country...And none of you can deny that Damascus was, and is, in the region of Arabia, although now it belongs to what is called Syrophœnicia."[97]

After possibly traveling to Jerusalem by way of the usual shorter mountain pass from the Jordan, God warned them not to return by the same way. They would most likely have

---

97 [Roberts] (Chapter LXXVIII)

used the existing southern trade route which would have taken them back toward and along the western edge of Arabia.

THE STAR

What exactly was the "star" and can any of the details in the biblical narrative be used to give clarity to the date? Many have suggested various astronomical events: a comet, a super-nova, planetary conjunctions. Others consider a star that moves around in the sky and then stands still so preposterous that they either consider it a unique miraculous event or allegorize it completely away. The text in Matthew assumes a natural phenomenon since the super natural elements are clearly described (i.e. various angelic visions which occur throughout the narrative).

There have been proposals trying to connect the star with planetary conjunctions in 2-3 BC. However, these theories erroneously transfer modern astrological methods and concepts to an ancient culture which would not have understood them in the same way.

Another proposal which considers the star as a planetary conjunction is put forward in Molnar's book "The Star of Bethlehem." He considers the significance of the heavenly bodies involved and their astrological symbolism from a more accurate cultural and historical viewpoint. His research shows that this event occurred in 6 BC.

Molnar traces how the Magi continued to improve their understanding of astronomy over the centuries from the empires of Babylon, Persia and eventually adopting Greek influences.[98] This Greek-influenced astrology is recorded around 150 AD in the works of Claudius Ptolemy who collected infor-

---

98 [Molnar] p. 34-36

mation from first century BC sources.[99] Ptolemy's work contains details of how nations and regions were symbolized by their own unique astrological zodiac sign. The Syrian region, including Judea, was symbolized by Aries, the ram. Molnar gives evidence of this by describing the history and including images of Syrian coins which were minted several times during the early decades of the first century which prominently featured the sign of Aries and a star on one side.[100]

Molnar goes on to describe the astronomical phenomena that the Magi would have considered astrologically significant. Jupiter as a regal planet was occulted by and emerged from behind the moon on April 17, 6 BC. At this exact time, Jupiter rose above the eastern horizon – a helical rising – as a star rising in the east. In addition, Jupiter, Saturn, the Sun, and the Moon all were significantly located in the sign of Aries – the symbol of the region of Judea.[101]

The term "went before" that is in Matthew's narrative has been found in Ptolemy's writings where it is used to refer to retrograde motion of the planets. Planets, in their orbits as viewed from the earth, slow to a stop, move backwards relative to the other objects in the sky, then again slow to a stop and finally begin moving in their normal direction and speed. During 6 BC, Jupiter slowed and stopped on August 23 for about a week. It began to move westward in the night sky and re-entered the sign of Aries on October 27. It again stopped and stood still for a week on December 19 and then resumed its eastward motion in early January of 5 BC.[102] Matthew's account paraphrased by Molnar to contain astronomical lan-

---

99 [Molnar] p. 44
100 [Molnar] p. 51
101 [Molnar] p. 101
102 [Molnar] p. 93-94

guage is: "And behold the planet which they had seen at its heliacal rising went retrograde and became stationary above in the sky (which showed) where the child was."[103]

These various astrological elements were based on uniquely positioned astronomical observations during that year. Although conjunctions such as these happen roughly every sixty years, the exact combinations that occurred during 6 BC are extremely rare.[104]

EARLY CHRISTIAN ASSUMPTION

Al-Biruni, although a moslem scholar, also engaged in an in-depth discussion of the various aspects of the 70 Weeks prophecy of Daniel. He states a very intriguing fact in his writings: "Further, Jews and Christians unanimously suppose that the birth of Jesus the son of Mary took place Anno Alexandri 304."[105] He determines that using this date does not work out for the number of Weeks as stated in the prophecy and concludes that both the Jews and Christians have modified the Bible to hide the truth.

As discussed in Part 1, Al-Biruni based the start of the Anno Alexandri era at the point when Alexander the Great entered Jerusalem in 330 BC. However, the commonly used Seleucid Era dating begins from 311-310 BC which he never seems to recognize in his long and very detailed work.

330 BC + 304 years = 26 BC

The result of 26 BC is much too early to be correct. But by redoing the calculation starting with the Seleucid era instead, the resulting date is 7-6 BC; a date that is extremely relevant. Al-

---

103 [Molnar] p. 96
104 [Molnar] p. 102
105 [Sachau] p. 21

Biruni states that the number of '304' was commonly known in the Christian community of his time. It is possible that the era was misrepresented and instead of Anno Alexandri, it should have actually been counted from the beginning of the Seleucid Era.

Unfortunately, there are no definitive historical records that shed light as to Jesus' exact date of birth. However, there is enough plausible evidence in the topics discussed that point to the mid first decade BC and more specifically to 6 BC as the year. The end of the 62 Weeks proposed does fit into this time period.

Chapter 16

The Year of Christ's Sacrifice

Unlike the account of Jesus' birth where there are no details that specify an exact date, the account of the days leading up to when Jesus was sacrificed does allow for an exact date to be determined. The crucifixion occurred during the Jewish Passover which always occurs on Nisan 14 each year. The activities recorded in the Gospels are quite detailed. However, readers do see contradictions in these details which cause a lot of debate. Once the specifics of the Hebrew calendar are taken into account, what some consider as contradictions vanish.

It must be mentioned that Church tradition is a powerful thing. By several centuries after the event, Christianity had developed the tradition of memorializing the Crucifixion on Friday with the Resurrection occurring early on Sunday morning – at dawn. But Church leadership was not much concerned with historical accuracy. This can be seen in Al-Biruni's description of the calculations of when Easter should occur (it was still called Passover by Christians of that eastern region).

"In the first year of the cycle they fixed Passover on the 25th of Adhar, because in the year when Christ was crucified it must have fallen on this date....And this is to serve as a help and precaution against that which is mentioned in the 7th Canon of the Canones Apostolorum : " Whatever bishop, or presbyter, or diaconus celebrates the feast of Passover before the equinox together with the Jews, shall be deposed from his rank."" [106]

The month called Adhar was the month before Nisan so as of the writing of the above quote circa 1000 AD, the Church had lost sight of the biblical directive that Passover should always occur on Nisan 14. They were more concerned with separating themselves from the feasts as they were celebrated by the Jews.

Anderson's and Hoehner's interpretation of the 70 Week prophecy recognize and restore the important detail of the Nisan 14 date for Passover. The generally accepted date in current Christian scholarship is Friday, April 3, 33 AD.

33 AD

	Su	M	Tu	W	Th	F	Sa	Su	M	Tu	W	Th	F	Sa	
	24	25	26	27	28	29	1	15	16	17	18	19	20	21	March
Nisan	2	3	4	5	6	7	8	22	23	24	25	26	27	28	
	9	10	11	12	13	14	15	29	30	31	1	2	3	4	April
	16	17	18	19	20	21	22	5	6	7	8	9	10	11	
	23	24	25	26	27	28	29	12	13	14	15	16	17	18	

THE FIG TREE

A fig tree might seem to be a strange place to begin when determining an exact date for the crucifixion. However, just as we discovered with barley, the fig tree has its own peculiar life cycle which reveals some interesting details. The day after the triumphal entry into Jerusalem, Jesus was journeying with His disciples:

106[Sachau] p. 300

"In the morning, as he was returning to the city, he became hungry. And seeing a fig tree by the wayside, he went to it and found nothing on it but only leaves. And he said to it, "May no fruit ever come from you again!" And the fig tree withered at once." (Matthew 21: 18-19)

"On the following day, when they came from Bethany, he was hungry. And seeing in the distance a fig tree in leaf, he went to see if he could find anything on it. When he came to it, he found nothing but leaves, for it was not the season for figs. And he said to it, "May no one ever eat fruit from you again." And his disciples heard it." (Mark 11: 12-14)

Mark includes the detail that it "was not the season for figs" at the time when Jesus was expecting to eat some ripe figs. At first this seems quite unreasonable until you discover that figs have two separate phases of ripening. Quite quickly after leafing out at the end of March, flower bracts develop which have both male and female flowers. Depending on the variety of fig, up to half of the female flowers can be sterile. These sterile flowers go through a very fast growth phase and ripen in about three weeks. The remaining fertile female flowers continue to develop and await a symbiotic relationship with a certain species of wasp. This wasp only starts to emerge in June and the second period of figs ripen a few weeks later. This second harvest is the main fig harvest for the year.[107]

When Jesus approached the fig tree and saw nothing but leaves, he knew that not only were there no ripe early figs available, but there would be no ripe figs either at the later main harvest.

107[Galil]

This early fig season in Judea would have been from mid to late April. The narrative has provided an overlooked clue that the assumed early date of April 3, 33 AD for the Crucifixion is most likely not the correct date.

Options for a Friday Date

Are there other options in the surrounding years that allow for a Passover to occur on a Friday and later in April? Since Passover always occurs on Nisan 14, we have to look for years when Nisan 1 occurred on a Saturday, two weeks before. Using the modern rules for the Jewish calendar, the only other option occurred in 26 AD; too early for the Crucifixion of Jesus to have taken place. This can be determined when considering the ministry of John the Baptizer. His ministry started in the fifteenth year of Tiberius Caesar (Luke 3:1). Tiberius became Caesar in 14 AD with his fifteenth year in 28 AD. Even if taking into account the year of succession method that some scholars include, the year would be 29 AD. There is debate as to which method Luke was using for his dates but both dates are later than 26 AD.

3 Days and 3 Nights

But does a Friday Passover actually match the biblical account? Jesus specifically pointed to Jonah as a sign for three days and three nights:

> "An evil and adulterous generation seeks for a sign, but no sign will be given to it except the sign of the prophet Jonah. For just as Jonah was **three days and three nights** in the belly of the great fish, so will the Son of Man be

> **three days and three nights** in the heart of the earth." (Matthew 12:39-40) [emphasis added]

The enemies of Jesus thought it important enough to post guards for three days:

> "...the chief priests and the Pharisees gathered before Pilate and said, "Sir, we remember how that impostor said, while he was still alive, '**After three days** I will rise.' Therefore order the tomb to be made secure until **the third day.**"" (Matthew 27:62-64) [emphasis added]

This has always been a question of the traditional view of the sequence of events from Friday to Sunday. How can three days and three nights be counted between those days? Why are the many times that Jesus referred to this specific number of days not taken literally? (Matthew 17:23, 20:19, 26:61, 27:40; Mark 8:31, 9:31, 10:34, 14:58, 15:29; Luke 9:22, 18:33, 24:7; John 2:19)

There is a Fast of Nineveh celebrated by eastern Christians. Al-Biruni describes the event in his writings circa 1000 AD:

> "The fast of Nineveh is called from the Syrian town of that name, which is also the town of the prophet Jonah (May God bless him). The name Jonah is a Greek one; according to the Christians he spent three days and three nights in a fish's belly, and this is regarded as a sign that Jesus would remain three days and three nights under the earth. This fast lasts for three days and precedes the great feast by three weeks beginning on a Monday."[108]

When this was written, the length of this Christian fast consisting of three twenty-four hour days was still symbolically connected with the burial period of Jesus. This is a notable inconsistency since already the Church's Easter celebration included

---

108[Wright] p. 177

Good Friday – not a period of three literal days. However, no descriptions of the modern practice of the Fast of Nineveh can be found that make any connection with Jesus' burial.

EVE OF THE PASSOVER

There is an important time cue that is used in all four Gospels. This is the Greek word "paraskeué" (S#3904) defined as "the day of Preparation".

"The next day, that is, after the day of Preparation..." (Matthew 27:62)

Matthew does not give an explanation about the term. He assumes the reader knows what he is referring to.

"And when evening had come, since it was the day of Preparation, that is, the day before the Sabbath..." (Mark 15:42)

Mark includes an additional detail which explains the term. This is the single Greek word "prosabbaton" (S#4315) or "day before the Sabbath." It is the only time the word occurs in the New Testament. He uses the word to describe the same day. One word is directly linked with the name of the day and the other is linked with the Jewish religious customs for the day.

"It was the day of Preparation, and the Sabbath was beginning." (Luke 23:54)

Luke connects the term with the Sabbath day that followed.

"Now it was the day of Preparation of the Passover." (John 19:14)

John connects the term with the Passover feast.

"Since it was the day of Preparation, and so that the bodies would not remain on the cross on the Sabbath (for that Sabbath was a high day)..." (John 19:31)

John includes the detail that there was something special about that particular Sabbath.

"So because of the Jewish day of Preparation..." (John 19:42)

John includes the detail that this was specifically connected with Jewish religious customs.

These passages show that "day of Preparation" was a proper term in the Greek language for that particular day. Josephus also makes use of the term in his writings:

> "...it seemed good to me and my counsellors, according to the sentence and oath of the people of Rome, that the Jews have liberty to make use of their own customs, according to the law of their forefathers, as they made use of them under Hyrcanus the high priest of the Almighty God; and that their sacred money be not touched, but be sent to Jerusalem, and that it be committed to the care of the receivers at Jerusalem; and that they be not obliged to go before any judge on the **Sabbath day**, nor on the **day of the preparation** to it, after the ninth hour..."[109] [emphasis added]

One of the most well known aspects of Judaism is that worship occurs on the seventh day of the week – the Sabbath.

109[Josephus] Antiquities 16, 163

Since a lot of the passages just quoted mention the Sabbath, it is traditionally assumed that the seventh day of the week is meant. However, this is not necessarily accurate. Most forget that the regular feast days throughout the Jewish year are also considered as Sabbaths and follow the same religious customs and restrictions as the weekly Sabbath. This is outlined in Leviticus – admittedly not a very well read book:

> "These are the appointed feasts of the Lord that you shall proclaim as holy convocations; they are my appointed feasts. Six days shall work be done, but on the **seventh day is a Sabbath** of solemn rest, **a holy convocation**. You shall do no work. It is a Sabbath to the Lord in all your dwelling places. These are the appointed **feasts of the Lord, the holy convocations**, which you shall proclaim at the time appointed for them. In the first month, on the fourteenth day of the month at twilight, is the Lord's Passover. And on the fifteenth day of the same month is the Feast of Unleavened Bread to the Lord; for seven days you shall eat unleavened bread. **On the first day you shall have a holy convocation; you shall not do any ordinary work.** But you shall present a food offering to the Lord for seven days. On the seventh day is a holy convocation; you shall not do any ordinary work." (Leviticus 23:2-8) [emphasis added]

Although the weekly Sabbath, by definition, always occurs on the same day of the week, the Feast Days as Sabbaths can occur on any day of the week – not just on the seventh day. Due to the calendar arrangement where the month will start on a different weekday each month, the Feast Days also occur on different days of the week every year. It must be remembered that the timing is based on the new moon which results in months having either twenty-nine or thirty days. In addition, the lunar year cycles of 354 days are periodically synchronized with the 365.25 day solar cycles by adding an additional month.

It is not well known by Christians of the West that there exist New Testament manuscripts just as ancient as the Greek New Testament manuscripts. The Peshitta used by Christians of the East, written in Aramaic, is culturally closer to Hebrew than the Greek is. We have already examined the Aramaic version of the Old Testament when considering the Hebrew and Aramaic used in the book of Daniel. There are those who consider the widespread use of Aramaic in the first century AD as significant enough evidence for the New Testament to have been first written in Aramaic and not in Greek. This view is called Aramaic Primacy – a view that had much more vigorous debate through the nineteenth century when ancient Aramaic manuscripts were regularly being found throughout the Middle East during that time. However, New Testament Greek language scholars through to modern times consider this a ridiculous view. This is understandable since Western Christianity's translations of the Bible have been mainly based on the Greek manuscripts. There was not much amicable communication between Eastern and Western Christianity for many centuries.

There is actually compelling evidence to prove either view but no matter which was first, the other language was certainly translated very soon afterward. An eminent scholar of Aramaic describes the situation this way:

> "Black began his work with the assumption that "At the basis of the Greek Gospels ... there must lie a Palestinian Aramaic tradition, at any rate of the sayings and teaching of Jesus, and this tradition must at one time have been translated from Aramaic into Greek" ... Taking a "linguistic approach" Black reviewed grammatical features (syntax, grammar, and vocabulary), poetic features (parallelism, alliteration), and various indicators of translation of Aramaic. He hoped to clarify difficult passages and in many cases contribute to the exegetical

task. He concluded that the evidence points decidedly to an "Aramaic origin" of the Gospels and Acts. Although, "whether that source was written or oral, it is not possible from the evidence to decide.""[110]

Another scholar writing in 1915 says of the Peshitta:

"The great value of this translation depends on its high antiquity, on the competence and fidelity of the translators, and on the near affinity of its language to that spoken by our Lord and his Apostles. In all these respects it stands pre-eminent among the numerous versions of the New Testament."[111]

Torrey, an Aramaic primacist scholar says:

"This is the most significant item in the whole great chain of evidence; the Greek never gets away from the Aramaic, even for a single clause. Greek idioms which have no counterpart or standing equivalent in the Semitic original are not to be found in the Gospels. Everything that is said in this 'Greek' can be said in similar words in idiomatic Aramaic. This extremely important fact has of course been unknown to the experts in NT Greek."[112]

"Was not Luke capable of saying this in intelligible language? He does not do so, but instead reproduces the words and order of his source. In place of clear and classical Aramaic we have muddy Greek."[113]

"There is however ... an authority behind the Greek, and behind the Aramaic or Hebrew, which is quite untouched by any conjectures or conclusions as to the literary history of these records. It might conceivably have

---

110[Evans] p. v-vi
111[Hall] p. 490
112[Torrey 1991] p. 108
113[Torrey 1933] p. 268

been the divine purpose that in the latter days men in various parts of the world should pay attention not only to Greek, the language of the early Gentile church, but also to Aramaic, the language of Jesus and his disciples. It would seem, after all, to be a question of fact rather than of dogma."[114]

It is not the intent here to prove Aramaic primacy but only to shed some light into a debate of which many might not even be aware. There is much value in investigating the New Testament written in Aramaic and how it compares with the usually consulted Greek manuscripts. Porter, in his collection "The Language of the New Testament – Classic Essays" published in 1991, says:

> "Whereas there has been significant work in this area for well over the near one hundred years surveyed by this collection, many engaged in academic biblical studies are unaware of even the major contours of the debate. The result is often uncritical acceptance of a position which may not in fact be as well supported as some believe. Those who can recount the major positions of the last one hundred years are all too aware that consensus on its many topics is still lacking."[115]

Returning to the discussion, the Gospel passages quoted earlier as they are found in the Peshitta do not make use of a word translated as "day of Preparation." Instead, an entirely different term is used: "ruwb,t'a" meaning "eve." The phrase is either "eve of the Passover" or "eve of the Sabbath." "Eve of the Sabbath" is actually the common name for the day of Friday in Aramaic. It is worth noting that the Greek word "day of Preparation" is a reference to the religious customs that occurred on

---

114[Torrey 1933] p. 285
115[Porter] p. 12

the particular day and the Aramaic term is purely a reference to time.

The question is whether the term "eve" was also technically used to describe the day before a Feast Day occurring on any day of the week and not just used to refer to the day of Friday. There are two extra-biblical sources that shed light on this. An entry in the *International Standard Bible Encyclopedia Online* describes the Jewish story of Judith written during the time of the Maccabees. Even though the book is not part of Scripture, examination of the words used at the time can shed light on common terms in the culture. The book was most likely written in Hebrew since the idioms which are used match that of Hebrew and not Aramaic[116]

> "And she fasted all the days of her widowhood, save the eves of the sabbaths, and the sabbaths, and the eves of the new moons, and the new moons and the feasts and solemn days of the house of Israel." (Judith 8:6)

Instead of the term "day of Preparation", the phrase "eves of the sabbaths" is found. In addition, there is "eves of the new moons." These days definitely did not all fall on the 6th day of the week. Therefore, we see that the use of "eve" was used to refer to other days than just of Friday.

Secondly, there is a passage found in the Munich Talmud, a Hebrew manuscript from 1343 AD which contains words censored out of later printed editions.[117] The original Talmud writings date from early third century AD. Jesus of Nazareth is mentioned in the text but this has been partially erased.[118]

116[BibEnc]
117[Instone-Brewer] p. 269
118[Instone-Brewer] p. 272

1 לא: והתניא בערב הפסח תלאוהו לישו הנוצרי והכרוז יום ישר הנוצרי
יוצא לפניו ארבעים יוצא ליסקל על שכיסף
2 והיסית והידיח את ישראל כל מי שיודע לו זכות יבא
וילמד עליו זכות ולא מצאו לו זכות ותלאוהו בערב פסח אמר עולא
3 ותסברא הנוצרי בר הפוכי זכות הוא מסית הוא ורחמנא אמר: לא תחמול
ולא תכסה עליו שאני ישו הנוצרי דקרוב למלכות
4 הוה   ת"ר. דמשה תלמידים היו לו לישו הנוצרי.
מתאי. נקאי נצר ובוני ותודדה. אתיווה למתי. אמד להו: מתי
5 יהרג? הכתיב מתי אבוא ואראה פני אלהים ־ אמרו לו: אין.
מתי יהרג דכתיב מתי ימות ואבד שמו. אתידהן לנקאי. אמר לדו: נקאי
6 יהרג? הכתיב ונקי וצדיק אל תהרג ־ אמרו לו: אין, נקאי יהרג.
דכתיב במסתרים יהרג נקי. אתיוה לנצר, אמר: נצר יהרג? הכתיב ונצר

"It was taught:

On the Eve of Passover they hung Yeshu the Notzarine. And the herald went out before him for 40 days [saying]: "Yeshu the Notzarine will go out to be stoned for sorcery and misleading and enticing Israel [to idolatry]. Any who knows [anything] in his defense must come and declare concerning him." But no-one came to his defense so they hung him on the Eve of Passover."[119]

There is debate whether or not this reflects an historically accurate account of the trial of Jesus of Nazareth. However, textually, the Hebrew phrase "eve of Passover" occurs twice in this Jewish religious text. It is used as a technical term describing the day before the Passover meal which occurred at twilight. Therefore, "eve" is not just used as a substitute for referring to the sixth day of the week. This is strong evidence that the Gospel account is not necessarily referring to a Friday crucifixion.

119[Instone-Brewer] p. 275

SET TIMES FOR TEMPLE SACRIFICES

Jesus Christ suffered for hours while hanging on the cross. The narrative in Matthew states the following:

> "Now from the sixth hour there was darkness over all the land until the ninth hour. And about the ninth hour Jesus cried out with a loud voice." (Matthew 27:45-46)

There are some intriguing details recorded in the Jewish Mishnah or the "Oral Torah." These are writings outlining how the Jewish religion functioned during the era of the second temple:

> "The daily offering was slaughtered half an hour after the eighth hour, and sacrificed half an hour after the ninth hour; but **on the day before Passover**, whether that happened to be on the week or a Sabbath-day, it was slaughtered half an hour after the seventh hour, and **sacrificed half an hour after the eighth hour.** When the day before Passover happened on Friday, it was slaughtered half an hour after the sixth hour, sacrificed half an hour after the seventh hour, and the Passover sacrifice after it."[120] [emphasis added]

The Mishnah specifies that normal daily sacrifices occur at half past the ninth hour. If the Preparation Day occurred on a Friday, the sacrifice should occur earlier, at half past the seventh hour. However, if the Preparation Day was on any other day than Friday, then the sacrifice should occur half past the eighth hour. The time of day detail that Jesus yielded his spirit around the ninth hour could be indicative that Matthew was showing how Jesus died right at the time when the prescribed sacrifice was to be offered in the temple. When Jesus died, there was a great earthquake and the temple curtain was torn (Matt. 27:51).

120[DeSola] p. 107

This would have interrupted the usual religious sacrifice happening right at that very moment.

Although this is not clear evidence, it does strongly suggest that the Day of Preparation was not on a Friday but was on some other day of the week based on the directives in this portion of the Mishnah and how they related to Matthew's narrative.

SEQUENCE OF EVENTS

It is possible to arrive at an accurate sequence of events by arranging the time cues mentioned in all the Gospel accounts. A few things have to be kept in mind. The Jewish day started after sundown; at twilight. The Passover was part of a week-long Feast of Unleavened Bread which specified a Sabbath on the first and last days of the Feast:

> "In the first month, on the fourteenth day of the month at twilight, is the Lord's Passover. And on the fifteenth day of the same month is the Feast of Unleavened Bread to the Lord; for seven days you shall eat unleavened bread. On the **first day** you shall have a **holy convocation;** you shall not do any ordinary work." (Leviticus 23: 5-7) [emphasis added]

NISAN 13 - DAY BEFORE PASSOVER

> "Then came the day of Unleavened Bread, on which the Passover lamb had to be sacrificed. So Jesus sent Peter and John, saying, "Go and prepare the Passover for us, that we may eat it."" (Luke 22:7-8)

> "Now before the Feast of the Passover, when Jesus knew that his hour had come to depart out of this world

to the Father, having loved his own who were in the world, he loved them to the end. During supper..." (John 13:1-2a)

In the daylight portion of Nisan 13 before the day of Passover (Nisan 14) started, they prepare for the evening feast.

николаев 14 - Preparation Day/Eve of Passover

Nisan 14 began at sundown and they had the evening meal at the beginning of the day. The events in the garden, the trial and then the crucifixion unfold. This is throughout the night into the daylight portion of the day. Jesus Christ is sacrificed and dies in the afternoon. This was the Preparation Day for the Holy Convocation occurring on the next day, Nisan 15.

> "Since it was the day of Preparation, and so that the bodies would not remain on the cross on the **Sabbath (for that Sabbath was a high day)**, the Jews asked Pilate that their legs might be broken and that they might be taken away." (John 19:31) [emphasis added]

> "And when **evening had come, since it was the day of Preparation,** that is, **the day before the Sabbath,** Joseph of Arimathea, a respected member of the council, who was also himself looking for the kingdom of God, took courage and went to Pilate and asked for the body of Jesus." (Mark 15:42-43) [emphasis added]

> "When it was **evening,** there came a rich man from Arimathea, named Joseph, who also was a disciple of Jesus. He went to Pilate and asked for the body of Jesus. Then Pilate ordered it to be given to him. And Joseph took the body and wrapped it in a clean linen shroud..." (Matthew 27:57-59) [emphasis added]

> "Then he took it down and wrapped it in a linen shroud and laid him in a tomb cut in stone, where no one had

ever yet been laid. It was **the day of Preparation, and the Sabbath was beginning."** (Luke 23: 53-54) [emphasis added]

NISAN 15 - FIRST DAY OF UNLEAVENED BREAD / HOLY CONVOCATION SABBATH

"The **next day, that is, after the day of Preparation,** the chief priests and the Pharisees gathered before Pilate...Therefore order the tomb to be made secure **until the third day...**" (Matthew 27:62, 64) [emphasis added]

Keep in mind that the day began after sunset and not, as is the usual assumption, after dawn. These religious leaders were well acquainted with the significant statements that had been made regarding "three days."

NISAN 16 - SECOND DAY OF UNLEAVENED BREAD

"When **the Sabbath was past,** Mary Magdalene, Mary the mother of James, and Salome **bought spices**, so that they might go and anoint him." (Mark 16: 1) [emphasis added]

The women bought spices after the Sabbath. This could not be after the normal weekly Sabbath because they go to the tomb before dawn (as we'll see) when the shops are not open. There had to be a day available in order for this activity to take place.

"Then they [the women] ... prepared spices and ointments. On the **Sabbath** they rested according to the commandment." (Luke 23: 56) [emphasis added]

THIRD DAY OF UNLEAVENED BREAD / WEEKLY SABBATH – NISAN 17

The disciples and the women observe the weekly seventh day as a Sabbath.

NISAN 18 - FOURTH DAY OF UNLEAVENED BREAD / THE OFFERING OF FIRSTFRUITS OF BARLEY HARVEST

"Now **on the first day of the week** Mary Magdalene came to the tomb early, **while it was still dark**, and saw that the stone had been taken away from the tomb." (John 20:1) [emphasis added]

"Now **after the Sabbath, toward the dawn of the first day of the week,** Mary Magdalene and the other Mary went to see the tomb." (Matthew 28:1) [emphasis added]

"But on **the first day of the week, at early dawn**, they went to the tomb, **taking the spices they had prepared**." (Luke 24:1) [emphasis added]

"And **very early on the first day of the week, when the sun had risen**, they went to the tomb." (Mark 16: 2) [emphasis added]

"Now when he rose **early on the first day of the week,** he [Jesus] appeared first to Mary Magdalene, from whom he had cast out seven demons..." (Mark 16:9) [emphasis added] (This is included for completeness though some manuscripts don't include this section)

When the time cues of the all the narratives are arranged in this manner, the discrepancies vanish and the literal three days and three nights become very evident. Between the Crucifixion and the first day of the week, there occurred Nisan 15, Nisan 16, and Nisan 17.

TIME CUES IN THE PESHITTA

An important point must be made about the events that happened at dawn on the first day of the week. The ubiquitous tradition exists that Jesus Christ resurrected at dawn on Sunday. The passages from each of the Gospels listed above do not state this. In fact, John's narrative specifically states that it was still dark when Mary arrived at the uncovered and empty tomb. All the accounts tie the dawn time cue with the arrival of the women to the tomb. However, the English translations of the Greek are inconsistent in their details whether it was before or after sunrise when the women arrived.

John 20:1

John's narrative contains three specific details: it was the first day of the week, it was early in the day, and it was still dark. The words used in the Aramaic Peshitta have exactly the same connotation.[121]

Matthew 28:1

Matthew's narrative contains three specific details: it was after the Sabbath, dawn was just beginning, and it was the first day of the week. The words used in the Aramaic Peshitta specify: after the evening of the Sabbath, the dawn light was shining, and it was the first day of the week.[122]

Luke 24:1

Luke's narrative contains two specific details: it was the first day of the week and it was at the very early part of dawn.[123] The words used in the Aramaic Peshitta specify: it was the first day of the week and it was at daybreak. It also in-

---

121 [Dukhrana] John 20:1
122 [Dukhrana] Matthew 28:1
123 [BibleHub] biblehub.com/text/luke/24-1.htm

cludes one additional important detail not found in the Greek: while it was still dark.[124]

Mark 16: 2

Mark's narrative contains three specific details: it was very early in the day, it was the first day of the week, the sun had risen. This last detail is very clear using the aorist form.[125] The words used in the Aramaic Peshitta have exactly the same connotation for the first two details. However, for the last detail, two words are used that both have multiple meanings. The first is "k'ad" which can mean "when, just as, or after." The second is "d'naH" which is "to shine or to rise." Although the sense given in the Greek of "after the sun rose" matches, the Aramaic can just as easily mean "just as the sun shone."[126] Is this a case of Aramaic primacy? If so, there would not be any apparent contradiction with the other Gospels.

Mark 16:9

Translations such as the ESV show an error in punctuation – they put the comma in the wrong spot. Instead of "Now when he rose early on the first day of the week, he appeared...", it should be "Now having risen, early on the first day of the week he appeared...." The verb is the very first word of the phrase and is in aorist form – the action was already complete.[127]

The Aramaic Peshitta has a different word order but the verb is still translated as "having risen." It reads: "Then at dawn on the first day of the week having risen he appeared..."[128]

---

124 [Dukhrana] Luke 24:1
125 [BibleHub] biblehub.com/text/mark/16-2.htm
126 [Dukhrana] Mark 16:2
127 [BibleHub] biblehub.com/text/mark/16-9.htm
128 [Dukhrana] Mark 16:9

THE EMMAUS ROAD

There is some confusion regarding the account of the conversation on the Emmaus road during Sunday. The phrase in question is: "the third day since."

"Then one of them, named Cleopas, answered him, "Are you the only visitor to Jerusalem who does not know the things that have happened there in these days?" And he said to them, "What things?" And they said to him, "Concerning Jesus of Nazareth, a man who was a prophet mighty in deed and word before God and all the people, and how our chief priests and rulers delivered him up to be condemned to death, and crucified him. But we had hoped that he was the one to redeem Israel. Yes, and besides all this, **it is now the third day since these things happened.** Moreover, some women of our company amazed us. They were at the tomb early in the morning, and when they did not find his body, they came back saying that they had even seen a vision of angels, who said that he was alive." (Luke 24:18-23) [emphasis added]

They are recounting the events that have happened in Jerusalem regarding Jesus. If one assumes the common understanding that the crucifixion occurred on Friday, then Sunday should be considered the second day since the events of Friday. But if one assumes that the crucifixion occurred on Wednesday, then Sunday should be considered the fourth day since the events of Wednesday. This is one proof text that is used for the alternate view that the crucifixion occurred on Thursday.

However, the last event in Jerusalem was not the crucifixion on the Preparation Day but the event on the following day, the First day of Unleavened Bread, where the chief priests and Pharisees went to Pilate to set up a guard of soldiers at the tomb for three days. Only then, in verse 22, does the discussion get into the account that the body was not there and that Jesus was alive. Sunday, the First day of the week, was the third day since the last event on the First Day of Unleavened Bread.

In verse 21, the Greek uses the word "tritēn" (S#5154) or "third" along with the singular form of day (i.e. "third day"). The Aramaic Peshitta contains a notable difference. The Peshitta uses "t'lat,a" or "three" along with the plural "days" since all this happened.[129] It literally reads: "behold! three days behold from these all happened." The Aramaic does not include the current day (of Sunday) in the total number of days being referred to. There is no contradiction in the account as given in the Peshitta if one considers three days elapsed between Wednesday and Sunday.

THE OPTIONS FOR A DATE

As previously discussed, the combined timeline shows that three nights/three days occurred between Passover and the First day of the week (Sunday). This means that Passover (Nisan 14) occurred on a Wednesday. Counting 14 days prior, Nisan 1 occurred on a Thursday.

Using the modern Jewish calendar (even though we have determined this method was not in use during this period) and referring back to Table 3, the only possible option for a date is March 23, 30 AD for Nisan 1. However, if we need to take into account that the first figs would need to be ripe in the later part of April, then the date of Passover in 30 AD would be too early.

Now the importance of the abib based calendar becomes clearly evident. Remember that it was essential to ob-

---

129[Dukhrana] Luke 24:21

serve the state of the barley in order for there to be ripe grain by the time it was needed during this period of the Feasts. Referring to Table 3 and using the abib method, the year where Nisan 1 occurred on a Thursday was April 12, 31 AD. Passover, Nisan 14, occurred on Wednesday, April 25. The Resurrection then occurred three days and three nights later during the early night portion of April 28/29.

31 AD

	Su	M	Tu	W	Th	F	Sa	Su	M	Tu	W	Th	F	Sa	
Adar	7	8	9	10	11	12	13	18	19	20	21	22	23	24	
	14	15	16	17	18	19	20	25	26	27	28	1	2	3	March
	21	22	23	24	25	26	27	4	5	6	7	8	9	10	
	28	29	30	1	2	3	4	11	12	13	14	15	16	17	
Adar II	5	6	7	8	9	10	11	18	19	20	21	22	23	24	
	12	13	14	15	16	17	18	25	26	27	28	29	30	31	
	19	20	21	22	23	24	25	1	2	3	4	5	6	7	April
	26	27	28	29	1	2	3	8	9	10	11	12	13	14	
Nisan	4	5	6	7	8	9	10	15	16	17	18	19	20	21	
	11	12	13	14	15	16	17	22	23	24	25	26	27	28	
	18	19	20	21	22	23	24	29	30	1	2	3	4	5	May
	25	26	27	28	29	30	1	6	7	8	9	10	11	12	

This date in late April matches all the requirements that we have examined. Figs would be expected to be ripe. The winter barley would be ripe in order for it to be used in the Firstfruits offering. And there is a literal period of three days that match the words of Jesus exactly.

THE ECLIPSE

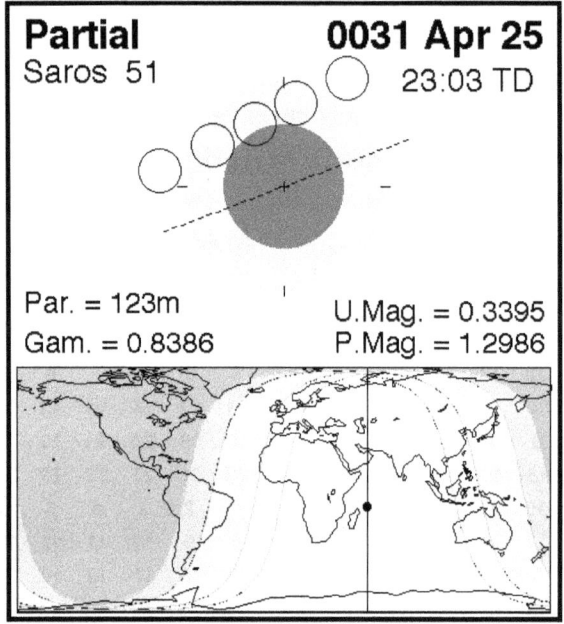

Five Millennium Canon of Lunar Eclipses (Espenak & Meeus)
NASA TP-2009-214172

Interestingly, there was an eclipse that happened on the traditional date of Friday April 3, 33 AD and an eclipse that happened on Wednesday, April 25, 31 AD. How do they compare? The one in 31 AD was directly over the Middle East during the night – between 9 pm and 11 pm (taking into account the TD time shown in the image).

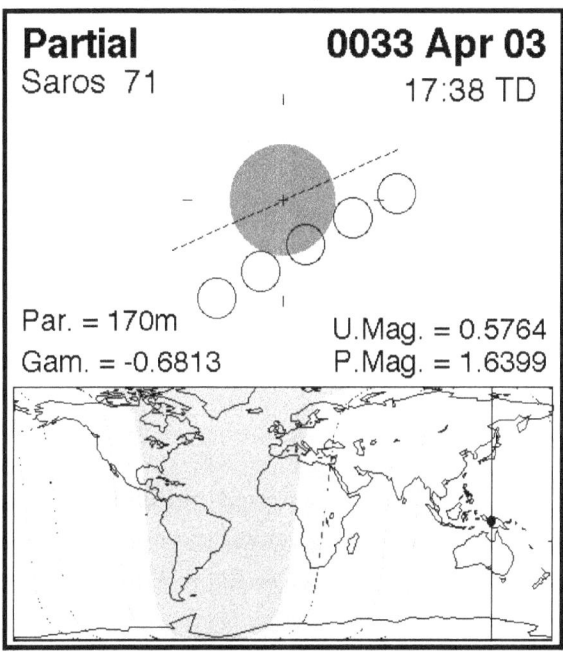

Five Millennium Canon of Lunar Eclipses (Espenak & Meeus)
NASA TP-2009-214172

The eclipse in 33 AD was in the afternoon between 3-5pm (taking into account the TD time shown in the image) and was not very visible to the people of Jerusalem.

There are records saying that an eclipse did take place during the evening after the Passover. Two scholars explain it this way:

> "There is some other evidence that on the evening of the day of the Crucifixion the moon appeared like blood. The so-called 'Report of Pilate', a New Testament apocryphal fragment states, 'Jesus was delivered to him by Herod, Archelaus, Philip, Annas, Caiphas, and all the people. At his Crucifixion the sun was darkened; the stars appeared and in all the world people lighted lamps

from the sixth hour till evening; the moon appeared like blood'.

Further evidence is provided by Cyril of Alexandria, the orthodox Patriarch of Alexandria in AD 412. After stating that there was darkness at the Crucifixion he adds, 'Something unusual occurred about the circular rotation of the moon so that it even seemed to be turned into blood', and notes that the prophet Joel foretold such signs. It is concluded that the 'Report of Pilate' and the words of Cyril may be used as secondary supporting evidence that the moon appeared like blood on the evening of the Crucifixion."[130]

The 33 AD eclipse occurred before the sunset and can not be associated with the previous quotes. This is further evidence that 31 AD is the correct year.

As a further explanation, a lunar eclipse does not darken the sky; only with a solar eclipse is that possible. A solar eclipse can not happen at the same time as a lunar eclipse since one occurs at the New Moon phase and the other at the Full Moon phase. Since the Passover is always at the time of the Full Moon, only a lunar eclipse is possible then. The eclipse can not be used as an explanation for the darkening of the daylight during the Crucifixion.

THE EARTHQUAKE

In 2011, research was published which examined layers in an earth core taken from Ein Gedi on the western shore of the Dead Sea. The authors were able to determine a very strong earthquake occurred which

---

130[Humphreys]

they dated to 31 BC – the time of Herod and which was documented by Josephus.

They went on to describe a smaller deformed sediment zone which occurred years later and which they dated circa 31 AD with a margin of error +/- five years. Their goal was not to specifically connect this with the Matthew 27 mention of an earthquake at the time of the Crucifixion but to determine what other options were available:

> "A date was assigned to the seismite based on varve[layer] counting alone. Then, an attempt was made to determine the accuracy of that varve count and to compare this with an analysis of the historical sources which reveals a less well defined date assignment than the dominant 33 AD date that is present in most of the catalogues."[131]

Their article includes two pages displaying very detailed images of the layers and their interpretation of the sediment changes year by year starting from 31 BC and ending at 31 AD. They show that the strata from 31 AD down to 28 AD was disturbed and that the normal cycle of sediment deposition began again after 31 AD. The significant point which must be emphasized is that they felt confident enough after their professional examination of the data that they included this as their estimated date in their publication.

Their discussion assumes the Friday, April 3, 33 AD date for the Crucifixion as the best scholarly proposal and they try to determine why their count lead to a different conclusion. They explain that a good number of the varve layers are difficult to differentiate – even through a microscope. They reference a previous study by Migowski that also counted the same core sample and which proposed a date of 33 AD.[132] However,

---

131 [Williams] p. 2
132 [Williams] p. 7

when one actually examines the source data from the earlier study, one notices that 'Year 0' has been included between 1 BC and 1 AD.[133] There exists no Year 0 between the two eras and therefore, Migowski's date should be later by one year. Although she includes a similar margin of error, the supposed verification of a seemingly significant year of 33 AD is not accurate.

These two studies serve as tantalizing evidence for the accuracy of the Gospel account of Matthew, at least over a small range of years. However, there is still no definitive agreement as to the exact year the earthquake occurred although Williams' publication does include 31 AD as a best guess.

THE LETTER OF PILATE

During the fourth century AD, a priest named Paul Orosius wrote a history of the Roman Empire. As with many other histories, original historical documents were referenced which have not survived through to our era. One of these documents is a letter by Pilate to Tiberius which caused significant turmoil in Rome:

> "After Christ the Lord had suffered, risen from the dead, and sent forth His disciples to preach, Pilate, the governor of the province of Palestine, made a report to the emperor Tiberius and the Senate concerning Christ's suffering, resurrection, and the miracles which then followed, both those performed by Himself in public and those performed by His disciples in His name. He also reported that He was believed to be God by the growing faith of a great number of men. Tiberius proposed, and

---

133[Migowski] p. A15

strongly recommended, to the Senate that Christ be considered as God, but the Senate was angry that this matter had not been brought to its notice first, as was the custom, in order that it might be the first to decree that a new cult be adopted. Therefore, it refused to consecrate Christ and passed a decree that Christians be completely extirpated from the City, above all because Tiberius's prefect, Sejanus, strongly opposed adopting the religion. Tiberius then passed a decree threatening death to those who denounced Christians. Because of these events, Tiberius gradually abandoned his praiseworthy moderation in order to take revenge on the Senate for opposing him – for whatever the king did by his own choice was pleasing to him, and so from the mildest of princes there blazed forth the most savage of wild beasts. He proscribed great numbers of the Senate and force them to their deaths; he left scarcely two of the 20 noble men whom he had chosen as his councilors alive, murdering the others on a variety of charges; he killed his prefect, Sejanus, when he was plotting revolution..."[134]

Tacitus, in his history of the Romans, along with other historians confirm the overall timing of events for Tiberius and Sejanus in the account. However, confirmation of motivations which connect to Christian events does not exist. Orosius sought to give clarity to the underlying dispute between Tiberius and Sejanus. His goal was not to prove a date but as an unintended result, he does provide for an exact date. Sejanus lived from 20 BC and was executed by Tiberius on October 18, 31 AD. If Pilate's letter is historically accurate, then the events of the Crucifixion happened earlier that spring and confirm that particular year.

---

134 [Fear] p. 325-326

THE ORDER OF DAYS

There are two other surprising evidences that bolster the Wednesday date for the Crucifixion – the evidences of the order of days. Recall that we examined how the calendar was set up at the time of the Exodus (see Chapter 2). The Exodus and the Feasts of the LORD instituted during that time are a type; the purposes of the Feasts were fulfilled during the crucifixion, death and resurrection of the Messiah. The amazing thing about the specific day order of that first Exodus Passover month is that Passover, Nisan 14, fell on a Wednesday – just like its fulfillment in 31 AD. And Nisan 1 as the start of both months fell on a Thursday.

We also investigated the day order of the Creation Week with the sun, moon and stars having been created on the Fourth Day. The first sliver of the New Moon would have occurred on the Fifth Day or Thursday signaling the first day of the first month of that first year. This particular day order also matches that of 31 AD. It would seem that Creation Week signals a prophetically significant day order for that month which continues through the year for the rest of the Feast Days. The first group of Jewish feasts occur in the first month and they saw fulfillment during 31 AD in Jesus Christ. The second main grouping of Jewish feasts occur later in the year during the autumn period which suggests that they also have day order significance for the future when their purposes are fulfilled.

Summary

For a person who has affected history in such a profound way, it is truly unbelievable that the date of Jesus Christ's birth and death/resurrection are not known with absolute certainty. There exist traditionally accepted dates; however, there are demonstrable doubts associated with them.

The date of His birth can be narrowed down to a small range of years – from 8 BC to 3 BC – with 6 BC as a very real possibility. The probable dates of His crucifixion and resurrection can be determined with more accuracy. Synthesizing various details in the Gospel accounts such as Jesus' own words, the life cycle of the fig, the order of events in the accounts, the likely calendar of the time, the order of days and eclipse data, results in the date of Wednesday, April 25, 31 AD as the date of His sacrifice and His resurrection three literal days later on April 28th in the evening. This throws the traditionally accepted sequence of events into question (i.e. Good Friday) but even tradition should be held up against the details found in the Scriptures.

This completes an investigation into dating the major historical events associated with the 70 Weeks prophecy. Many resources and ancient records are needed when validating historical events. If only there was a single trustworthy method to accurately date these events. We investigate that next.

Part 4
Eclipse Event Signs

Overview

Up until this point, chronology and dates have been determined by taking the biblical record literally and by using historical sources where needed. We have examined the intersections of Jewish history with the 70 Weeks prophecy. There is one additional very unique and fascinating proof that can be layered in. But first, a brief discussion about what is and what is not astrology is needed.

> "And beware lest you raise your eyes to heaven, and when you see the sun and the moon and the stars, all the host of heaven, you be drawn away and bow down to them and serve them, things that the Lord your God has allotted to all the peoples under the whole heaven." (Deuteronomy 4:19)

This passage is a warning against using the objects in the heavens for guidance in how to live life instead of worshiping God who created them in the first place. But sometimes, in the attempt to remove anything that might seem at all astrological, even the godly uses for His creation are ignored. God did create the sun, moon and stars for specific reasons:

"And God said, "Let there be lights in the expanse of the heavens to separate the day from the night. And let them be for signs and for seasons, and for days and years."" (Genesis 1:14)

The word translated "signs" is the Hebrew word "oth" (S# 226) which is defined as "a signal (literally or figuratively), as a flag, beacon, monument, omen, prodigy, evidence, etc. -- mark, miracle, (en-)sign, token." Some aspect of the interaction between the earth, moon, and sun is considered a mark in history of some work or miracle of God that has taken place. This is not related to individual lives as astrology would wrongly dictate. But it is an evidence as to what God is and has been doing with and for His chosen nation as a whole throughout history.

Chapter 17

Feasts of the LORD

We'll begin with a brief overview of the Jewish Feast Days which God calls the "Feasts of the LORD" (Leviticus 23:2). We have already examined the start of the Jewish year as it relates to the first group of feasts: Passover, the Feast of Unleavened Bread and the Feast of Firstfruits. Those are the first three feasts described in Leviticus 23. Fifty days after the Feast of Firstfruits, the single Feast of Weeks occurs. It always occurs on the first day of the week since it is counted from a Sabbath. The third group of feasts occurs in the autumn period. The first of this group is the Feast of Trumpets which is a Sabbath and is always on the first day of the seventh month, Tishri. The tenth day of that month is the Day of Atonement; also a Sabbath. On the fifteenth, the eight day long Feast of Booths begins. It has a Sabbath on the first and the last days of the feast.

The Feasts of the LORD

Spring Feasts (In First month)

Passover	Nisan 14
Feast of Unleavened Bread	Nisan 15 (for 7 days)
First Fruits	Day after the weekly Sabbath that occurs during the 7 days
Feast of Weeks (Pentecost)	50th day after First Fruits

Autumn Feasts (In Seventh month)

Feast of Trumpets	Tishri 1
Day of Atonement	Tishri 10
Feast of Booths	Tishri 15 (for 7 days)
The Eighth Day	Tishri 22

Chapter 18

The Blood Moon Phenomenon

During the autumn of 2009 as I was investigating the 70 Weeks prophecy, I came across a very intriguing topic. I had missed the excitement that had been generated in the biblical prophecy circles. In 2008, Pastor Mark Biltz discovered a connection between Jewish Feast Days coinciding with "blood moons" or total lunar eclipses. On the surface, it wasn't really a surprising coincidence since lunar eclipses are very common and Jewish Feasts are tied to lunar phases; this happens relatively frequently. What was uncommon, however, was a tetrad of blood moons; that is, a group of four total eclipses in a row that coincided with the feasts. He also found that there were solar eclipses that occurred within this time period that also matched feast days. Looking through the eclipse records on the NASA website, he found that several tetrads matched significant dates for the Jewish people: the 1948 rebirth of Israel and the 1967 Six Day War. The next future tetrad (and the last for a long time) would occur in 2014/2015. Initially, as Biltz's information became known, people began to declare that 2008 would be the start of the expected seven Year Tribulation period. Joel 2:31 was quoted as proof of this: "The sun shall be turned to darkness, and the moon to blood, before the great and awesome day of the Lord comes." However, this view quickly died down after nothing biblically significant occurred. As 2014 approached, there again was an increasing frenzy of debate as to what the significance for the 2014/2015 group was and people were attributing it as a sign of the "end of the age" and offering many outlandish expectations.

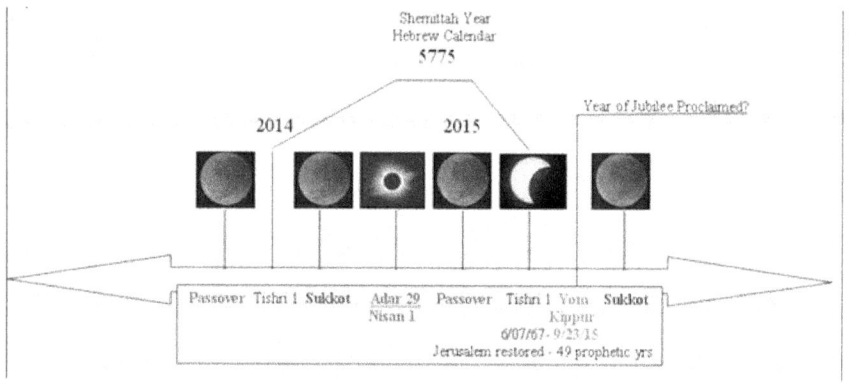

Illustration 2: 2014/2015 Eclipses on Jewish Feast days first posted by Biltz in 2008 [Biltz]

	Greatest Eclipse	T.D.	Type	Saros	Lunation	Member	Gamma	Pen.	Umb.	Pen.	Par.	Tot.
AD	2014-Apr-15	7:46:46	T	1129	122	56	-0.3016	2.3198	1.2915	343.7	214.6	77.9
AD	2014-Oct-08	10:55:42	T	1135	127	42	0.3825	2.147	1.1666	317.7	199.3	58.9
AD	2015-Apr-04	12:01:22	T	1141	132	30	0.4458	2.0805	1.0015	357.9	209.2	6.5
AD	2015-Sep-28	2:48:15	T	1147	137	26	-0.3295	2.2311	1.2773	310.3	199.6	71.9

Table 8: "Blood moon" tetrad 2014-2015 (estimated 2009) source: http://transit.savage-garden.org/en/lunar.html?centuryId=21

For additional proof, there was mention of searching through the eclipse data for other significant tetrads matching historical dates with the year 1493 AD given as an example.

However, the twentieth century matches very much intrigued me. The eclipse data was generated by NASA since eclipses are very predictable through the interaction of orbital properties. The data couldn't be fabricated and modified to fit any particular religious notions and anyone at any time could verify the information for themselves. But the timing of the eclipse matches around the rebirth of Israel bothered me. The lunar tetrad began with the eclipse of April 13, 1949. This was one year *after* the proclamation of May 15, 1948 (Iyar 5). If the matching eclipse was supposed to be prophetically significant then why didn't it match up exactly in the year it happened?

Referencing the NASA website, there are actually two additional lunar eclipses that fell on the Feast Days in 1948: April 23 and October 18. But they are not "blood moons" or total lunar eclipses and therefore, they didn't match the system that Biltz had determined and he didn't include them. Yet, the fact that these eclipses exist during that particularly significant year was very intriguing since God is not just *close* but is always *exact*. In comparison, the total lunar eclipse tetrad of 1967 begins in the year that the Six Day War occurred which then is an exact event/timing match.

Chapter 19

Eclipse Event Signs

As I'm sure almost everyone who first learns about these "blood moon"/Feast Day matches does, I started searching through the NASA lunar and solar eclipse tables. There are very few tetrads of total eclipses that match the "correct" days. I then expanded my search for any type of eclipse that would coincide with the Jewish Feast Days. Sometimes there indeed was a cluster around significant historical dates. But then, checking where the Feasts fell in the Jewish calendar for that year, I found that the intercalation pattern didn't allow for those matches to be significant. However, here is the payoff for investigating how the ancient Hebrew calendar was actually determined.

If one uses the method of calendar construction based on the abib state of the winter barley harvest, suddenly there are many significant **Eclipse Event Signs** which match historical events of the Jewish people. I will use the phrase Eclipse Event Sign to describe this phenomenon. Eclipses on their own are not significant. Eclipses coinciding with Jewish Feasts are not significant. Only those eclipses coinciding with Feast Days that occur during a significant historical event for the Jewish people are significant; and only the first year of that grouping is the year of significance. One could not and cannot determine whether a grouping of matches is significant ahead of time – it is not astrology.

Chapter 20

Eclipse Event Signs of the Recent Past

Now, having a clear definition of an Eclipse Event Sign, we can go through the NASA lunar and solar eclipse tables for the the twentieth century and discover what groupings exist. Eclipses coinciding with Jewish Feast days occur quite regularly; roughly every ten to fifteen years. Some groupings consist of more matches than others. Some have more lunar eclipse matches and others more solar eclipse matches. They do not occur exactly on the day of the Feasts but within a one to two day window. Some groupings were significant; others, not.

1902-1904 AD

Eclipse	Eclipse Type	Date (AD)
Solar	partial	Tuesday, April 08, 1902
Lunar	total	Tuesday, April 22, 1902
Lunar	total	Friday, October 17, 1902
Solar	annular	Sunday, March 29, 1903
Lunar	partial	Sunday, April 12, 1903
Solar	total	Monday, September 21, 1903
Lunar	partial	Tuesday, October 06, 1903
Solar	annular	Thursday, March 17, 1904
Lunar	penumbral	Thursday, March 31, 1904
Solar	total	Friday, September 09, 1904
Lunar	penumbral	Saturday, September 24, 1904

AD	AM		New Moon Conjunction + 18 hr		Abib Barley Method		Modern Method
1902	5662	Nisan 1	Apr 9, 1902 09:50:AM	WE	● Apr 9, 1902 W	●	Apr 8, 1902 TU
		Nisan 14 – Passover			● Apr 22, 1902 TU	●	Apr 21, 1902 MO
	5663	Tishri 1 – Trumpets	Oct 2, 1902 01:09:PM	TH	● Oct 3, 1902 F	●	Oct 2, 1902 TH
		Tishri 15 – Tabernacles			● Oct 17, 1902 F	●	Oct 16, 1902 TH
1903		Nisan 1	Mar 30, 1903 07:26:PM	M	● Mar 30, 1903 M	●	Mar 29, 1903 SU
		Nisan 14 – Passover			● Apr 12, 1903 SU	●	Apr 11, 1903 SA
	5664	Tishri 1 – Trumpets	Sep 22, 1903 10:31:PM	TU	● Sep 22, 1903 TU	●	Sep 22, 1903 TU
		Tishri 15 – Tabernacles			● Oct 6, 1903 TU	●	Oct 6, 1903 TU
1904		Nisan 1	Mar 18, 1904 01:39:AM	F	● Mar 19, 1904 SA	●	Mar 17, 1904 TH
		Nisan 14 – Passover			● Apr 1, 1904 F	●	Mar 30, 1904 W
	5665	Tishri 1 – Trumpets	Sep 10, 1904 04:43:PM	SA	● Sep 11, 1904 SU	●	Sep 10, 1904 SA
		Tishri 15 – Tabernacles			● Sep 25, 1904 SU	●	Sep 24, 1904 SA

● = Eclipse Event Match

This first series is the start of the Eclipse Event Signs for the twentieth century. The first year of the grouping, 1902, would be the significant year that coincides with an event. One can make the case that the significance is that twenty-nine Jewish settlements were started in what was the ancient Jewish homeland after thousands of years of dispersion.

The upper chart lists all the lunar and solar eclipses that potentially could match Feast Days. The lower chart shows how they match both the abib method calendar and the modern calendar method. As a reminder, the main difference between the calendars is the intercalation method being used. It will become clear that the abib method is the accurate method to be used for Eclipse Event Signs.

1912-1913 AD

Eclipse	Eclipse Type	Date (AD)
Lunar	partial	April 1, 1912
Solar	hybrid	April 17, 1912
Lunar	partial	September 26, 1912
Solar	total	October 10, 1912
Lunar	total	March 22, 1913
Solar	partial	April 6, 1913
Solar	partial	August 31, 1913
Lunar	total	September 15, 1913

AD	AM		New Moon Conjunction + 18 hr	Abib Barley Method	Modern Method
1912	5672	Nisan 1	Mar 19, 1912 06:08:PM TU	Mar 20, 1912 W	Mar 19, 1912 TU
		Nisan 14 – Passover		• Apr 2, 1912 M	• Apr 1, 1912 SU
	5673	Tishri 1 – Trumpets	Sep 12, 1912 11:48:PM TH	Sep 13, 1912 F	Sep 12, 1912 TH
		Tishri 15 – Tabernacles		• Sep 27, 1912 F	• Sep 26, 1912 TH
1913		Nisan 1	Apr 7, 1913 01:48:PM M	• Apr 8, 1913 TU	• Apr 8, 1913 TU

• = Eclipse Event Match

This series of potential matches contains a relatively large grouping of lunar and solar eclipses. However, due to the arrangement of the calendar, not all coincide with Feast Days. There is no obvious significance for this set of eclipse matches. 1912 would contain the significant event if this were a Sign.

Here is an example that not all series of matches will have significance. If this Eclipse Event Sign phenomenon would have been known at the time, one still could not predict its significance ahead of time.

1921-1923 AD

Eclipse	Eclipse Type	Date (AD)
Solar	annular	April 8, 1921
Lunar	total	April 21, 1921
Solar	total	October 1, 1921
Lunar	partial	October 16, 1921
Solar	annular	March 28, 1922
Lunar	penumbral	April 11, 1922
Solar	total	September 21, 1922
Lunar	penumbral	October 6, 1922
Solar	annular	March 17, 1923
Solar	total	September 10, 1923

AD	AM		New Moon Conjunction + 18 hr		Abib Barley Method		Modern Method
1921	5681	Nisan 1	Apr 9, 1921 04:05:AM SA	•	Apr 10, 1921 SU	•	Apr 9, 1921 SA
		Nisan 14 – Passover		•	Apr 23, 1921 SA	•	Apr 22, 1921 F
	5682	Tishri 1 – Trumpets	Oct 2, 1921 08:26:AM SU	•	Oct 3, 1921 M	•	Oct 3, 1921 M
		Tishri 15 – Tabernacles		•	Oct 17, 1921 M	•	Oct 17, 1921 M
1922		Nisan 1	Mar 29, 1922 09:03:AM W	•	Mar 30, 1922 TH	•	Mar 30, 1922 TH
		Nisan 14 – Passover		•	Apr 12, 1922 W	•	Apr 12, 1922 W
	5683	Tishri 1 – Trumpets	Sep 22, 1922 12:38:AM SA	•	Sep 23, 1922 SA	•	Sep 23, 1922 SA
		Tishri 15 – Tabernacles		•	Oct 7, 1922 SA	•	Oct 7, 1922 SA
1923		Nisan 1	Mar 18, 1923 08:51:AM SU	•	Mar 19, 1923 M	•	Mar 18, 1923 SU
	5684	Tishri 1 – Trumpets	Sep 11, 1923 04:52:PM TU	•	Sep 12, 1923 W	•	Sep 11, 1923 TU

• = Eclipse Event Match

This set of potential matches contains quite a large number of eclipses. They do coincide with the majority of possible Feast Days over this period of years. 1921 is the significant year and marked the creation of Trans-Jordan and Palestine, meant by the British to make good on their promise of a national home for the Jewish people. This event marked the end of the Ottoman Empire in the twentieth century and of its influence over the region.

1930-1931 AD

Eclipse	Eclipse Type	Date (AD)
Lunar	partial	April 13, 1930
Lunar	partial	October 7, 1930
Lunar	total	April 2, 1931
Solar	partial	September 12, 1931
Lunar	total	September 26, 1931

AD	AM		New Moon Conjunction + 18 hr		Abib Barley Method		Modern Method	
1930	5690	Nisan 1	Mar 31, 1930 01:36:AM	M		Apr 1, 1930 TU		Mar 30, 1930 SU
		Nisan 14 – Passover			●	Apr 14, 1930 M	●	Apr 12, 1930 SA
	5691	Tishri 1 – Trumpets	Sep 23, 1930 07:41:AM	TU		Sep 24, 1930 W		Sep 23, 1930 TU
		Tishri 15 – Tabernacles			●	Oct 8, 1930 W	●	Oct 7, 1930 TU
1931		Nisan 1	Mar 20, 1931 03:50:AM	F		Mar 21, 1931 SA		Mar 19, 1931 TH
		Nisan 14 – Passover			●	Apr 3, 1931 F	●	Apr 1, 1931 W
	5692	Tishri 1 – Trumpets	Sep 13, 1931 12:26:AM	SU		Sep 14, 1931 M		Sep 12, 1931 SA
		Tishri 15 – Tabernacles			●	Sep 28, 1931 M	●	Sep 26, 1931 SA

● = Eclipse Event Match

This grouping of potential matches doesn't seem to be significant.

1940-1942 AD

Eclipse	Eclipse Type	Date (AD)
Solar	annular	April 7, 1940
Lunar	penumbral	April 22, 1940
Solar	total	October 1, 1940
Lunar	penumbral	October 16, 1940
Solar	annular	March 27, 1941
Solar	total	September 21, 1941
Solar	partial	March 16, 1942
Solar	partial	Sep 10, 1942

AD	AM		New Moon Conjunction + 18 hr		Abib Barley Method		Modern Method
1940	5700	Nisan 1	Apr 8, 1940 04:18:PM M	●	Apr 9, 1940 TU	●	Apr 9, 1940 TU
		Nisan 14 – Passover		●	Apr 22, 1940 M	●	Apr 22, 1940 M
	5701	Tishri 1 – Trumpets	Oct 2, 1940 08:41:AM W	●	Oct 3, 1940 TH	●	Oct 3, 1940 TH
		Tishri 15 – Tabernacles		●	Oct 17, 1940 TH	●	Oct 17, 1940 TH
1941		Nisan 1	Mar 28, 1941 04:14:PM F	●	Mar 29, 1940 SA	●	Mar 29, 1941 SA
	5702	Tishri 1 – Trumpets	Sep 22, 1941 12:38:AM M	●	Sep 23, 1941 TU	●	Sep 22, 1941 M
1942		Nisan 1	Mar 17, 1942 07:50:PM TU	●	Mar 18, 1942 W	●	Mar 19, 1942 TH
	5703	Tishri 1 – Trumpets	Sep 11, 1942 11:53:AM F	●	Sep 12, 1942 SA	●	Sep 12, 1942 SA

● = Eclipse Event Match

This Eclipse Event Sign is very significant. It contains a large group of eclipses coinciding with Feast Days and notice that the majority are solar eclipse matches. More research is needed in order to determine if the relative number of matching solar eclipses has an additional significance.

1940 contained the infamous start of the "Final Solution" against the Jewish people by the Nazis. This is the year the camp at Auschwitz was constructed and of the first deportation to Poland.

1948-1950 AD

Eclipse	Eclipse Type	Date (AD)
Lunar	partial	April 23, 1948
Lunar	penumbral	October 18, 1948
Lunar	total	April 13, 1949
Lunar	total	October 7, 1949
Solar	annular	March 18, 1950
Lunar	total	April 2, 1950
Solar	total	September 12, 1950
Lunar	total	September 26, 1950

AD	AM		New Moon Conjunction + 18 hr		Abib Barley Method		Modern Method	
1948	5708	Nisan 1	Apr 10, 1948 09:17:AM	SA		Apr 11, 1948 TU		Apr 10, 1948 SA
		Nisan 14 – Passover			●	Apr 24, 1948 SA	●	Apr 23, 1948 F
	5709	Tishri 1 – Trumpets	Oct 3, 1948 03:42:PM	SU		Oct 4, 1948 M		Oct 4, 1948 M
		Tishri 15 – Tabernacles			●	Oct 18, 1948 M	●	Oct 18, 1948 M
1949		Nisan 1	Mar 30, 1949 01:11:AM	W		Mar 31, 1949 TH		Mar 31, 1949 TH
		Nisan 14 – Passover			●	Apr 13, 1949 W	●	Apr 13, 1949 W
	5710	Tishri 1 – Trumpets	Sep 23, 1949 08:21:AM	TU		Sep 24, 1949 W		Sep 24, 1949 SA
		Tishri 15 – Tabernacles			●	Oct 8, 1949 SA	●	Oct 8, 1949 SA
1950		Nisan 1	Mar 19, 1950 11:20:AM	SU	●	Mar 20, 1950 M	●	Mar 19, 1950 SU
		Nisan 14 – Passover			●	Apr 2, 1950 SU	●	Apr 1, 1950 SA
	5711	Tishri 1 – Trumpets	Sep 12, 1950 11:29:PM	TU	●	Sep 13, 1950 W	●	Sep 12, 1950 TU
		Tishri 15 – Tabernacles			●	Sep 27, 1950 W	●	Sep 26, 1950 TU

● = Eclipse Event Match

Much has been made of the eclipses that match Feast Days during this time period. It is easily the most significant event in the twentieth century for the Jewish people which saw the rebirth of their nation of Israel. The so-called "blood moon" tetrad began in 1949.

Notice that the significant event occurred in the first year of the group of matching eclipses. 1948 contained the Eclipse Event Sign. This is evidence that, although spectacular, the tetrad of total eclipses is only of minor importance as part of the complete phenomenon of signs in the heavens.

1967-1968 AD

Eclipse	Eclipse Type	Date (AD)
Lunar	total	April 24, 1967
Lunar	total	October 18, 1967
Solar	partial	March 28, 1968
Lunar	total	April 13, 1968
Solar	total	September 22, 1968
Lunar	total	October 6, 1968
Solar	annular	March 18, 1969
Solar	annular	September 11, 1969

AD	AM		New Moon Conjunction + 18 hr		Abib Barley Method		Modern Method	
1967	5727	Nisan 1	Apr 10, 1967 06:20:PM	M		Apr 11, 1967 TU		Apr 11, 1967 TU
		Nisan 14 – Passover			•	Apr 24, 1967 M	•	Apr 24, 1967 M
	5728	Tishri 1 – Trumpets	Oct 4, 1967 04:24:PM	W		Oct 5, 1967 TH		Oct 5, 1967 TH
		Tishri 15 – Tabernacles			•	Oct 19, 1967 TH	•	Oct 19, 1967 TH
1968		Nisan 1	Mar 29, 1968 06:48:PM	F	•	Mar 30, 1968 SA	•	Mar 30, 1968 SA
		Nisan 14 – Passover			•	Apr 12, 1968 F	•	Apr 12, 1968 F
	5729	Tishri 1 – Trumpets	Sep 23, 1968 07:08:AM	M	•	Sep 24, 1968 TU	•	Sep 23, 1968 M
		Tishri 15 – Tabernacles			•	Oct 8, 1968 TU	•	Oct 7, 1968 M
1969		Nisan 1	Mar 19, 1969 12:51:AM	W	•	Mar 20, 1969 TH	•	Mar 20, 1969 TH
	5730	Tishri 1 – Trumpets			•	Sep 13, 1969 SA	•	Sep 13, 1969 SA

• = Eclipse Event Match

This period contains probably the second most significant event of the twentieth century for the Jewish people. As a result of the 6 Day War in 1967, Israel expanded her borders and gained complete control over Jerusalem. Again, much has been made of the tetrad of total lunar eclipses which occurred in 1967. As is being evidenced, the Eclipse Event Sign must take into account the entire grouping of all types of eclipse which coincide with Feast Days over the period of years.

1977-1978 AD

Eclipse	Eclipse Type	Date (AD)
Lunar	partial	April 4, 1977
Lunar	pen	September 27, 1977

AD	AM		New Moon Conjunction + 18 hr	Abib Barley Method	Modern Method
1977	5737	Nisan 1	Mar 20, 1977 02:33:PM SU	Mar 21, 1977 M	Mar 20, 1977 SU
		Nisan 14 – Passover		● Apr 3, 1977 SU	● Apr 2, 1977 SA
	5738	Tishri 1 – Trumpets	Sep 14, 1977 05:23:AM W	Sep 15, 1977 TH	Sep 13, 1977 TU
		Tishri 15 – Tabernacles		● Sep 29, 1977 TH	● Sep 27, 1977 TU

● = Eclipse Event Match

This period contains a very small group of matching eclipse events. The significance is most likely marking the peace process of Egyptian President Anwar Sadat and Israeli Prime Minister Menachim Begin in 1977.

1986-1987 AD

Eclipse	Eclipse Type	Date (AD)
Solar	partial	April 9, 1986
Lunar	total	April 24, 1986
Solar	pen	October 3, 1986
Lunar	total	October 17, 1986
Solar	hybrid	March 29, 1987
Lunar	pen	April 14, 1987
Solar	annular	September 23, 1987
Lunar	pen	October 7, 1987

AD	AM		New Moon Conjunction + 18 hr		Abib Barley Method		Modern Method
1986	5746	Nisan 1	Apr 10, 1986 02:08:AM	TH	• Apr 11, 1986 F	•	Apr 10, 1986 TH
		Nisan 14 – Passover			• Apr 24, 1986 TH	•	Apr 23, 1986 W
	5747	Tishri 1 – Trumpets	Oct 4, 1986 02:55:PM	SA	• Oct 5, 1986 SU	•	Oct 4, 1986 SA
		Tishri 15 – Tabernacles			• Oct 19, 1986 SU	•	Oct 18, 1986 SA
1987		Nisan 1	Mar 30, 1987 08:45:AM	M	• Mar 31, 1987 TU	•	Mar 31, 1987 TU
		Nisan 14 – Passover			• Apr 13, 1987 M	•	Apr 13, 1987 M
	5748	Tishri 1 – Trumpets	Sep 23, 1987 11:08:PM	W	• Sep 24, 1987 TH	•	Sep 24, 1987 TH
		Tishri 15 – Tabernacles			• Oct 8, 1987 TH	•	Oct 8, 1987 TH

• = Eclipse Event Match

This period contains quite a large grouping of potential matching eclipse events. However, it is not clear what, if any, historically significant event this Eclipse Event Sign would be marking. The significant year would be 1986. Here is a reminder that not every such grouping is actually significant. It could possibly be a sign that Israel had developed nuclear weapon capability since during this year a former nuclear-plant technician revealed information to this effect. Nuclear weapon use seems to be hinted at in the prophecies of the yet future Last Days and this could be a sign of Israel's technical ability in this area.

1995-1996 AD

Eclipse	Eclipse Type	Date (AD)
Lunar	partial	April 15, 1995
Lunar	pen	October 8, 1995
Lunar	total	April 4, 1996
Lunar	total	September 27, 1996

AD	AM		New Moon Conjunction + 18 hr		Abib Barley Method		Modern Method	
1995	5755	Nisan 1	Mar 31, 1995 10:09:PM	F		Mar 31, 1995 F		Apr 1, 1995 SA
		Nisan 14 – Passover			•	Apr 13, 1995 TH	•	Apr 14, 1995 F
	5756	Tishri 1 – Trumpets	Sep 25, 1995 12:55:PM	M		Sep 26, 1995 TU		Sep 25, 1995 M
		Tishri 15 – Tabernacles			•	Oct 10, 1995 TU	•	Oct 9, 1995 M
1996		Nisan 1	Mar 20, 1996 06:45:AM	W		Mar 21, 1996 TH		Mar 21, 1996 TH
		Nisan 14 – Passover			•	Apr 3, 1996 TH	•	Apr 3, 1996 W
	5757	Tishri 1 – Trumpets	Sep 13, 1996 07:07:PM	F		Sep 14, 1996 SA		Sep 14, 1996 SA
		Tishri 15 – Tabernacles			•	Sep 28, 1996 SA	•	Sep 28, 1996 SA

• = Eclipse Event Match

This period is another smaller set of potential eclipse matches, containing only lunar eclipses. There are two significant events which happened in 1995. The first is the signing of the Oslo II Agreement – the Interim Agreement on the West Bank and the Gaza Strip. Israel was willing to give up a portion of her land. Secondly, this year saw the assassination of Prime Minister Rabin.

2005-2007 AD

Eclipse	Eclipse Type	Date (AD)
Solar	partial	April 19, 2004
Lunar	total	May 4, 2004
Solar	partial	October 14, 2004
Lunar	total	October 28, 2004
Solar	hybrid	April 8, 2005
Lunar	penumbral	April 24, 2005
Solar	annular	October 3, 2005
Lunar	partial	October 17, 2005
Solar	total	March 29, 2006
Solar	annular	September 22, 2006
Solar	partial	March 19, 2007
Solar	partial	September 11, 2007

AD	AM		New Moon Conjunction + 18 hr		Abib Barley Method		Modern Method
2005	5765	Nisan 1	Apr 9, 2005 04:32:PM SA	●	Apr 10, 2005 SU	●	Apr 10, 2005 SU
		Nisan 14 – Passover		●	Apr 23, 2005 SA	●	Apr 23, 2005 SA
	5766	Tishri 1 – Trumpets	Oct 4, 2005 06:28:AM TU	●	Oct 5, 2005 W	●	Oct 4, 2005 TU
		Tishri 15 – Tabernacles		●	Oct 19, 2005 W	●	Oct 18, 2005 TU
2006		Nisan 1	Mar 30, 2006 06:15:AM TH	●	Mar 31, 2006 F	●	Mar 30, 2006 TH
		Nisan 14 – Passover			Apr 13, 2006 TH		Apr 12, 2006 W
	5667	Tishri 1 – Trumpets	Sep 23, 2006 07:45:AM SA	●	Sep 24, 2006 SU	●	Sep 23, 2006 SA
2007		Nisan 1	Mar 19, 2007 10:43:PM M	●	Mar 20, 2007 TU	●	Mar 20, 2007 TU
		Nisan 14 – Passover			Apr 2, 2007 M		Apr 2, 2007 M
	5668	Tishri 1 – Trumpets	Sep 12, 2007 08:44:AM W	●	Sep 13, 2007 TH	●	Sep 13, 2007 TH

● = Eclipse Event Match

This period is a good example of the use of the abib barley observation for the calendar in determining Eclipse Event Signs. Notice that the grouping of potential matching eclipses includes four eclipses during 2004. They look like they would coincide during the right time of Jewish Feast Days. However, the winter barley in Israel was in abib state already in early March and so an intercalation year did not need to be added.[135]

The result was that 2005, not 2004, was the start of a potential Eclipse Event Sign. The year of 2005 was significant and saw the relinquishing of Israeli occupied land; they gave up land which God has promised them in His covenant. The removal of settlers from the Gaza Strip and the West Bank occurred in August. The year also contained the "World Without Zionism" conference where the President of Iran called for the complete destruction of Israel and that she should be "wiped off the map."

2014-2015 AD

Eclipse	Eclipse Type	Date (AD)
Lunar	penumbral	April 25, 2013
Lunar	penumbral	October 18, 2013
Lunar	total	April 15, 2014
Lunar	total	October 8, 2014
Solar	total	March 20, 2015
Lunar	total	April 4, 2015
Solar	partial	September 13, 2015
Lunar	total	September 28, 2015

135[ABIB001]

AD	AM		New Moon Conjunction + 18 hr		Abib Barley Method		Modern Method	
2014	5774	Nisan 1	Mar 31, 2014 02:45:PM	M		Apr 1, 2014 TU		Apr 1, 2014 TU
		Nisan 14 – Passover			•	Apr 14, 2014 M	•	Apr 14, 2014 M
	5775	Tishri 1 – Trumpets	Sep 25, 2014 02:14:AM	TH		Sep 26, 2014 F		Sep 25, 2014 TH
		Tishri 15 – Tabernacles			•	Oct 10, 2014 F	•	Oct 9, 2014 TH
2015		Nisan 1	Mar 21, 2015 05:36:AM	SA	•	Mar 22, 2015 SU	•	Mar 21, 2015 SA
		Nisan 14 – Passover			•	Apr 4, 2015 SA	•	Apr 3, 2015 F
	5776	Tishri 1 – Trumpets	Sep 14, 2015 02:41:AM	M	•	Sep 15, 2015 TU	•	Sep 14, 2015 M
		Tishri 15 – Tabernacles			•	Sep 29, 2015 TU	•	Sep 28, 2015 M

• = Eclipse Event Match

This period of potential matching eclipses contains two eclipses in 2013. However, the abib state of the winter barley for that year was early and an intercalation did not need to be added[136] and therefore, the eclipses did not fall on the Feast Days in that year.

The year 2014 is the year of significance. Much has been made of the series of four total lunar eclipses ("blood moons") in a row. Since the popularization of the phenomenon, each eclipse that occurred saw a flurry of discussion announcing all sorts of outlandish apocalyptic predictions. Although it is very evident that the fulfillment of God's prophecies in the Bible is coming into clearer focus, this is not the purpose for these eclipses.

136[ABIB002]

As the charts have shown, there seems to be a distinct rule in play: if the coincidence of any type of eclipse with Jewish Feast Days has significance, it is *only the first year of that group that marks the significant event.*

The first year of the group, 2014, would seem to mark the restoration of the Islamic Caliphate. Practically out of nowhere during that year, the group called ISIS or ISIL or Daesh announced their goal and began a concerted effort to revive the Islamic-based empire over the entire region and ultimately over the world. Compare this significant event with the Eclipse Event Sign of 1921 which marked the dissolution and end of the previous caliphate of the Islamic Ottoman Empire which had control over the region up until that point.

Chapter 21

Eclipse Event Signs of Jesus Christ

The previous chapter listed Eclipse Event Signs for the recent past. Some groups of eclipse/Feast Day matches turned out to be significant, others didn't. If a grouping does coincide with an event in the life of the Jewish people, then it is the first year of the group that marks the historical event.

In the chapters which discussed the life of Jesus Christ, the proposal was made that His birth occurred in 6 BC and the death/resurrection occurred in 31 AD. If, as we have seen, significant events have been marked with Eclipse Event Signs in the recent past, it would stand to reason that other important events throughout ancient history would also be marked in the same fashion. In fact, they have been. However, the modern Jewish calendar cannot be used to determine this. This is the reason for the detailed discussion explaining how the ancient Hebrew calendar functioned and how it can be reconstructed in order to unveil these ancient Eclipse Event Signs.

THE BIRTH OF JESUS CHRIST

6-5 BC

Eclipse	Eclipse Type	Date (BC)
Lunar	partial	April 4, 6
Lunar	partial	September 27, 6
Lunar	total	March 23, 5
solar	penumbral	April 6, 5
Lunar	total	September 15, 5
solar	penumbral	October 1, 5

BC	AM		New Moon Conjunction + 18 hr		Abib Barley Method		Modern Method
6	3755	Nisan 1	Mar 20, 6 BC 05:28:PM	SA	Mar 21, 6 BC SU		Mar 20, 6 BC SA
		Nisan 14 – Passover			● Apr 3, 6 BC SA	●	Apr 2, 6 BC F
	3756	Tishri 1 – Trumpets	Sep 14, 6 BC 06:39:AM	TU	Sep 15, 6 BC W		Sep 13, 6 BC M
		Tishri 15 – Tabernacles			● Sep 29, 6 BC W	●	Sep 27, 6 BC M
5		Nisan 1	Apr 7, 5 BC 12:51:PM	F	● Apr 8, 5 BC SA		Mar 9, 5 BC TH
	3757	Tishri 1 – Trumpets	Oct 2, 5 BC 05:16:AM	M	● Oct 3, 5 BC TU		Aug 31, 5 BC SA

● = Eclipse Event Match

If the 62 Weeks of the 70 Weeks prophecy start from the reconstruction of Jerusalem in 440 BC, then 6 BC is the terminus. This year would signify the coming of the awaited Messiah, Jesus of Nazareth. The grouping shown is the only set of eclipse/Feast Day matches during this particular decade. Although other years have been proposed for the birth, 6 BC is the significant year which matches this sign consisting of the orbital relationships of objects in the heavens. It becomes increasingly difficult to rationalize from the modern secular worldview.

In addition, the full set of eclipse/Feast day matches only occur if making use of the abib method of calendar construction. The modern method has Nisan begin too early in March, 5 BC.

THE HISTORY CHANGING SACRIFICE

31-33 AD

Eclipse	Eclipse Type	Date (AD)
Lunar	partial	April 25, 31
Lunar	partial	October 19, 31
Solar	partial	March 29, 32
Lunar	total	April 14, 32
Solar	partial	September 23, 32
Lunar	total	October 7, 32
Solar	total	March 19, 33
Lunar	partial	April 3, 33
Solar	annular	September 12, 33
Lunar	partial	September 27, 33

BC	AM		New Moon Conjunction + 18 hr		Abib Barley Method		Modern Method	
31	3791	Nisan 1	Apr 11 07:33AM	W		Apr 12, 31 AD TH		Mar 13, 31 AD TU
		Nisan 14 – Passover			•	Apr 25, 31 AD W		Mar 26, 31 AD M
	3792	Tishri 1 – Trumpets	Oct 05 10:52PM	F		Oct 5, 31 AD F		Sep 6, 31 AD TH
		Tishri 15 – Tabernacles			•	Oct 19, 31 AD F		Sep 20, 31 AD TH
32		Nisan 1	Mar 30 04:01PM	SU	•	Mar 31, 32 AD M	•	Apr 1, 32 AD TU
		Nisan 14 – Passover			•	Apr 13, 32 AD SU	•	Apr 14, 32 AD M
	3793	Tishri 1 – Trumpets	Sep 24 05:15AM	W	•	Sep 25, 32 AD TH	•	Sep 25, 32 AD TH
		Tishri 15 – Tabernacles			•	Oct 9, 32 AD TH	•	Oct 9, 32 AD TH
33		Nisan 1	Mar 20 06:39AM	F	•	Mar 21, 33 AD SA	•	Mar 21, 33 AD SA
		Nisan 14 – Passover			•	Apr 3, 33 AD F	•	Apr 3, 33 AD F
	3794	Tishri 1 – Trumpets	Sep 13 05:43AM	SU	•	Sep 14, 33 AD M	•	Sep 14, 33 AD M
		Tishri 15 – Tabernacles			•	Sep 28, 33 AD M	•	Sep 28, 33 AD M

• = Eclipse Event Match

As one of the most important events in history, if not the most important, this date has been hidden from view. The significant year of the Eclipse Event Sign begins in 31 AD. It is not possible to find a Wednesday to Sunday day order coinciding with the Feasts in 31 AD using the current modern calendar. The dates only becomes visible when applying the biblical calendar rules regarding the abib state of the barley harvest. In addition, notice that the traditional date of 33 AD is actually the last year of the grouping.

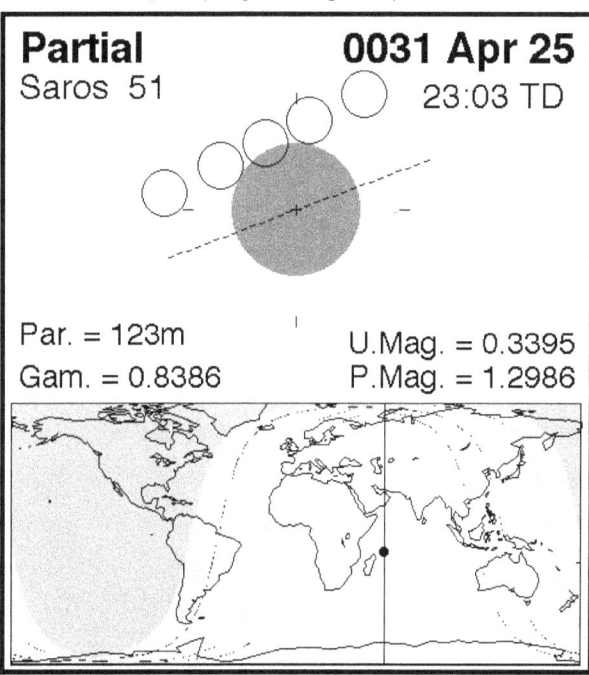

Five Millennium Canon of Lunar Eclipses (Espenak & Meeus)
NASA TP-2009-214172

In the discussion of the events of the Crucifixion, it was already stated that this lunar eclipse during Wednesday night was at a time in the evening when it could have been noticed by the population. We saw references in ancient writings regarding this. An additional significant property of this lunar eclipse is that it is of the same Saros cycle as the eclipse in 6 BC (Saros 51). Actually, the whole series of matching lunar eclipses in the group are in their same corresponding Saros cycles: 51, 56, 61, 66, 71, 76. A Saros is the time period between two eclipses that share very similar geometry; roughly eighteen years, eleven days and eight hours apart.[137] The significance is

---

137[Espenak (Saros)]

that the arrangement of the sun, earth and moon were extremely similar at both His birth and His death/resurrection. It also means that Jesus Christ was not thirty-three at this time, but instead was thirty-five and in His thirty-sixth year.

In addition, this grouping of Saros cycles is the same as in 709 BC. This is the time of King Hezekiah and it is theorized that in this year the Miracle of the Reversed Sun Dial could have occurred (2 Kings 20 and Isaiah 38). The calendar of many cultures was modified after this time and it is interesting to discover the high probability that the eclipse geometry matched the geometry during both events of Christ. More research is needed to determine what the significance of this would be, if any.

START OF THE GREAT DIASPORA

One of the other major events described after the end of the 62 Weeks is they "shall destroy the city and the sanctuary. Its end shall come with a flood, and to the end there shall be war. Desolations are decreed." (Daniel 9:26b)

Jesus also predicted this:

And while some were speaking of the temple, how it was adorned with noble stones and offerings, he said, "As for these things that you see, the days will come when there will not be left here one stone upon another that will not be thrown down." (Luke 21:5)

For such a monumental event there would surely have to be a sign from God in history if the Eclipse Event Sign pattern that is being presented is consistent. There is.

69-70 AD

Eclipse	Eclipse Type	Date (AD)
Solar	total	April 10, 69
Lunar	partial	April 25, 69
Solar	annular	October 4, 69
Lunar	partial	October 18, 69
Solar	total	March 30, 70
Lunar	penumbral	April 14, 70
Solar	annular	September 23, 70
Lunar	penumbral	October 8, 70
Solar	hybrid	March 20, 71
Solar	hybrid	September 12, 71

BC	AM		New Moon Conjunction + 18 hr		Abib Barley Method		Modern Method
69	3829	Nisan 1	Apr 11, 69AD 10:17:PM TU	•	Apr 12, 69 AD W		Mar 12, 69 AD SU
		Nisan 14 – Passover		•	Apr 25, 69 AD TU		Mar 25, 69 AD SA
	3830	Tishri 1 – Trumpets	Oct 04, 69AD 08:41:PM W	•	Oct 5, 69 AD TH		Sep 5, 69 AD TU
		Tishri 15 – Tabernacles		•	Oct 19, 69 AD TH		Sep 19, 69 AD TU
70		Nisan 1	Mar 31, 70AD 03:19:PM SA	•	Apr 1, 70 AD SU	•	Mar 31, 70 AD SA
		Nisan 14 – Passover		•	Apr 14, 70 AD SA	•	Apr 13, 70 AD F
	3831	Tishri 1 – Trumpets	Sep 23, 70AD 10:10:PM SU	•	Sep 23, 70 AD SU	•	Sep 24, 70 AD M
		Tishri 15 – Tabernacles		•	Oct 7, 70 AD SU	•	Oct 8, 70 AD M
71		NIsan 1	Mar 21, 71AD 05:18:AM TH	•	Mar 22, 71 AD F	•	Mar 21, 71 AD TH
	3832	Tishri 1 – Trumpets	Sep 13, 71AD 06:44:AM F	•	Sep 14, 71 AD SA	•	Sep 14, 71 AD SA

• = Eclipse Event Match

This is a large grouping of matching eclipses. It is another case where relying on the modern calendar does not provide for all the possible matches. The date of March 12, 69 AD is too early for the usual start of Nisan which means that Nisan began in April allowing for the eclipse matches. However, the immediate realization is that the destruction of Jerusalem occurred in 70 AD but the eclipse/Feast Day matches begin one year prior. According to what has been presented, it is always the first year of the grouping that marks the significant event.

There are two possible ways to consider this time period. First, as we have seen with more recent Eclipse Event Signs, the abib state of barley is variable. Although it usually occurs after mid March, there are some years where environmental conditions are such that the barley could flower early and no intercalation would be required. It is possible that 69 AD was one such year and the potential eclipse matches might not have occurred leaving 70 AD as the first year of the Eclipse Event Sign. However, without existing historical records, it is impossible to be certain.

The second possibility is to determine what the actual historical trigger for this Eclipse Event Sign was. God states in the book of Exodus that the ancient calendar should begin in the spring season when Passover is to be observed. By the start of Nisan in what we consider as 70 AD, the Roman forces had already begun their move against Jerusalem; the judgement of God was already occurring. The previous year's Nisan to Nisan (starting 69 AD) was the year that contained the move of God's judgement against Jerusalem – the first year of the grouping. The Roman forces began their campaign at the end of 69 AD and into the beginning of 70 AD culminating in the destruction of the city later that summer.

Chapter 22

Eclipse Event Signs of the Babylonian Exile

Continuing with the examination of the eclipse tables, more ancient historical events are discovered to match with Eclipse Event Signs. The previously described interpretation of the 70 Week prophecy is bolstered by these matches during the Exile period.

611-610 BC

Eclipse	Eclipse Type	Date (BC)
Lunar	penumbral	April 2, 611
Solar	total	April 17, 611
Lunar	penumbral	May 1, 611
Lunar	penumbral	Sep 27, 611
Solar	annular	Oct 11, 611
Lunar	penumbral	Oct 26, 611
Lunar	partial	Mar 22, 610
Solar	annular	April 7, 610
Lunar	partial	Sep 16, 610
Solar	total	Sept 30, 610

BC	AM		New Moon Conjunction + 18 hr		Abib Barley Method		Modern Method	
611	3150	Nisan 1	Apr 18, 611 BC 11:00 AM	SU	• Apr 19, 611 BC	M	Mar 20, 611 BC	SA
		Nisan 14 – Passover			• May 2, 611 BC	SU	• Apr 2, 611 BC	F
	3151	Tishri 1 – Trumpets	Oct 11, 611 BC 02:53 PM	TU	• Oct 12, 611 BC	W	Sep 13, 611 BC	M
		Tishri 15 – Tabernacles			• Oct 26, 611 BC	W	• Sep 27, 611 BC	M
610		Nisan 1	Apr 8, 610 BC 08:25 PM	F	• Apr 9, 610 BC	SA	Mar 8, 610 BC	TU
		Nisan 14 – Passover			Apr 22, 610 BC	F	Mar 21, 610 BC	M
	3152	Tishri 1 – Trumpets	Oct 1, 610 BC 03:55 AM	SA	• Oct 2, 610 BC	SU	Sep 1, 610 BC	TH
		Tishri 15 – Tabernacles			Oct 16, 610 BC	SU	Sep 15, 610 BC	TH

• = Eclipse Event Match

The year of 611 BC marked the ending of the Assyrian empire. Nineveh, its capital city, was burned by a coalition of Babylonian, Persian, Medes and Scythian forces that year. Nabopolassar was the ruler of Babylon and Nebuchadnezzar, a general in the army, was his son.

Notice that only the abib based calendar method results in a full series of eclipse event signs.

602-601 BC

Eclipse	Eclipse Type	Date (BC)
Solar	partial	April 8, 602
Lunar	total	April 22, 602
Solar	partial	October 1, 602
Lunar	total	October 17, 602
Solar	annular	March 28, 601
Lunar	partial	April 11, 601
Solar	total	September 20, 601
Lunar	partial	October 5, 601

BC	AM		New Moon Conjunction + 18 hr	Abib Barley Method	Modern Method
602	3159	Nisan 1	Apr 9, 602 BC 09:37 AM TU	• Apr 10, 602 BC W	Mar 10, 602 BC SU
		Nisan 14 – Passover		• April 23, 602 BC TU	Mar 23, 602 BC SA
	3160	Tishri 1 – Trumpets	Oct 2, 602 BC 12:34 PM W	• Oct 3, 602 BC TH	Sep 3, 602 BC TU
		Tishri 15 – Tabernacles		• Oct 17, 602 BC TH	Sep 17, 602 BC TU
601		Nisan 1	Mar 28, 601 BC 04:50 PM SA	• Mar 29, 601 BC SU	• Mar 28, 601 BC SA
		Nisan 14 – Passover		• April 11, 601 BC SA	• April 10, 601 BC F
	3161	Tishri 1 – Trumpets	Sep 21, 601 BC 02:04 AM M	• Sep 22, 601 BC TU	• Sep 21, 601 BC M
		Tishri 15 – Tabernacles		• Oct 6, 601 BC TU	• Oct 5, 601 BC M

• = Eclipse Event Match

The year of 602 BC marked the year that King Jehoiakim of Judah rebelled against Babylon. Since the death of King Josiah in 609 BC, Judah had become a vassal state, first under the Egyptians, then in 605 BC, under Babylon. Despite warnings from godly prophets (especially Jeremiah), Judah rebelled which prompted a swift response by Nebuchadnezzar.

Notice that only the abib based calendar method results in a full series of eclipse event signs.

This 602 BC date as the start of God's further judgement will be examined in a later chapter.

592 BC

Eclipse	Eclipse Type	Date (BC)
Solar	annular	April 17, 592
Solar	partial	October 10, 592

BC AM		New Moon Conjunction + 18 hr		Abib Barley Method	Modern Method
592 3170 Nisan 1		Apr 17, 592 BC 03:22 AM	TU	● Apr 18, 592 BC W	Mar 20, 592 BC TU
	Tishri 1 – Trumpets	Oct 10, 592 BC 12:33 PM	M	● Oct 11, 592 BC TU	Sep 13, 592 BC TH

● = Eclipse Event Match

According to the dates found in Ezekiel Chapters 8-10, this is the year in which the Glory of God departed from the temple.

Notice that only the abib based calendar method results in a series of eclipse event signs. It is also significant that this grouping consists only of solar eclipses.

537-535 BC

Eclipse	Eclipse Type	Date (BC)
Lunar	partial	May 5, 538
Lunar	partial	October 29, 538
Lunar	total	April 23, 537
Lunar	total	October 17, 537
Solar	annular	March 28, 536
Lunar	partial	April 13, 536
Solar	annular	September 22, 536
Lunar	partial	October 6, 536
Solar	total	March 18, 535
Lunar	penumbral	April 2, 535
Solar	annular	September 11, 535
Lunar	penumbral	September 26, 535

BC	AM		New Moon Conjunction + 18 hr	Abib Barley Method	Modern Method
537	3224	Nisan 1	Apr 9, 537 BC 09:30 AM SU	Apr 10, 537 BC M	Mar 11, 537 BC SA
		Nisan 14 – Passover		• Apr 23, 537 BC SU	Mar 24, 537 BC F
	3225	Tishri 1 – Trumpets	Oct 3, 537 BC 0 7:28 PM TU	Oct 4, 537 BC W	Sep 4, 537 BC M
		Tishri 15 – Tabernacles		• Oct 18, 537 BC W	Sep 18, 537 BC M
536		Nisan 1	Mar 29, 536 BC 0 1:53 PM TH	• Mar 30, 536 BC F	• Mar 29, 536 BC TH
		Nisan 14 – Passover		• Apr 12, 536 BC TH	• Apr 11, 536 BC W
	3226	Tishri 1 – Trumpets	Sep 23, 536 BC 0 5:57 AM SU	• Sep 24, 536 BC M	• Sep 22, 536 BC SA
		Tishri 15 – Tabernacles		• Oct 8, 536 BC M	• Oct 6, 536 BC SA
535		Nisan 1	Mar 19, 535 BC 0 1:23 AM TU	• Mar 20, 535 BC W	• Mar 19, 535 BC TU
		Nisan 14 – Passover		• Apr 2, 535 BC TU	• Apr 1, 535 BC M
	3227	Tishri 1 – Trumpets	Sep 12, 535 BC 0 9:17 AM TH	• Sep 13, 535 BC F	• Sep 12, 535 BC TH
		Tishri 15 – Tabernacles		• Sep 27, 535 BC F	• Sep 26, 535 BC TH

• = Eclipse Event Match

Babylon was defeated by Cyrus and the Medo-Persians in 539 BC. In 538 BC, Cyrus proclaimed the end of the Jewish exile. 537 BC marks the return to Jerusalem and the start of the rebuilding of the temple as fulfillment of the prophecies given by Jeremiah.

Once again, notice that only the abib-based calendar method results in a full series of eclipse event signs.

518-516 BC

Eclipse	Eclipse Type	Date (BC)
Lunar	total	May 5, 519
Solar	partial	October 14, 519
Lunar	total	October 28, 519
Solar	annular	April 9, 518
Lunar	total	April 24, 518
Solar	annular	October 3, 518
Lunar	partial	October 17, 518
Solar	total	March 28, 517
Lunar	penumbral	April 13, 517
Solar	annular	September 22, 517
Lunar	penumbral	October 6, 517
Solar	total	March 18, 516
Solar	annular	September 11, 516

BC	AM		New Moon Conjunction + 18 hr		Abib Barley Method		Modern Method	
518	3243	Nisan 1	Apr 10, 518 BC 09:06:PM	TH	● Apr 11, 518 BC	TH	Mar 12, 518 BC	TU
		Nisan 14 – Passover			● Apr 24, 518 BC	W	Mar 25, 518 BC	M
	3244	Tishri 1 – Trumpets	Oct 4, 518 BC 01:59:PM	F	● Oct 5, 518 BC	SA	Sep 5, 518 BC	TH
		Tishri 15 – Tabernacles			● Oct 19, 518 BC	SA	Sep 19, 518 BC	TH
517		Nisan 1	Mar 29, 517 BC 0 9:05:AM	SU	● Mar 30, 517 BC	M	● Mar 29, 517 BC	SU
		Nisan 14 – Passover			● Apr 12, 517 BC	SU	● Apr 11, 517 BC	SA
	3245	Tishri 1 – Trumpets	Sep 22, 517 BC 04:49:PM	TU	● Sep 23, 517 BC	W	● Sep 22, 517 BC	TU
		Tishri 15 – Tabernacles			● Oct 7, 517 BC	W	● Oct 6, 517 BC	TU
516		Nisan 1	Mar 19, 517 BC 01:31:AM	F	● Mar 20, 517 BC	SA	● Mar 18, 516 BC	TH
	3246	Tishri 1 – Trumpets	Sep 11, 517 BC 04:30:PM	SA	● Sep 12, 517 BC	SU	● Sep 11, 516 BC	SA

● = Eclipse Event Match

The year of 518 BC marked the decree of Darius 1 proclaiming that the rebuilding of the temple could continue. The temple was finished and dedicated during this period.

444-442 BC

Eclipse	Eclipse Type	Date (BC)
Lunar	penumbral	April 15, 444
Lunar	partial	Oct 10, 444
Lunar	total	April 4, 443
Lunar	total	September 29, 443
Solar	annular	March 11, 442
Lunar	total	March 25, 442
Solar	total	September 3, 442
Lunar	partial	September 18, 442

BC	AM		New Moon Conjunction + 18 hr		Abib Barley Method	Modern Method
444	3317	Nisan 1	Apr 2, 444 BC 12:46:AM	TH	April 3, 444 BC F	April 1, 444 BC W
		Nisan 14 – Passover			● April 16, 444 BC TH	● April 14, 444 BC TU
	3318	Tishri 1 – Trumpets	Sep 25, 444 BC 06:43:AM	F	Sep 26, 444 BC SA	Sep 26, 444 BC SA
		Tishri 15 – Tabernacles			● Oct 10, 444 BC SA	● Oct 10, 444 BC SA
443		Nisan 1	Mar 22, 444 BC 02:09:PM	M	Mar 23, 444 BC TU	Mar 23, 444 BC TU
		Nisan 14 – Passover			● Apr 5, 444 BC M	● Apr 5, 444 BC M
	3319	Tishri 1 – Trumpets	Sep 14, 444 BC 04:03:PM	TU	Sep 15, 444 BC W	Sep 16, 444 BC TH
		Tishri 15 – Tabernacles			● Sep 29, 444 BC W	● Sep 30, 444 BC TH

● = Eclipse Event Match

The year of 444 BC marked the decree of Artaxerxes when Nehemiah petitioned him and asked to return to Jerusalem and rebuild the walls and the city.

Chapter 23

Eclipse Event Sign for Creation Week

This next discussion should be considered especially speculative, but it's still fun to think about. There are two passages stating that a day in God's view is like a thousand years:

> For a thousand years in your sight are but as yesterday when it is past, or as a watch in the night. (Psalm 90:4)

> But do not overlook this one fact, beloved, that with the Lord one day is as a thousand years, and a thousand years as one day. (2 Peter 3:8)

What results if this is applied literally through recorded history? The numbering of the Jewish year is at roughly 6000 years of history where 2015 AD = 5775 AM. If this number of years is split up so that it roughly matches the BC/AD time period and add in the future expected period of the Millennial Kingdom this is the result:

4000 + 2000 + 1000 = 7000 total years

The BC/AD year numbering is counted from what was assumed to be the birth of Jesus Christ. However, that event is arguably not the main event in the history of the world – His sacrifice and resurrection is *the* central important event of human history. If this event is taken to be the four-thousandth year of history, where does the first year occur?

3970 BC + 4000 years = 31 AD

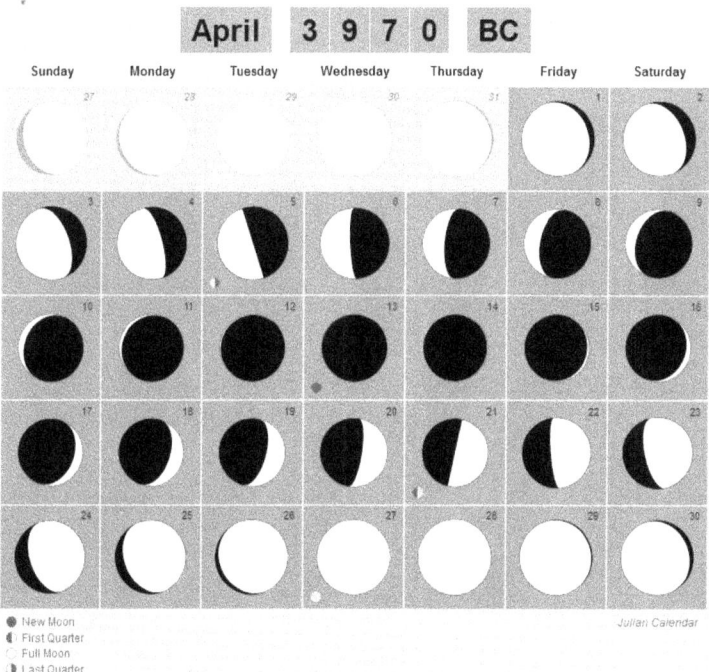

*Illustration 3: Lunar phases for April 3970 BC
source http://www.paulcarlisle.net/mooncalendar/*

What is fascinating to discover, is that in March/April of 3970 BC, the first sliver of the New Moon would have been visible on Thursday, March 31; Day 5 of Creation as the start of the new month of Nisan. This matches the Creation Week day order exactly with the sun, moon, and stars being created on the fourth day of that week.

Of course, one cannot be absolutely sure of this so far back into history. The accumulated errors of astronomical orbits increase the further back one looks. The other issue is how to take into account at least two events described in the Bible that most likely affected the conjunction cycles. These include Joshua's Long Day and the Miracle of the Reversed Sundial of Hezekiah.

However, it is still very intriguing to see potential confirmation such as this. It would be interesting to determine if any eclipse event signs occurred starting during this year and following.

Summary

Throughout this section, many technical charts have been presented. They show that groups of eclipses coinciding with Feast Days do mark significant events in the long history of the Jewish people. These significant events are evidence of God's amazing orchestration of history allowing His overarching plan to be accomplished. One of the most exciting things is to realize that here is confirmation of exactly when Jesus Christ was alive on this Earth. It is also evidence that God is using the heavens to give us signs of His unbroken timeline throughout history.

Part 5
Rhythms of the Future

Overview

What has been presented is very controversial since it requires setting aside many commonly held traditions in Christianity. The following section will be even more so and I have continually debated whether or not to include it. As you read the following section, it is very important to take into account all that has been discussed up to this point. What has been presented has incrementally built on concepts found in the Bible and fit together like an intricate clockwork throughout history. There are biblical prophecies that have yet to be fulfilled. If those which have already been fulfilled are consistent with the rules that have been presented, then it only stands to reason that the future fulfillment will also be consistent with these rules. The signs which have marked historical events already existed from the time God first set the orbits of the sun, moon and earth in motion. Therefore, the future fulfillments are also in motion at this point. Can these be seen from our place in the present?

Immediately, the objection will be raised that no one knows the day or the hour because there have been many false predictions seen through the years – and some even sounded plausible at the time.

"Therefore, stay awake, for you do not know on what day your Lord is coming. But know this, that if the master of the house had known in what part of the night the thief was coming, he would have stayed awake and would not have let his house be broken into. Therefore you also must be ready, for the Son of Man is coming at an hour you do not expect." (Matthew 24: 42)

"Now concerning the times and the seasons, brothers, you have no need to have anything written to you. For you yourselves are fully aware that the day of the Lord will come like a thief in the night. While people are saying, "There is peace and security," then sudden destruction will come upon them as labor pains come upon a pregnant woman, and they will not escape. But you are not in darkness, brothers, for that day to surprise you like a thief. For you are all children of light, children of the day." (I Thessalonians 5:1-5a)

Both of these passages talk about a thief coming at an unknown hour. But they both contrast this event with those that do know the expected time of the event and that it is possible to be ready for it. There are intriguing patterns of future Eclipse Event Signs that match possible years – but not the day or the hour. There is also a reason why, even after considering these future years, the exact timing could still be unexpected.

To be clear and very specific – I am not making any predictions. I am merely pointing out existing patterns that already exist which seem to be highly significant. As a reader, please study and come to your own conclusions whether or not these observations have merit.

Chapter 24

Eclipse Event Signs for Gabriel's 1 Week

FEAST ECLIPSES IN THE 21ST CENTURY

We have seen that major events in the life of the Jewish people have been marked by God using the arrangement of objects in the heavens. The various time periods described by Gabriel in the 70 Weeks prophecy have all been connected with Eclipse Event Signs in history. Could the final and yet future 1 Week also be marked in this way? What follows are charts of the groups of eclipses which are expected to match with Jewish Feast Days throughout the 21st century. We must also take into account what Jesus said:

> "So also, when you see these things taking place, you know that he is near, at the very gates. Truly, I say to you, this generation will not pass away until all these things take place." (Mark 13:29-30)

2052-2053 AD

Eclipse	Eclipse Type	Date (AD)
Solar	total	March 30, 2052
Lunar	total	April 14, 2052
Solar	annular	September 22, 2052
Lunar	total	October 8, 2052
Solar	annular	March 20, 2053
Solar	total	September 12, 2053

AD	AM		New Moon Conjunction + 18 hr	Abib Barley Method	Modern Method
2052	5812	Nisan 1	Mar 31, 2052 02:27:PM SU	● Apr 1, 2052 M	● Mar 31, 2052 SU
		Nisan 14 – Passover		● Apr 14, 2052 SU	● Apr 13, 2052 SA
	5813	Tishri 1 – Trumpets	Sep 23, 2052 07:33:PM M	● Sep 24, 2052 TU	● Sep 24, 2052 TU
		Tishri 15 – Tabernacles		● Oct 8, 2052 TU	● Oct 8, 2052 TU
2053		Nisan 1	Mar 21, 2053 03:11:AM F	● Mar 22, 2053 SA	● Mar 20, 2053 TH
	5814	Tishri 1 – Trumpets	Sep 13, 2053 05:36:AM SA	● Sep 14, 2053 SU	● Sep 13, 2053 SA

● = Eclipse Event Match

2060-2062 AD

Eclipse	Eclipse Type	Date (AD)
Lunar	pen	April 15, 2060
Lunar	pen	October 9, 2060
Lunar	total	April 4, 2061
Lunar	total	September 29, 2061
Lunar	total	March 25, 2062

AD	AM		New Moon Conjunction + 18 hr		Abib Barley Method		Modern Method	
2060	5820	Nisan 1	Apr 1, 2060 09:38:PM	TH		Apr 1, 2060 TH		Apr 1, 2060 TH
		Nisan 14 – Passover			●	Apr 14, 2060 W	●	Apr 14, 2060 W
	5821	Tishri 1 – Trumpets	Sep 25, 2060 11:54:AM	SA		Sep 26, 2060 SU		Sep 25, 2060 SA
		Tishri 15 – Tabernacles			●	Oct 10, 2060 SU	●	Oct 9, 2060 SA
2061		Nisan 1	Mar 22, 2061 01:23:PM	TU		Mar 23, 2061 W		Mar 22, 2061 TU
		Nisan 14 – Passover			●	Apr 5, 2061 TU	●	Apr 4, 2061 M
	5822	Tishri 1 – Trumpets	Sep 14, 2061 04:38:PM	W		Sep 15, 2061 TH		Sep 15, 2061 TH
		Tishri 15 – Tabernacles			●	Sep 29, 2061 TH	●	Sep 29, 2061 TH

● = Eclipse Event Match

2079-2080 AD

Eclipse	Eclipse Type	Date (AD)
Lunar	partial	April 16, 2079
Lunar	total	October 10, 2079
Solar	partial	March 21, 2080
Lunar	total	April 4, 2080
Solar	partial	September 13, 2080
Lunar	total	September 29, 2080

AD	AM		New Moon Conjunction + 18 hr		Abib Barley Method		Modern Method
2079	5839	Nisan 1	Apr 2, 2079 09:31:PM	SU	Apr 3, 2079 M		Apr 2, 2079 SU
		Nisan 14 – Passover		•	Apr 16, 2079 SU	•	Apr 15, 2079 SA
	5840	Tishri 1 – Trumpets	Sep 26, 2079 01:07:AM	TU	Sep 27, 2079 W		Sep 26, 2079 TU
		Tishri 15 – Tabernacles		•	Oct 11, 2079 W	•	Oct 10, 2079 TU
2080		Nisan 1	Mar 22, 2080 08:07:AM	F •	Mar 23, 2080 SA	•	Mar 21, 2080 TH
		Nisan 14 – Passover		•	Apr 5, 2080 F	•	Apr 3, 2080 W
	5841	Tishri 1 – Trumpets	Sep 14, 2080 12:26:PM	SA •	Sep 15, 2080 SU	•	Sep 14, 2080 SA
		Tishri 15 – Tabernacles		•	Sep 29, 2080 SU	•	Sep 28, 2080 SA

• = Eclipse Event Match

All of these eclipse/Feast Day groupings follow the rules that have been laid out in previous chapters. If these have any significance, it would be the first year of the grouping that would mark the event.

I purposely left out two other future matches for reasons that will soon become evident. We'll focus on them next.

2025 AD

Eclipse	Eclipse Type	Date (AD)
Lunar	total	March 25, 2024
Lunar	total	September 18, 2024
Solar	partial	March 29, 2025
Solar	partial	September 21, 2025

AD	AM	New Moon Conjunction + 18 hr		Abib Barley Method		Modern Method
2025	5785 Nisan 1	Mar 30, 2025 0 6:58:AM SU	●	Mar 31, 2025 M	●	Mar 30, 2025 SU
	5756 Tishri 1 – Trumpets	Sep 22, 2025 03:54:PM W	●	Sep 23, 2025 TU	●	Sep 23, 2025 TU

● = Eclipse Event Match

This grouping of eclipse/Feast Day matches is the next expected series. There are two lunar eclipses which will occur in 2024 AD. Fourteen days prior to the first match would be the potential start of Nisan 1 around March 11. This is most likely too early for the abib state of winter barley to exist. However, this cannot be verified until that year arrives and for observation to happen so at this point, we can only assume that there will be an intercalation added to the 2024 calendar based on the abib method. This intercalation would mean that the eclipses of 2024 would not match with any Feast Days and the following year of 2025 would be the potential significant year. Notice that this sequence would consist of a very small grouping of solar eclipse matches.

2032-2034 AD

Eclipse	Eclipse Type	Date (AD)
Lunar	total	April 25, 2032
Lunar	total	October 18, 2032
Solar	total	March 30, 2033
Lunar	total	April 14, 2033
Lunar	total	October 8, 2033
Solar	total	March 20, 2034
Lunar	partial	April 3, 2034
Solar	annular	September 12, 2034
Lunar	partial	September 28, 2034
Solar	annular	March 9, 2035

AD	AM		New Moon Conjunction + 18 hr		Abib Barley Method		Modern Method
2032	5792	Nisan 1	Apr 10, 2032 10:39:PM SA		Apr 11, 2032 SU		Mar 13, 2032 SA
		Nisan 14 – Passover		•	Apr 24, 2032 SA		Mar 26, 2032 F
	5793	Tishri 1 – Trumpets	Oct 5, 2032 09:27:AM TU		Oct 6, 2032 W		Sep 6, 2032 M
		Tishri 15 – Tabernacles		•	Oct 20, 2032 W		Sep 20, 2032 M
2033		Nisan 1	Mar 31, 2033 01:52:PM TH	•	Apr 1, 2033 F	•	Mar 31, 2033 TH
		Nisan 14 – Passover		•	Apr 14, 2033 TH	•	Apr 13, 2033 W
	5794	Tishri 1 – Trumpets	Sep 24, 2033 09:40:AM SA		Sep 25, 2033 SU		Sep 24, 2033 SA
		Tishri 15 – Tabernacles		•	Oct 9, 2033 SU	•	Oct 8, 2033 SA
2034		Nisan 1	Mar 21, 2034 06:14:AM TU		Mar 22, 2034 W	•	Mar 21, 2034 TU
		Nisan 14 – Passover		•	Apr 4, 2034 TU	•	Apr 3, 2034 M
	5795	Tishri 1 – Trumpets	Sep 13, 2034 12:14:PM W		Sep 14, 2034 TH		Sep 14, 2034 TH
		Tishri 15 – Tabernacles		•	Sep 28, 2034 TH	•	Sep 28, 2034 TH

• = Eclipse Event Match

2032 AD

	Su	M	Tu	W	Th	F	Sa		Su	M	Tu	W	Th	F	Sa	
	22	23	24	25	26	27	28		29	30	31	1	2	3	4	September
Elul	29	30	1	2	3	4	5		5	6	7	8	9	10	11	
	6	7	8	9	10	11	12		12	13	14	15	16	17	18	
	13	14	15	16	17	18	19		19	20	21	22	23	24	25	
	20	21	22	23	24	25	26		26	27	28	29	30	1	2	October
Tishri	27	28	29	1	2	3	4		3	4	5	6	7	8	9	
	5	6	7	8	9	10	11		10	11	12	13	14	15	16	
	12	13	14	15	16	17	18		17	18	19	20	21	22	23	
	19	20	21	22	23	24	25		24	25	26	27	28	29	30	

If 2025 AD proves to be a significant year, seven years later will be the next grouping of eclipse/Feast Day matches starting in 2032 AD. The very important thing to notice is that the modern calendar method places the start of Nisan in early March for 2032 AD. Taking into account that the abib state of barley is usually evident later in March, this would require an intercalation for that year and push Nisan 1 into April. This would allow for the expected eclipse/Feast Day matches for that year. It is also significant that this group has the greatest number of matching eclipses for this century.

If the modern fixed method of determining the month has not changed by that year, the eclipse event signs will be at a time when people do not expect them; they will be expecting the eclipse signs to begin a year later.

Notice that if the full sequence of eclipses is determined by using the abib method calendar then another lunar tetrad begins in 2032 AD. In addition, there are two total solar eclipses as part of the series making it a series of six total eclipses in a row. This is extremely rare. The sequences in

1948 AD, 1967 AD and 2014 AD had at most five total eclipses as part of their series.

It is very intriguing to notice that the expected Feast dates for 2032: April 11, April 24, October 6, and October 20 are extremely similar to the Feast dates of 31 AD: April 12, April 25, October 5, October 19. The dates in 31 AD are based on the Julian calendar but even when converted to the Gregorian equivalent, the similar dates would be: April 10, April 23, October 3, October 17 for 31 AD.

If Christ's birth occurred in 6 BC and His sacrifice occurred in 31 AD, then notice that the autumn feasts of 6 BC occurred on a Wednesday, the Passover of 31 AD occurred on a Wednesday and the autumn Feasts of 2032 AD are also expected to occur on a Wednesday. This also means that the calendar weekday order of Christ's first coming in 6 BC would be repeated exactly in the expected calendar weekday order of 2032 AD.

70 Weeks and the Gaps

In the discussions of the 70 Weeks prophecy, the case was made that each period of Weeks outlined in the prophecy is separated by an unspoken gap of years. The first 7 Weeks occurred between 587 BC and 538 BC. The second group, that of 62 Weeks, occurred between 440 BC and 6 BC. The first gap consisted of ninety-eight years which is fourteen weeks (7 x 14). Therefore, if the fulfillment of the prophecy is consistent, then the remaining gap starting from 6 BC should also be a multiple of Weeks of years. The prophecy states that the last period would consist of 1 Week or seven years. The time period between 2025 AD and 2032 AD is seven years. The time period between 6 BC and 2025 AD is a period of 2030 years or exactly 290 Weeks.

7 x 290 Weeks = 2030 years

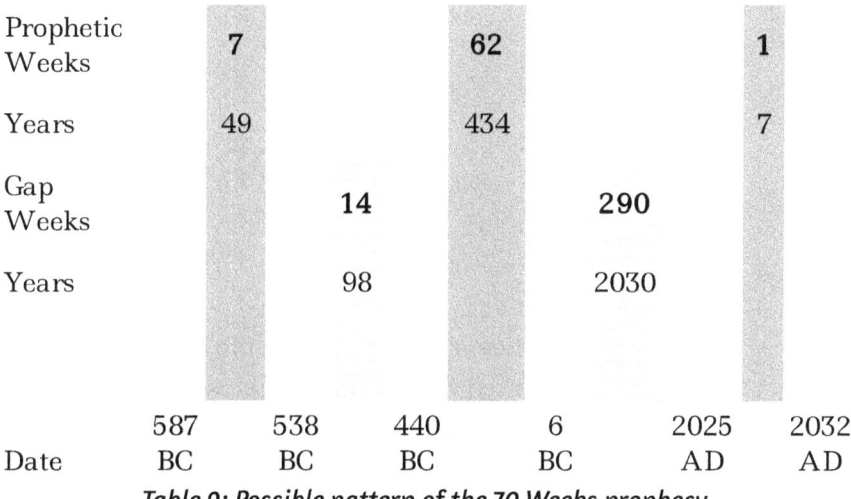

Table 9: Possible pattern of the 70 Weeks prophecy.

Chapter 25

Days of the Lord

This short chapter revisits the discussion of the assumed 6000 years of elapsed human history. If 31 AD is considered as the end of the fourth 1000 year Day of the Lord, looking back 4000 years, the calendar of April 3970 BC does place a significant New Moon lunar phase on the expected day order of that year. I expressed that this relationship cannot be absolutely confirmed.

If 31 AD is considered the start of the next couple of Days of the Lord, 2031 AD would be the end of the sixth day and the seventh day would begin in 2032 AD. This year would not only contain the beginning of the millennial kingdom but would be a literal fulfillment of the prophetic phrase "day of the Lord" used so often in Scripture. Again, no predictions are being made. These are merely potentially significant relationships that exist.

Chapter 26

The 430 Day Prophecy of Ezekiel

If the previous chapters describing the expected highly significant relationships haven't already left your mind exclaiming, "That's impossible!", then here is one more significant area to investigate: Ezekiel's 430 Day prophecy.

Historical Background

In 609 BC, King Josiah of Judah felt threatened as the Egyptian army marched past his territory on their way to engage the Babylonians at Carchemish. Josiah decided to attack but was killed by an Egyptian archer (2 Chronicles 35-20-24). The Egyptians continued on but were beaten back and during their retreat, they conquered Judah and turned it into a vassal state. Judah and the surrounding area were under the judgement of God as Babylon was now the dominant power in the region (2 Chronicles 34:22-28). Three times throughout Jeremiah's writings, God refers to Nebuchadnezzar as "my servant" (Jeremiah 25:9, 27:6, 43:10). The pagan king, along with his Babylonian empire, were being used by God for His special purposes.

Judah's next king, Jehoiakim, was warned to accept this time of God's discipline. In 605 BC, Jeremiah wrote his entire career of prophecies on a scroll and had them read in the temple. It caused such a stir that Jehoiakim wanted to hear it for himself:

> "...and the king was sitting in the winter house, and there was a fire burning in the fire pot before him. As Jehudi read three or four columns, the king would cut them off with a knife and throw them into the fire in the fire pot, until the entire scroll was consumed in the fire that was in the fire pot. Yet neither the king nor any of his servants who heard all these words was afraid, nor did they tear their garments." (Jeremiah 35:22-24)

Jeremiah's prophecies were quite specific:

> "Because you have not obeyed my words, behold, I will send for all the tribes of the north, declares the Lord, and for Nebuchadnezzar the king of Babylon, my servant, and I will bring them against this land and its inhabitants, and against all these surrounding nations." (Jeremiah 25:8-9)

> "So I took the cup from the Lord's hand, and made all the nations to whom the Lord sent me drink it: Jerusalem and the cities of Judah, its kings and officials, to make them a desolation and a waste..." (Jeremiah 25:17-18)

> "And if they refuse to accept the cup from your hand to drink, then you shall say to them, 'Thus says the Lord of hosts: You must drink!'" (Jeremiah 25:28)

That very year, Nebuchadnezzar conquered Judah, made them pay tribute to him instead and carted off some of the prized temple artifacts (2 Chronicles 35:6-7). Jehoiakim went along with this arrangement for three years, but then rebelled.

> "In his days, Nebuchadnezzar king of Babylon came up, and Jehoiakim became his servant for three years. Then he turned and rebelled against him. And the Lord sent against him bands of the Chaldeans and bands of the Syrians and bands of the Moabites and bands of the Ammonites, and sent them against Judah to destroy it, according to the word of the Lord that he spoke by his servants the prophets. Surely this came upon Judah at the command of the Lord, to remove them out of his sight, for the sins of Manasseh, according to all that he had done, and also for the innocent blood that he had shed. For he filled Jerusalem with innocent blood, and the Lord would not pardon." (2 Kings 24: 1-4)

This rebellion against the judgement of God marked the start of the further prophesied judgements that Jeremiah had spoken of. The eclipse event sign of 602 BC marks this pivotal event[138]. By 597 BC, Jehoiakim had been killed and Jehoiachin, his son, along with ten thousand others were deported to Babylon and Zedekiah was made ruler in Jerusalem.

Jeremiah again warned the people that they needed to accept this allotted time of judgement. Jeremiah 27 is a prophecy given at the beginning of the reign of Zedekiah:

> "Now I have given all these lands into the hand of Nebuchadnezzar, the king of Babylon, my servant, and I have given him also the beasts of the field to serve him. All the nations shall serve him and his son and his grandson, until the time of his own land comes. Then many nations and great kings shall make him their slave.

---

138 Refer to the chart in Chapter 22

> But if any nation or kingdom will not serve this Nebuchadnezzar king of Babylon, and put its neck under the yoke of the king of Babylon, I will punish that nation with the sword, with famine, and with pestilence, declares the Lord, until I have consumed it by his hand." (Jeremiah 27:6-8)
>
> "To Zedekiah king of Judah I spoke in like manner: "Bring your necks under the yoke of the king of Babylon, and serve him and his people and live. Why will you and your people die by the sword, by famine, and by pestilence, as the Lord has spoken concerning any nation that will not serve the king of Babylon? Do not listen to the words of the prophets who are saying to you, 'You shall not serve the king of Babylon,' for it is a lie that they are prophesying to you. I have not sent them, declares the Lord, but they are prophesying falsely in my name, with the result that I will drive you out and you will perish, you and the prophets who are prophesying to you." (Jeremiah 27:12-15)

King Zedekiah was not happy about hearing this type of message. There were plenty of prophets who told him what he wanted to hear instead. But they were proven not to be speaking for the true God. For example, Hananiah prophesied that within two years, the period of judgement on the nations by Babylon would be over. Jeremiah informed him that he would die because of his false predictions. It turned out that he didn't even last the two years to see that his prophecy was wrong; he died two months later.

However, Zedekiah did not submit and their rebellion was even worse:

> "He did what was evil in the sight of the Lord his God. He did not humble himself before Jeremiah the prophet, who spoke from the mouth of the Lord. He also rebelled

against King Nebuchadnezzar, who had made him swear by God. He stiffened his neck and hardened his heart against turning to the Lord, the God of Israel. All the officers of the priests and the people likewise were exceedingly unfaithful, following all the abominations of the nations. And they polluted the house of the Lord that he had made holy in Jerusalem." (2 Chronicles 36:12-14)

Nebuchadnezzar returned once again and set up a multi-year siege against Jerusalem which resulted in horrific deaths and suffering. The city fell in 586 BC and the remaining majority of the population was deported.

THE PROPHECY

Meanwhile, the prophet Ezekiel was living in exile in Babylon after the deportation of Jehoiachin in 597 BC (Ezekiel 1:2). In 593 BC, God gave him a strange set of activities to perform as an object lesson.

"And you, son of man, take a brick and lay it before you, and engrave on it a city, even Jerusalem. And put siegeworks against it, and build a siege wall against it, and cast up a mound against it. Set camps also against it, and plant battering rams against it all around. And you, take an iron griddle, and place it as an iron wall between you and the city; and set your face toward it, and let it be in a state of siege, and press the siege against it. This is a sign for the house of Israel.

"Then lie on your left side, and place the punishment of the house of Israel upon it. For the number of the days that you lie on it, you shall bear their punishment. For I assign to you a number of days, 390 days, equal to the number of the years of their punishment. So long shall you bear the punishment of the house of Israel. And when you have completed these, you shall lie down a second time, but on your right side, and bear the punishment of the house of Judah. Forty days I assign you, a day for each year. And you shall set your face toward the siege of Jerusalem, with your arm bared, and you shall prophesy against the city. And behold, I will place cords upon you, so that you cannot turn from one side to the other, till you have completed the days of your siege." (Ezekiel 4: 1-8)

The object lesson was for both the house of Israel and the house of Judah. It is stated twice in the passage that the number of days represent the number of years: 390 years for Israel and 40 years for Judah – a total number of 430 years. It is stated multiple times that this represents the years of their punishment.

INTERPRETATIONS

This passage is a difficult one to interpret and there are many ideas. A very intriguing possibility is similar to the Anderson interpretation of the 70 Weeks. The years are converted to 360 day "prophetic" years and the date is then made to coincide with the May 1948 AD rebirth of Israel. I emphasize "made to coincide" because it is not clear what the exact date and year should be from which to start. There is nothing significant that marks the start of the period in their calculations.[139] In addition, the years in the prophecy are stated to represent the punishment of the Jewish people. If the prophecy ended in 1948, has all the punishment for the Jewish people ended? At the present time, they as a na-

---

139 [Bloomfield] pp. 174-178

tion still do not acknowledge their true Messiah. Let's consider the prophecy more fully.

DATING THE PROPHECY

There are very specific dates given through this entire narrative in Chapters 1 through 10. The first date is when Ezekiel's initial vision took place preparing him for his prophetic ministry. It was in the fifth year of exile of Jehoiachin, the fourth month and on the fifth day (Ezekiel 1:1-2). Using the "Babylonian Chronology", the exact date can be determined[140] which also matches the abib method calendar.

Tammuz 5 on Saturday, July 1, 593 BC
(1505011.5 Julian date)

Ezekiel then spends seven days recovering and on the eighth day he begins the prophecy of 430 Days (Ezekiel 3:16).

Tammuz 13 on Sunday, July 9, 593 BC
(1505019.5 Julian date)

The first period is 390 days for the house of Israel. That year included an intercalation and Nisan 1 occurred on April 19, 592 BC. The end date was:

Tammuz 19 on Friday, August 3, 592 BC
(1505409.5 Julian date)

The next period was 40 days for the house of Judah and the end of the entire 430 days:

Elul 1 on Thursday, September 13, 592 BC
(1505449.5 Julian date)

Chapter 8 lists the next date as Ezekiel is supernaturally transported to Jerusalem, witnesses another Passover where the

---

140[Parker] p. 26

idolaters who haven't been marked on their foreheads are killed and the Glory of the Lord departs from the temple. This is in the sixth year of Jehoiachin's exile, the sixth month and the fifth day:

>Elul 5 on Monday, September 17, 592 BC
>(1505454.5 Julian date)

That year of 592 BC contained two solar eclipse event signs – eclipses that coincided with the Feast days, April 17, 592 BC and October 10, 592 BC[141]. This grouping consisted solely of solar eclipses, which seems to signify an especially important judgement from God. Both the end of the 430 Day prophecy and the Glory departing from the temple occur within this year.

430 Day Prophecy Interpretation

How should the riddle of prophetic time periods be interpreted? First, the stated purpose for each period is the same: the periods are "equal to the number of the years of their punishment" (Ezekiel 4:5). God had determined that the remaining Jewish nation and the surrounding nations would be under a period of seventy years of discipline starting in 609 BC in which He used Babylon as His agent. Jehoiakim and Judah rebelled against this in 602 BC – after only seven years. The 430 year time of prophesied judgement demonstrated by Ezekiel began at this point of rebellion against God.

However, even after they started to experience the judgements for rebellion which Jeremiah had prophesied, Zedekiah, along with the rest of Judah, continued to rebel against God. God put into effect His rule of judgement found in Leviticus 26. Multiple times in that chapter, God states that if

---

141 Refer to the chart in Chapter 22

the nation will not listen after a period of discipline, then there will be a further period of discipline that is multiplied seven fold.

> "Then if you walk contrary to me and will not listen to me, I will continue striking you, sevenfold for your sins." (Leviticus 26:21)

The remaining portion of the 430 years would be multiplied seven fold before their entire time of judgement would be over.

a. The portion of the initial 70 years of judgement served starting from their rebellion:

    602 BC   -   539 BC   =   63 years

b.   430   -   63   =   367 years
    years of   years original   remaining
    judgement   judgement

c.   367   x   7   =   2569 years
    years   (God   seven fold
         multiplies   total
         judgement)

d.   538 BC   +   2569 years   +   1 year   =   2032 AD
    start of additional judgement   (no 0
    begins after end of 70 years   BC/AD
    of judgement for nations   year)

e. 2032 AD as the end of the judgement against Israel

Both the 70 Weeks spoken of by Gabriel and the 430 Days of Ezekiel have possible fulfillment in the same year. It is intriguing to notice that the starting points of these various judgements from God against Israel cluster around 600 BC. This is an observation that has not been noticed by most scholars of the prophetic. Most concentrate on the termination of the seventy years ending at the fall of Babylon and assume significant starting dates after that point. However, arguably one of the most significant events in the history of the Jewish people until that point occurred when God removed Himself from dwelling in the temple. He had been living in the midst of His chosen people since the time of the Exodus – for many centuries. This was first as a pillar of fire and smoke, then associated with the Ark of the Covenant and then finally inside the temple. It is very significant that the prophecy of Ezekiel's 430 years occurred right at this point. Gabriel also indicated that the start of the 70 Weeks was set to start during this time. In addition, God uniquely singles out two pagan rulers for this period: Cyrus described as "His anointed" and Nebuchadnezzar described as "His servant." The timelines of both prophecies not only seem to share a similar starting point but also a similar proposed end date.

Many times throughout Scripture there is the requirement for multiple witnesses in order to establish judgement and of a resulting sentence. For example:

> "Only on the evidence of two witnesses or of three witnesses shall a charge be established." (Deuteronomy 19:15b)

God used Daniel and Ezekiel as two faithful prophetic witnesses in order to lay out the same period of judgement in two uniquely different ways.

Chapter 27

Other Significant Numbers in Daniel

Very late in the development of this book and without any preconceived notions, I decided to investigate the other significant numbers that occur in the passages surrounding the 70 Weeks prophecy. It was not my intention to develop an exhaustive treatment of all the prophesies contained in the book of Daniel. Throughout my research, I had read many various interpretations of these enigmatic numbers and had yet to come across one with a convincing coherent argument. They were usually based on some fantastic leaps of logic that were not consistent with the overall treatment of the text which have left them historically vulnerable to mocking and derision. I took Daniel 8:27 to heart: "...but I was appalled by the vision and did not understand it." However, the thought came to mind that if what has been presented in previous chapters is, in fact, valid, then what will investigation of the other numbers reveal? This chapter presents those findings.

The Numbers

There are three passages which contain time periods related to the abomination of desolation and the removal of the offerings and include the specific numbers: 2,300, 3½, 1,290, 1,335. It is quite the riddle of numbers.

> "Then I heard a holy one speaking, and another holy one said to the one who spoke, "For how long is the vision concerning the regular burnt offering, the transgression that makes desolate, and the giving over of the sanctuary and host to be trampled underfoot?" And he said to me, "For 2,300 evenings and mornings. Then the sanctuary shall be restored to its rightful state.""
> (Daniel 8:13-14)

> "...he raised his right hand and his left hand toward heaven and swore by him who lives forever that it would be for a time, times, and half a time, and that when the shattering of the power of the holy people comes to an end all these things would be finished."
> (Daniel 12:7)

> "And from the time that the regular burnt offering is taken away and the abomination that makes desolate is set up, there shall be 1,290 days. Blessed is he who waits and arrives at the 1,335 days." (Daniel 12:11, 12)

The first assumption is that all these passages have yet to see final fulfillment. Although each chapter contains prophecy that was yet future to the time when Daniel penned it, much is now past history from our point of view. However, these numbers when taken in context all have to do with a yet future "time of the end" (Daniel 8:17, 12:9).

THE STRUCTURE

The structure of each passage and the order that the information is presented is significant. Notice that the start and the terminus vary. In Daniel 8, the answer is given by stating the number first until the terminus at the event (restored sanctuary). Daniel 12 starts from the event (regular offerings cease) and moves forward a certain number and then further forward to the final number which promises a blessing. The three and a half years in Daniel 12 states a more general period of time until the prophecy and "all these things" described is completed.

Taking this order into account, the following sequence in time can be constructed. Start from the date of the restored sanctuary and work backwards 2,300 evening/morning units until when the regular offerings ceased. From this known date, move forward 1,290 days. Then continue forward until 1335 days is reached. The missing piece is at what date to start from when the sanctuary will be restored.

THE TEXT

It is essential to examine the text in the original language for a complete and accurate understanding. There are two words used in Hebrew to describe the terminus event in Daniel 8:14. The first is from the root word "tsadeq" (S# 6663) or "to cleanse, make righteous." The second is "qodesh" (S# 6944) or "holy" which is usually used of the sanctuary in the temple but also of the holy people. The Aramaic Peshitta uses the word "zky" meaning "to be pure, wholo; to overcome, gain possession" and the word "zdeq" meaning "that which is due" referring to offering rituals from a root meaning "to justify."[142]

The next assumption now comes into play. The spring Feast Days in the Jewish calendar saw fulfillment during the first coming of the Messiah. The expectation is that the autumn Feasts will be fulfilled during the second coming of Jesus Christ. One Feast left unfulfilled which solely concerns cleansing and being made righteous is the Day of Atonement. This is observed every year during the seventh month and specified to begin on the ninth day at twilight through to the tenth day ending at twilight (Leviticus 23:26-32). The entire sixteenth chapter of Leviticus outlines how the Feast Day should be observed:

> "For on this day shall atonement be made for you to cleanse you. You shall be clean before the Lord from all your sins...He shall make atonement for the holy sanctuary, and he shall make atonement for the tent of meeting and for the altar, and he shall make atonement for the priests and for all the people of the assembly." (Leviticus 16:30, 33)

The ultimate event of the "cleansing of the holy" in Daniel 8:14 will fulfill the purposes of the Day of Atonement Feast.

As described previously, there seem to be several biblical prophecies connecting with and possibly having fulfillment in 2032 AD. In Chapter 24, the abib calendar method was used and the date for the Day of Atonement is listed as Wednesday, October 14/15, 2032 (Julian day 2463520.5). This date is not seen using the fixed calculations of the modern Jewish calendar method.

If this date is considered the terminus then Daniel 8:14 states to move backwards and reach 2,300 *evening/morning units*. I use this term specifically since some interpret these as

---

142 [CAL] Daniel 8:14

a number of years and some as a number of days but hardly any recognize the significance of the Hebrew term. Some popular English translations include the word "days." Most translations are more accurate and instead use "evenings and mornings." However, the two words in Hebrew are not plural, they are singular and there is no conjunction "and" used. Only Young's Literal Translation accurately represents the text out of all popular translations in English. The Aramaic Peshitta also represents the two words as singular and without a conjunction.[143] The Hebrew language is not stingy when using the "and" conjunction elsewhere. Therefore, if it is absent here, then that is a significant detail in the text.

Several verses later, Daniel 8:26 also mentions the evening/morning unit. Here again most translations use the plural form of the words but many do recognize that the words are singular and represent them in this manner. The Hebrew text includes the definite article ("the") for both words and also uses the conjunction "and." They function as adjectives to describe the vision and literally state "the vision [of] the evening and the morning that was told [is] true." Whatever these terms refer to, they are to be understood singularly as time markers and are of the same essence so that 2,300 in total can be counted.

These terms are given in answer to the question posed in Daniel 8:13: "For how long is the vision concerning the regular burnt offering, the transgression that makes desolate, and the giving over of the sanctuary and host to be trampled underfoot?" When looking at the context of all these passages, the significance of the temple and the sanctuary is of utmost importance. The term "regular burnt offering" occurs multiple times throughout. "Regular" does not imply "ordinary" but is the Hebrew word "tamid" (S# 8548) meaning "continual." Numbers

---

143 [CAL] Daniel 8:14

28:1-8 contain the instructions regarding these continual sacrifices occurring "day by day, as a regular offering" (verse 3). Each daily offering was the same and consisted of two male lambs, one offered after dawn and the other at twilight along with food and drink offerings. The same Hebrew words for morning and evening are used. Once these offerings can no longer take place, the number of sequential continual offerings that will not happen are given as 2,300 total.

$$2300 \text{ evening/morning sacrifices} \ / \ 2 \text{ per day} = 1150 \text{ days}$$

THE DATES

From the terminus date, move backward a total of 1150 days.

October 14/15, 2032 - 1150 days = August 21/22, 2029
2463520.5   2462370.5
Julian day   Julian day

In the modern Jewish calendar, August 21/22, 2029 is Elul 11 – no obvious significance. However, the abib method calendar based on the biblical instructions must be taken into account. Using this method, in 2029 AD, the potential first day of Nisan 1 on March 17 would be too early for abib barley. An intercalation month will be needed which will push Nisan into April and will affect each subsequent month. The beginning of the fifth month of Av will be related to the New Moon phase on August 10, 01:56 (UT). Adding an additional eighteen hours for observation of the first sliver of the moon results in 21:56 (Jerusalem time). Av 1 will most likely occur on August 12 and Tuesday/Wednesday, August 21/22 would be Av 11. This would be the start of the 2,300 missed continual offerings. The day before, Av 10th, would be the day that the sacrifices are caused to cease.

2029 AD

	Su	M	Tu	W	Th	F	Sa	Su	M	Tu	W	Th	F	Sa	
Tammuz	24	25	26	27	28	29	30	5	6	7	8	9	10	11	August
Av	1	2	3	4	5	6	7	12	13	14	15	16	17	18	
	8	9	**10**	11	12	13	14	19	20	**21**	22	23	24	25	
	15	16	17	18	19	20	21	26	27	28	29	30	31	1	
	22	23	24	25	26	27	28	2	3	4	5	6	7	8	September

Anyone who is familiar with Jewish history will immediately recognize the extreme importance of the infamous date of the 10th of Av. Both the first and second temples were destroyed on that date and Jewish tradition marks Av 9/10 as a day of mourning and fasting.

> "In the fifth month, on the tenth day of the month—that was the nineteenth year of King Nebuchadnezzar, king of Babylon—Nebuzaradan the captain of the bodyguard, who served the king of Babylon, entered Jerusalem. And he burned the house of the Lord, and the king's house and all the houses of Jerusalem; every great house he burned down." (Jeremiah 52:12-13)

> "In the fifth month, on the seventh day of the month—that was the nineteenth year of King Nebuchadnezzar, king of Babylon—Nebuzaradan, the captain of the bodyguard, a servant of the king of Babylon, came to Jerusalem. And he burned the house of the Lord and the king's house and all the houses of Jerusalem; every great house he burned down." (2 Kings 25:8-9)

Although these very similar passages seem to contradict which day is being discussed, it is usually interpreted that the 7th was the day the destruction began and the 10th saw its completion.

Josephus records the destruction details of the second temple:

> But as for that house, God had, for certain, long ago doomed it to the fire; and now that fatal day was come, according to the revolution of ages; it was the tenth day of the month Lous, [Ab,] upon which it was formerly burnt by the king of Babylon[144]

Here is another Av 10 tragedy seemingly pointing to when sacrifices will cease and the desolation of the holy sanctuary. Notably, this date is in the middle of the week which would be a double fulfillment of Daniel 9:27 which specifically mentions the time period of half a week. Not only would it be at the middle of a seven year week but also in the middle of a seven day week.

Beginning from this Av 10 date, both numbers of days in Daniel 12 can now be applied.

August 20/21, 2029 + 1290 days = March 3, 2033
2462369.5   2463659.5
Julian day   Julian day

The end of the 1,290 days would be on Wednesday/Thursday, March 3, 2033 AD. This would be the beginning of the last month of that Jewish year. No other significance is obvious.

August 20/21, 2029 + 1335 days = April 17, 2033
2462369.5   2463704.5
Julian day   Julian day

144[Josephus] Wars 6, 249

The date of expectant longing would be on Saturday/Sunday, April 17, 2033 AD. This would be the Day of Firstfruits during the Feast of Unleavened Bread for that new year – the first spring Feasts of the Lord in what may be the millennial kingdom.

2033 AD

	Su	M	Tu	W	Th	F	Sa	Su	M	Tu	W	Th	F	Sa	
	27	28	29	30	1	2	3	27	28	1	2	3	4	5	March
Adar	4	5	6	7	8	9	10	6	7	8	9	10	11	12	
	11	12	13	14	15	16	17	13	14	15	16	17	18	19	
	18	19	20	21	22	23	24	20	21	22	23	24	25	26	
Nisan	25	26	27	28	29	1	2	27	28	29	30	31	1	2	April
	3	4	5	6	7	8	9	3	4	5	6	7	8	9	
	10	11	12	13	14	15	16	10	11	12	13	14	15	16	
	17	18	19	20	21	22	23	17	18	19	20	21	22	23	
	24	25	26	27	28	29	30	24	25	26	27	28	29	30	

Passover is expected to occur on April 14 followed by the Convocation of Unleavened Bread the next day with the regular weekly Sabbath on the following day. The first day of the week and Firstfruits round out that close cluster of Feast Days.

It is significant to note that a total lunar eclipse is expected on April 14 at around 21:00 (Jerusalem time) and will be directly visible over Israel. This would be during the evening when the Passover meal is celebrated and would spectacularly highlight the event.

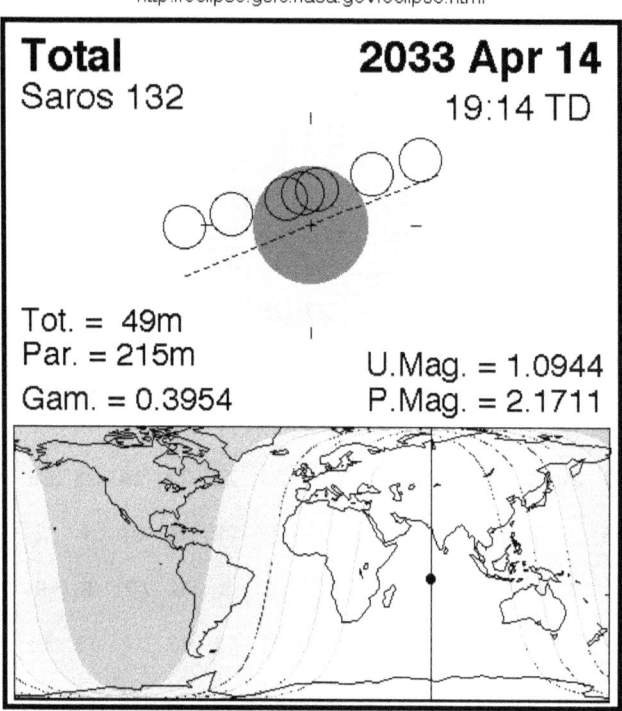

Five Millennium Canon of Lunar Eclipses (Espenak & Meeus)
NASA TP-2009-214172

The Feast of Firstfruits has a significant connection with Daniel 12:12. Gabriel says that the people are to be blessed, happy, congratulated (S# 835) who reach and arrive at the 1,335th day. They have waited, from the verb "chakah" (S# 2442), which also includes the sense of expectant longing. On the Feast of Firstfruits the priest takes the first and best of the peoples' harvest and waves it before the Lord in order that He may "ratson" (S# 7522) them or accept, show them favor, delight in them and bless them (Leviticus 23:9-11). Here again is a possible ultimate fulfillment of a Feast of the Lord as those who have been purified and refined (Daniel 12:10) are presented by Jesus, the High Priest on the Day of Firstfruits and receive blessing.

The usual assumption is that the verse following of Daniel 12:13 has no direct connection with the previous verse and is merely a concluding statement: "But go your way till the end. And you shall rest and shall stand in your allotted place at the end of the days." However, the verb "amad" (S# 5975) or "to rise and stand" takes on added significance if connected with the raising and waving of the Firstfruits. Even the Aramaic Peshitta confirms this understanding in the following transliteration of verse 13: "And you, then Daniel, continue on to the end (appointed death) and rest (be at peace) and rise, stand, be raised up at the time (era) of resurrection at the end of days."[145]

The question remains whether or not these are valid and significant dates and relationships. As with any future prophetic fulfillment, it is foolish to be dogmatic about anything. However, experimenting with the calendar math on other years does not result in similar results. Subtracting 1150 days from other Day of Atonement dates does end up at Av 10 for other years. But, nothing significant is forward the 1,290 or 1,335 days. Starting from 2031 AD leads to similar significant dates; however, the proposed start of Nisan is too early in March if taking into account the abib barley rules.

The previous discussion seeks to determine interpretation from the concepts contained within the prophecies themselves and use Jewish culture and law in developing a coherent understanding.

---

145 [CAL] Daniel 12:13

Summary

This section has presented many possible significant patterns for future years. Again, there are no predictions being made. For those familiar with biblical prophecy, it should be very intriguing that these patterns are visible. With many relationships pointing to the year 2032 AD, will that actually prove to be one of the most significant years in history?

Another interesting observation is that eclipse event signs which mainly consist of solar eclipses seem to signify an especially difficult time of God's judgement. 592 BC contained the Glory of God departing the temple. 69-71 AD saw the destruction of Jerusalem and the dispersion of the Jewish people. 1940 AD was the beginning of the Jewish Holocaust. Is it significant that 2025 AD is another expected grouping entirely made up of solar eclipses?

Conclusion

What you have read is something that I have pondered over and sought the LORD about for seven years. It all started because I noticed what I thought was a mistake in a Bible translation. This began some very intense research into wide ranging subjects. My first thought was always that the Bible should be taken literally where it presents itself literally. The answers that I was discovering showed that many of my preconceptions and traditional understandings had to be reevaluated. I trust you will also put what you have read to the test of the Truth of Scripture.

The other thought and prayer I had was that if we are nearing the time of the final fulfillments of Scripture, then sealed prophecies have to start making sense. There are so many various and conflicting interpretations through the ages which has led to much confusion. However, true prophetic understanding should be consistent with all passages and fit together as a whole.

I discovered that the instructions God gave to the ancient Hebrews for how their calendar should function, are the key in understanding many things through the biblical historical record. In continually pointing this fact out, I'm not advocating that this is the only calendar we should be using. However, it does underline that God expects His Feasts to be celebrated at His proper time.

When God carved out the orbits of the earth, moon and sun, He initiated a series of predictable cycles spanning all of history. The Feast Days which He ordained are integrally tied to these cycles. It would seem that at certain points in this cyclical rhythm, there are syncopated beats which loudly proclaim His work with His chosen people. Anyone can verify this for themselves. This present generation is at a time in history where highly accurate eclipse tables and ancient dates are instantly available and, with some effort, these relationships can be relatively easily worked out. Previously, this type of information would be accessible to very few and the tables would have taken years of slow detailed work to complete. I am convinced that we have entered the period of unsealed prophecies.

Two of the most enigmatic prophecies that contain specific timelines have shown that their rhythms fit into the syncopated historical beats perfectly. The birth and the sacrifice of Jesus Christ also fits like clockwork into this rhythm. The temptation to think that God is no longer doing anything of consequence in our time suddenly evaporates when examining potential approaching drum beats. This is a true statement: "Steadfast love will be built up forever; in the heavens you will establish your faithfulness." (Psalm 89:2)

What do you do with this information now? If what has been presented is accurate, then it is evidence of the amazing way God has designed His Creation to manifest His complete plan throughout all of time. It verifies that His chosen nation of Israel is central to His work on earth. It strengthens our faith in Him since intricate fulfillment of ancient prophecy points to similar future faithful fulfillment of remaining prophecy. And with so many time relationships possibly being so near, these things move from our head to our heart and give us renewed purpose to be about the work of the Lord.

"Amen. Come, Lord Jesus!"

Appendix

APPENDIX 1

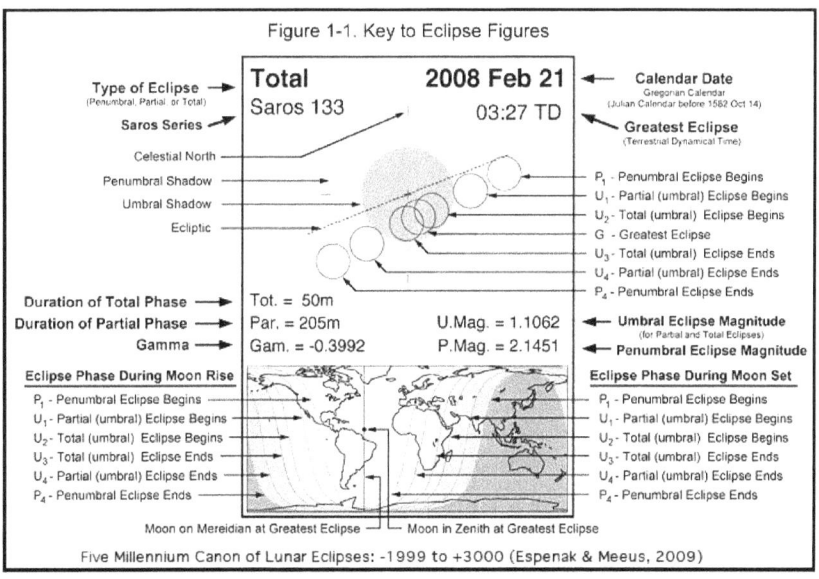

APPENDIX 2

The "abomination of desolation" and removal of the "continual" sacrifices are mentioned several times in the book of Daniel. Each time they are connected with a future ruler. The following pages contain an interlinear rendering of both Hebrew and Aramaic of those passages. These include:

Daniel 8:9-12

Daniel 8:23-25

Daniel 11:29-45

There are many who have never considered examining the text in the Hebrew. Similarly, hardly any are aware that manuscripts in Aramaic exist. When considering prophetic passages it is of utmost importance to examine ancient language structure, word choice and included details – sometimes not accurately represented in English translations.

The Hebrew is from the Westminster Leningrad Codex with English based on Strong's Concordance along with Brown-Driver-Briggs as provided by www.biblehub.com.

The Aramaic is based on the text in the Ambrosianus manuscript dating from the 6th or 7th century AD with English based on "A Compendious Syriac Dictionary" by J. Payne-Smith published in 1902 as provided at cal1.cn.huc.edu.

Appendix 297

S#	Translit	Hebrew	English	Morph	Aramaic	English
Daniel 8:9						
4480	ū-min-	וּמִן־	and out of	Prep	ܘܡܢ	and out from
259	hā-'a-ḥaṯ	הָאַחַת	one	Adj	ܚܕܐ	one
1992	mê-hem,	מֵהֶם	of them	Pro	ܡܢܗܘܢ	from them
3318	yā-ṣā	יָצָא	came forth	Verb	ܢܦܩ	issued/emerged
7161	qe-ren-	קֶרֶן־	a horn	Noun	ܩܪܢܐ	horn
259	'a-ḥaṯ	אַחַת	one	Adj	ܚܕܐ	one
4704	miṣ-ṣə-'î-rāh;	מִצְּעִירָה	little	Noun	ܙܥܘܪܬܐ	small
1431	wat-tiḡ-dal-	וַתִּגְדַּל־	and great	Verb	ܘܪܒܬ	and grew in size
3499	ye-ṯer	יֶתֶר	that became exceedingly	Noun	ܝܬܝܪܐܝܬ	especially
413	'el-	אֶל־	toward	Prep		
5045	han-ne-ḡeḇ	הַנֶּגֶב	the south	Noun	ܠܬܝܡܢܐ	to south
413	wə-'el-	וְאֶל־	and toward	Prep		
4217	ham-miz-rāḥ	הַמִּזְרָח	the east	Noun	ܘܠܡܕܢܚܐ	and to east
413	wə-'el-	וְאֶל־	and toward	Prep		
6643	haṣ-ṣe-ḇî.	הַצֶּבִי׃	the pleasant	Noun		
Daniel 8:10						
1431	wat-tiḡ-dal	וַתִּגְדַּל	And it became great	Verb	ܘܪܒܬ	and grew in size
5704	'aḏ-	עַד־	to	Prep	ܥܕܡܐ	as far as
6635	ṣə-ḇā	צְבָא	[even] the host	Noun	ܠܚܝܠܐ	to forces
8064	haš-šā-mā-yim;	הַשָּׁמָיִם	of heaven	Noun	ܕܫܡܝܐ	of heavens
5307	wat-tap-pêl	וַתַּפֵּל	and it cast down	Verb	ܘܐܪܡܝܬ	and caused to throw down/defeat
					ܥܠ	onto
776	'ar-ṣāh	אַרְצָה	to the ground	Noun	ܐܪܥܐ	earth
4480	min-	מִן־	of	Prep	ܘܡܢ	out of
6635	haṣ-ṣā-ḇā	הַצָּבָא	[some] the host	Noun	ܚܝܠܐ	forces
4480	ū-min-	וּמִן־	and of	Prep	ܘܡܢ	also from
3556	hak-kō-w-ḵā-ḇîm	הַכּוֹכָבִים	the stars/princes	Noun	ܟܘܟܒܐ	stars
7429	wat-tir-mə-sêm.	וַתִּרְמְסֵם׃	and stamped on	Verb	ܘܕܫܬ	and trampled/subdued
					ܐܢܘܢ	them

S#	Translit	Hebrew	English	Morph	Aramaic	English
Daniel 8:11						
5704	wə-'a□	וְעַד	and even to	Prep	ܘܥܕܡܐ	and as far as
8269	śar-	שַׂר־	[himself] the prince	Noun	ܠܪ̈ܒ	to general
6635	haṣ-ṣā-□ā	הַצָּבָא	of the host	Noun	ܚܝ̈ܠܐ	[of] forces
1431	hiḡ-dîl;	הִגְדִּ֑יל	he magnified	Verb	ܡܛܠܬ.	to reach
4480	ū-mim-men-nū	וּמִמֶּנּוּ	and by	Prep	ܘܡܢܗ	and causing
7311	(hū-ram q)	(הוּרַם ק)	was taken away him	Verb	ܐܪܝܡ	to exalt over/to eliminate
8548	hat-tā-mîḏ,	הַתָּמִ֔יד	the continual	Noun	ܐܡܝܢܘܬܐ	continual
7993	wə-huš-la□	וְהֻשְׁלַךְ	and was cast down	Verb	ܘܦܪܥܐ	and abolish/violate
4349	mə-□ō-wn	מְכוֹן	and the place/house	Noun	ܡܟܠܡ	place
4720	miq-dā-šōw.	מִקְדָּשׁוֹ׃	of His sanctuary	Noun	ܡܩܕܫܗ.	temple/sanctuary
Daniel 8:12						
6635	wə-□ā-□ā	וְצָבָא	And a host	Noun	ܘܚܝܠܐ	and a force
5414	tin-nā-ṯên	תִּנָּתֵן	was given	Verb	ܐܬܝܗܒ	was given/granted
5921	'al-	עַל־	against	Prep	ܥܠ	against
8548	hat-tā-mîḏ	הַתָּמִ֖יד	[him] the daily	Noun	ܐܡܝܢܘܬܐ	the continual
					ܒܚܘܒܐ.	during
6588	bə- p ā- š a';	בְּפָשַׁע	[sacrifice] by reason of transgression	Noun	ܘܐܫܬܪܝ	crime/time of vanquishing
7993	wə-□aš-lê□	וְתַשְׁלֵךְ	and it cast down	Verb		
571	'ĕ-meṯ	אֱמֶת	the truth	Noun	ܩܘܕܫܐ	holy place
					ܥܠ	over
776	'ar-ṣāh,	אַרְצָה	to the ground	Noun	ܐܪܥܐ	country/earth
6213	wə-'ā-śə-□āh	וְעָשְׂתָה	and it practiced	Verb	ܘܦܪܥ/ܘܥܒܕ	and violate/govern by force
6743	wə-hi□-lî-□āh.	וְהִצְלִ֥יחָה׃	and prospered	Verb	ܘܐܝܟ ܠܗ.	and prosper
Daniel 8:23						
319	ū-ḇə-'a-ḥă-rîṯ	וּבְאַחֲרִית	at the final end	Noun	ܘܒܣܘܦ	and at the final end
4438	mal-ḵū-□ām,	מַלְכוּתָם	of their rule	Noun	ܡܠܟܘܬܗܘܢ	reign
					ܗܕܐ	of this/therefore
8552	kə-hā-□êm	כְּהָתֵם	have come to the full	Verb	ܕܫܠܡܘ	so that fulfillment
6586	hap-pō-šə-'îm;	הַפֹּשְׁעִ֑ים	when the transgressors	Verb	ܚ̈ܘܒܐ	guilt/rebellions
5975	ya-'ă-mōḏ	יַעֲמֹד	shall stand up/rise	Verb	ܢܩܘܡ	will rise/appear

S#	Translit	Hebrew	English	Morph	Aramaic	English
4428	me-leḵ	מֶלֶךְ	a king	Noun	ܡܠܟܐ	king/ruler/caliph
5794	‘az-	עַז־	of fierce/strong	Adj	ܬܩܝܦ	strong/severe
6440	pā-nîm	פָּנִים	countenance/ insolence	Noun	ܐܦ̈ܐ	faces/manner
995	ū-mê-ḇîn	וּמֵבִין	and understanding	Verb	ܘܡܣܬܟܠ	and understand
2420	ḥî-□ō-w□.	חִידוֹת׃	riddles/intrigues	Noun	ܐܘܚܕ̈ܬܐ	enigmas
Daniel 8:24						
6105	wə-‘ā-□am	וְעָצַם	And shall be mighty	Verb	ܘܬܬܩܦ	and great/ strong/severe
3581	kō-ḥōw	כֹּחוֹ	his power	Noun	ܚܝܠܗ.	force/power
3808	wə-lō	וְלֹא	but not	Adv	ܘܠܐ	and not
3581	ḇə-ḵō-ḥōw,	בְּכֹחוֹ	by his own power	Noun	ܒܚܝܠܐ	of force/power
					ܕܢܦܫܗ	of himself
6381	wə- nip- lā-’ō-w	וְנִפְלָאוֹת	and extraordinarily	Verb	ܘܬܕܡܪ̈ܬܐ	and amazing surprising
7843	yaš-ḥî□	יַשְׁחִית	he shall destroy	Verb	ܢܚܒܠ	to destroy/damage
6743	wə-hi□-lî-a□	וְהִצְלִיחַ	and shall prosper	Verb	ܘܢܨܠܚ.	and prosper/succeed
6213	wə-‘ā-śāh;	וְעָשָׂה	and accomplish	Verb	ܘܢܥܒܕ	and violate
7843	wə-hiš-□î□	וְהִשְׁחִית	and shall destroy	Verb	ܘܢܚܒܠ	and destroy/damage
6099	‘ă-ṣū-mîm	עֲצוּמִים	the mighty/numerous	Adj	ܥܫܝ̈ܢܐ	strong/fortified
5971	wə-‘am-	וְעַם־	and the people	Noun	ܘܥܡܐ	also people
6918	qə-□ō-šîm.	קְדֹשִׁים׃	holy	Adj	ܕܩܕܝ̈ܫܐ	of holiness
Daniel 8:25						
5921	wə-‘al-	וְעַל־	And through	Prep	ܘܒܐܘܚܕܢܗ	and by his authority/power
7922	śiḵ-lōw,	שִׂכְלוֹ	his cunning/ shrewdness	Noun		
6743	wə-hi□-lî-a□	וְהִצְלִיחַ	and prosper/succeed	Verb	ܢܨܠܚ	will prosper/succeed
4820	mir-māh	מִרְמָה	deceit/treachery	Noun	ܢܟܠܐ	guile/conspiracy
3027	bə-yā-□ōw,	בְּיָדוֹ	by his influence	Noun	ܒܐܝܕܗ	by his power/control
3824	ū-ḇil-ḇā-ḇōw	וּבִלְבָבוֹ	in his heart	Noun	ܘܠܒܗ.	and secret heart
1431	yaḡ-dîl,	יַגְדִּיל	he shall boast	Verb	ܢܬܬܪܝܡ.	be exalted/haughty
7962	ū-ḇə-šal-wāh	וּבְשַׁלְוָה	and by prosperity/ complacency	Noun	ܘܒܫܠܝܐ	and at quiet/suddenly
7843	yaš-ḥî□	יַשְׁחִית	shall destroy	Verb	ܢܩܛܘܠ	kill/destroy
7227	rab-bîm;	רַבִּים	many	Adj	ܣܓܝ̈ܐܐ.	many/much
5921	wə-‘al-	וְעַל־	and against	Prep	ܘܥܠ	also against

S#	Translit	Hebrew	English	Morph	Aramaic	English
8269	śar-	שַׂר	the prince	Noun	ܫܠܝܛ	ruling
8269	śā-rîm	שָׂרִים	of princes	Noun	ܫܠܝܛܢܐ	rulers
5975	ya-'ă-mōḏ,	יַעֲמֹד	he shall also stand/rise up	Verb	ܢܩܘܡ	to rise up/stand
657	ū-ḇə-'e- pes	וּבְאֶפֶס	however, the end	Noun	ܘܕܐܚܪܢ	but in regards to
3027	yāḏ	יָד	power	Noun	ܐܚܝܕ	his captured possession
7665	yiš-šā-ḇêr.	יִשָּׁבֵר׃	shall be crushed/shattered	Verb	ܢܬܬܒܪ	be broken/routed

Daniel 11:29

4150	lam-mō-w-'êḏ	לַמּוֹעֵד	At the appointed	Noun		[there is
7725	yā-šūḇ	יָשׁוּב	he shall return	Verb		no matching
935	ū-ḇā	וּבָא	and come	Verb		text in
5045	ḇan-ne-ḡeḇ;	בַנֶּגֶב	into the South	Noun		the Aramaic]
3808	wə-lō-	וְלֹא־	but not	Adv	ܐܝܟ	like/as
1961	ṯih-yeh	תִהְיֶה	come to pass	Verb	ܕܩܕܡܝܬܐ	that of the first
7223	ḵā-ri-šō-nāh	כָרִאשֹׁנָה	like the first	Adj	ܐܦ	neither even
314	wə-ḵā-'a-ḥă-rō-nāh.	וְכָאַחֲרֹנָה׃	and the time after	Adj	ܕܒܬܪܟܢ	of time after

Daniel 11:30

935	ū-ḇā-'ū	וּבָאוּ	and shall come	Verb	ܘܢܐܬܘܢ	and to come
	ḇōw	בוֹ	in	Prep	ܥܠܘܗܝ	against/toward
6716	ṣi-yîm	צִיִּים	For the ships	Noun	ܚܝܠܘܬܐ	troops
3794	kit-tîm	כִּתִּים	of Kittim	Adj	ܕܟܬܝܐ	of Kittite
3512	wə-niḵ-'āh,	וְנִכְאָה	therefore he shall be grieved	Verb	ܘܢܬܒܕܪܘܢ	and break up/disperse
7725	wə-šāḇ	וְשָׁב	and return	Verb	ܘܢܗܦܟܘܢ	and turn/retreat
2194	wə-zā-'am	וְזָעַם	and be angry/enraged	Verb	ܘܢܪܓܙ	also be enraged
5921	'al-	עַל־	against	Prep	ܥܠ	against/toward
1285	bə-rîṯ-	בְּרִית־	covenant	Noun	ܩܝܡܐ	covenant
6944	qō-w-ḏeš	קוֹדֶשׁ	the holy	Noun	ܩܕܝܫܐ	holy
6213	wə-'ā-śāh;	וְעָשָׂה	so shall he do	Verb		
7725	wə-šāḇ	וְשָׁב	and turn to	Verb		
995	wə-yā-ḇên,	וְיָבֵן	and cunningly understand	Verb	ܘܢܣܬܟܠ	and understand/take note of
5921	'al-	עַל־	against/over	Prep	ܥܠ	with those
5800	'ō-zə-ḇê	עֹזְבֵי	those who forsake	Verb	ܕܫܒܩܘ	who leave/abandon
1285	bə-rîṯ	בְּרִית	covenant	Noun	ܩܝܡܐ	covenant
6944	qō-ḏeš.	קֹדֶשׁ׃	the holy	Noun	ܩܕܝܫܐ	holy

S#	Translit	Hebrew	English	Morph	Aramaic	English
Daniel 11:31						
2220	ū-zə-rō-'îm	וּזְרֹעִ ים	and forces	Noun	ܘܬܘܩܦܗܘܢ	and strong/angry force
4480	mim-men-nū	מִמֶּנּוּ	on his behalf	Prep	ܡܢܗܘܢ	belonging to him
5975	ya-'ă-mō-ḏū;	יַעֲמֹד ו	shall rise/stand	Verb	ܢܩܘܡ	establish/rise
2490	wə-ḥil-lə-lū	וְחִלְּלוּ	and shall pollute/defile	Verb	ܘܢܛܢܦܘܢ.	and defile/pollute
4720	ham-miq-dāš	הַמִּקְדָּשׁ	the sanctuary	Noun	ܡܩܕܫܐ	temple/holy place
4581	ham-mā-'ō-wz	הַמָּע וֹז	of strength/protection	Noun	ܥܫܝܢܐ	fortified/made strong
5493	wə-hê-sî-rū	וְהֵסִי רוּ	and shall remove/abolish	Verb	ܘܢܥܒܪܘܢ	and remove
8548	hat-tā-mîḏ,	הַתָּמִי ד	the continual	Noun	.ܡܘܪ̈ܒܐ	the continual
5414	wə-nā-ṯə-nū	וְנָתְנוּ	and shall install/place	Verb	ܘܢܬܠܘܢ	and place/turn into
8251	haš-šiq-qūṣ	הַשִּׁקּוּץ	the abomination	Noun	ܛܢܦܘܬܐ	abomination
8074	mə-šō-w-mêm.	מְשׁוֹמֵם	of desolation	Verb	ܠܚܒܠܐ	destruction/ruination
Daniel 11:32						
7561	ū-mar-šî-'ê	וּמַרְשִׁי עֵי	and those who act wickedly	Verb	ܘܐܝܠܝܢ	and those
					ܕܡܚܠܝܢ	who act against
					ܥܠ	concerning
1285	ḇə-rîṯ,	בְרִי ת	covenant	Noun	ܩܝܡܐ	the covenant
2610	ya-ḥă- nîp	יַחֲנִי ף	shall he corrupt	Verb	ܢܫܝܢ	be conquered
					ܐܢܘܢ	them
2514	ba-ḥă-laq-qō-wṯ;	בַּחֲלַקּוֹת	by smooth/flattery	Noun		
5971	wə-'am	וְעַם	but the people	Noun	ܘܥܡܐ	and people
3045	yō-ḏə-'ê	יֹדְעֵי	that do know	Verb	ܕܝ̈ܕܥܝܢ	who know/understand
430	'ĕ-lō-hāw	אֱלֹהָ י ו	their God	Noun	ܕܚܠܬܐ	the godly faith
2388	ya-ḥă-zi-qū	יַחֲזִקוּ ו	shall be strong/firm	Verb	ܢܬܩܦܘܢ	become strong
6213	wə-'ā-śū.	וְעָשׂוּ׃	be made into	Verb		
Daniel 11:33						
7919	ū-maś-kî-lê	וּמַשְׂכִּי לֵי	and they who have insight	Verb	ܘܙܕܝ̈ܩܘܗܝ	and the just/righteous
5971	'ām,	עָם	people	Noun	ܕܥܡܐ	of the people
995	yā-ḇî-nū	יָבִי נוּ	cause to understand	Verb	ܢܠܦܘܢ	to teach/instruct
7227	lā-rab-bîm;	לָרַבִּי ם	to the many	Adj	ܠܣܓܝ̈ܐܐ	for the many

302   Hidden Rhythms in Prophecy

S#	Translit	Hebrew	English	Morph	Aramaic	English
3782	wə-niṣ-šə-lū	וְנִכְשְׁלוּ	and yet they shall fall	Verb	ܘܢܬܬܩܠܘܢ	and be caused to stumble
2719	bə-ḥe-reḇ	בְּחֶרֶב	by sword	Noun	ܒܚܪܒܐ	by the sword
3852	ū-ḇə-le-hā-ḇāh	וּבְלֶהָבָה	and by flames	Noun	ܘܒܢܘܪܐ	also with fire
7628	biš-ḇî	בְשְׁבִי	by captivity	Noun	ܘܒܫܒܝܐ	also with captivity
961	ū-ḇə-ḇiz-zāh	וּבְבִזָּה	and by spoil/plunder	Noun	ܘܒܒܙܬܐ	also with plundering
3117	yā-mîm.	יָמִים׃	[many] days	Noun	ܝܘܡܬܐ	days
					ܐܠܦ	thousand

Daniel 11:34

					ܘܡܐ	and in any event
3782	ū-ḇə-hik-kā-šə-lām,	וּבְהִכָּשְׁלָם	when they shall fall	Verb	ܘܐܝܠܝܢ ܕܢܦܠܘ	and those who have fallen
5826	yê-'ā-zə-rū	יֵעָזְרוּ	they shall be helped/protected	Verb	ܢܬܥܕܪܘܢ	will be helped
5828	'ê-zer	עֵזֶר	help	Noun	ܥܘܕܪܢܐ	help
4592	mə-'āṭ;	מְעָט	with a little	Subst	ܩܠܝܠ	a little/short while
3867	wə-nil-wū	וְנִלְווּ	and shall cleave	Verb	ܘܢܬܠܘܘܢ	and gathered
5921	'ă-lê-hem	עֲלֵיהֶם	together	Prep	ܥܠܝܗܘܢ	together
7227	rab-bîm	רַבִּים	but many	Adj	ܣܓܝܐܐ	many
2519	ba-ḥă-laq-laq-qō-wṯ.	בַּחֲלַקְלַקּוֹת	in hypocrisy/treachery	Noun	ܒܚܠܘܛܐ	among with discord/fraud

Daniel 11:35

4480	ū-min-	וּמִן־	and of	Prep	ܘܡܢ	and of
7919	ham-maś-kî-lîm	הַמַּשְׂכִּילִים	those with insight	Verb	ܚܟܝܡܐ	the wise
3782	yik-kā-šə-lū,	יִכָּשְׁלוּ	shall fall	Verb	ܢܬܬܩܠܘܢ	be cast down
6884	liṣ-rō- wp	לִצְרוֹף	in order to refine	Verb	ܠܚܘܕܬܐ	for renewal/examination
	bā-hem	בָּהֶם	in them	Prep	ܒܗܘܢ	within
1305	ū-lə-ḇā-rêr	וּלְבָרֵר	and to purge/cleanse	Verb	ܘܠܣܘܟܠܐ	also for understanding
3835	wə-lal-bên	וְלַלְבֵּן	and to make white	Verb		
5704	'aḏ-	עַד־	to	Prep	ܥܕ	until
6256	'êṯ	עֵת	time	Noun	ܙܒܢܐ	set time
7093	qêṣ;	קֵץ	of the end	Noun	ܩܨܐ	end
3588	kî-	כִּי־	because	Conj	ܡܛܠ	because
5750	'ō-wḏ	עוֹד	yet	Subst	ܬܘܒ	that further
4150	lam-mō-w-'êḏ.	לַמּוֹעֵד׃	for an appointed time	Noun	ܐܝܬ	definite
					ܙܒܢܐ ܢܓܝܪܐ	long time
					ܕܥܠܡܐ	of eternity

S#	Translit	Hebrew	English	Morph	Aramaic	English
Daniel 11:36						
6213	wə-'ā-śāh	וְעָשָׂה	and shall do	Verb	ܘܢܥܒܕ	and behave/govern
7522	ḵir-ṣō-w-nōw	כִרְצוֹנוֹ	as he pleases	Noun	ܡܠܟܐ	king/ruler/caliph
					ܐܝܟ ܕ	like
4428	ham-me-leḵ,	הַמֶּלֶךְ	the king	Noun	ܨܒܝܢܗ.	his pleasure/will
7311	wə-yi□-rō-w-mêm	וְיִתְרוֹמֵם	and he shall exalt himself	Verb	ܘܢܬܬܪܝܡ	and exalt/lift up
1431	wə-yi□-gad-dêl	וְיִתְגַּדֵּל	and boast	Verb	ܥܠ	over
5921	'al-	עַל־	above	Prep		
3605	kāl-	כָּל־	every	Noun	ܟܠ	all
410	'êl,	אֵל	god	Noun	ܐܠܗܐ.	gods
5921	wə-'al	וְעַל	and against	Prep	ܐܠܗܐ	and over
410	'êl	אֵל	the God	Noun	ܐܠܗܐ	God
410	'ê-lîm,	אֵלִים	of gods	Noun	ܐܠܗ̈ܝܢ	of gods
1696	yə-□ab-bêr	יְדַבֵּר	shall speak	Verb	ܢܡܠܠ	speaking
6381	nip- lā-'ō-wṯ;	נִפְלָאוֹת	extraordinary/ miraculous	Verb	ܪܘܪܒܢ.	greatly/ of importance
6743	wə-hi□-lî-a□	וְהִצְלִיחַ	and shall prosper	Verb	ܘܢܨܠܚ	and prosper/succeed
5704	'aḏ-	עַד־	until	Prep	ܥܕ	until
3615	kā-lāh	כָּלָה	completion	Verb	ܢܫܠܡ	completion
2195	za-'am,	זַעַם	the fury	Noun	ܪܘܓܙܐ.	divine wrath
3588	kî	כִּי	that	Conj	ܡܛܠ	that
2782	ne-ḥĕ-rā-ṣāh	נֶחֱרָצָה	is determined	Verb	ܕܦܣܝܩܬܐ	which is decreed
6213	ne-'ĕ-śā-ṯāh.	נֶעֱשָׂתָה׃	is accomplished	Verb	ܐܬܥܒܕܬ	is done
Daniel 11:37						
5921	wə-'al-	וְעַל־	and above	Prep	ܘܒܐܠܗܐ	and about god
430	'ĕ-lō-hê	אֱלֹהֵי	the gods	Noun		
1	'ă-ḇō-ṯāw	אֲבֹתָיו	of his fathers	Noun	ܕܐܒܗ̈ܘܗܝ	of fathers
3808	lō	לֹא	not	Adv	ܠܐ	not
995	yā-ḇîn,	יָבִין	regard/ consider	Verb	ܢܬܒܝܢ.	observe/ consider
5921	wə-'al-	וְעַל־	and above	Prep	ܘܥܠ	and above
2532	ḥem-da□	חֶמְדַּת	the desire	Noun	ܪܓܬ	to desire
802	nā-šîm	נָשִׁים	of women	Noun	ܢܫ̈ܐ	women
5921	wə-'al-	וְעַל־	and above	Prep	ܘܥܠ	also above
3605	kāl-	כָּל־	all	Noun	ܟܠ	every
433	'ĕ-lō-w-ah	אֱלוֹהַּ	god	Noun	ܐܠܗܐ	god
3808	lō	לֹא	nor	Adv	ܠܐ	not

S#	Translit	Hebrew	English	Morph	Aramaic	English
995	yā-bîn;	יָבִין	regard/ consider	Verb	אתבונן	consider/think about
3588	kî	כִּי	for	Conj	אלא	rather
5921	'al-	עַל-	above	Prep	על	above
3605	kōl	כֹּל	all	Noun	כל	all
1431	yit-gad-dāl.	יִתְגַּדָּל׃	shall magnify/ boast	Verb	יתרברב	he will exalt/ boast

Daniel 11:38

433	wə-le-'ĕ-lō-ah	וְלֶאֱלֹהַּ	and the god	Noun	ולאלהא	and for god
4581	mā-'uz-zîm,	מָעֻזִּים	of fortresses	Noun	חסינא	strength/ fortified
5921	'al-	עַל-	in	Prep	על	of
3653	kan-nōw	כַּנּוֹ	his place/estate	Noun	באתריה	place/situation
3513	yə-ḵab-bêḏ;	יְכַבֵּד	shall he honor/glory	Verb	יוקר	to honor/ esteem
433	wə-le-'ĕ-lō-w-ah	וְלֶאֱלוֹהַּ	and a god	Noun	ולאלהא	and for god
834	'ă-šer	אֲשֶׁר	whom	Prt	דלא	who not
3808	lō-	לֹא-	not	Adv		
3045	yə-ḏā-'u-hū	יְדָעֻהוּ	knew/ acknowledged	Verb	ידעוהי	know/ experience
1 [e]	'ă-ḇō-ṯāw,	אֲבֹתָיו	his fathers	Noun	אבהתוהי	fathers
3513	yə-ḵab-bêḏ	יְכַבֵּד	shall he honor	Verb	יוקר	to honor/ esteem
2091	bə-zā-hāḇ	בְּזָהָב	with gold	Noun	בדהבא	with gold
3701	ū-ḇə-ḵe-sep̄	וּבְכֶסֶף	and silver	Noun	ובכספא	with silver/ money
68	ū-ḇə-'e-ḇen	וּבְאֶבֶן	and stones	Noun	ובאבנא	with gems
3368	yə-qā-rāh	יְקָרָה	with precious	Adj	טבא	valuable/ precious
2530	ū-ba-ḥă-mu-ḏō-wṯ:	וּבַחֲמֻדוֹת׃	and to desire/ covet	Verb	ובתאות	and with lustful desire

Daniel 11:39

6213	wə-'ā-śāh	וְעָשָׂה	to advance	Verb	ועבד	to overtake/ violate
4013	lə-miḇ-ṣə-rê	לְמִבְצְרֵי	strongholds/ fortifications	Noun	לכרכי	of walled cities
4581	mā-'uz-zîm	מָעֻזִּים	fortresses	Noun	חסינא	strong/ fortified
5973	'im-	עִם-	with	Prep	על	with
433	'ĕ-lō-w-ah	אֱלוֹהַּ	god	Noun	אלהא	gods
5236	nê-ḵār,	נֵכָר	strange/ foreign	Noun	נכראה	foreign/ different
834	'ă-šer	אֲשֶׁר	anyone who	Prt	דזכאין	those who realize/are victorious

S#	Translit	Hebrew	English	Morph	Aramaic	English
5234	Yak-kîr q	יַכִּיר ק	regarded/ respected -	Verb	ܘܢܫܠܛ	and rule/ dominate
7235	yar-beh	יַרְבֶּה	made great/ multiply	Verb	בܣܓܝܐܐ	among many
3519	kā-ḇō-wḏ;	כָבוֹד	with glory	Noun		
4910	wə-him-šî-lām	וְהִמְשִׁיל לָם	and make rule	Verb		
7227	bā-rab-bîm,	בָּרַבִּים	over the many	Adj		
127	wa-'ă-ḏā-māh	וְאֲדָמָה	and the land	Noun	ܘܐܪܥܐ	and land/ earth
2505	yə-ḥal-lêq	יְחַלֵּק	shall divide	Verb	ܢܦܠܓ	to divide
4242	bim-ḥîr.	בִּמְחִיר:	for a price	Noun	ܒܕܡܝܐ	for a price

Daniel 11:40

S#	Translit	Hebrew	English	Morph	Aramaic	English
6256	ū-ḇə-'êṯ	וּבְעֵת	and at the time	Noun	ܘܒܙܒܢܐ	and at the proper time
7093	qêṣ,	קֵץ	of the end	Noun	ܩܨܐ	end of the age
5055	yiṯ-nag-gaḥ	יִתְנַגַּח	push/ collide	Verb	ܢܬܟܬܫ	to fight/beat
5973	'im-mōw	עִמּוֹ	against	Prep	ܥܡܗ	with
4428	me-leḵ	מֶלֶךְ	king	Noun	ܡܠܟܐ	king/ruler/ caliph
5045	han-ne-ḡeḇ,	הַנֶּגֶב	of the south/ Negev	Noun	ܕܬܝܡܢܐ.	of south
8175	wə-yiś-tā-'êr	וְיִשְׂתָּעֵר	and will storm	Verb	ܘܢܕܠܚ	and terrorize/ disturb
5921	'ā-lāw	עָלָיו	against	Prep	ܥܠܘܗܝ,	against
4428	me-leḵ	מֶלֶךְ	the king	Noun	ܡܠܟܐ ܕ	king/ruler/ caliph
6828	haṣ-ṣā- p̄ōwn,	הַצָּפוֹן	of the north	Noun	ܓܪܒܝܐ.	of north
7393	bə-re-ḵeḇ	בְּרֶכֶב	with chariots	Noun	ܒܪܟܒܐ	with
					ܟ	2 horsed chariots
6571	ū-ḇə- pā-rā-šîm,	וּבְפָרָשִׁים	and with horsemen	Noun	ܘܒܦܪܫܐ	and with horsemen
591	ū-ḇā-'o-nî-yōwṯ	וּבָאֳנִיּוֹת	and ships	Noun	ܘܒܐܠܦܐ	and with ships
7227	rab-bōwṯ;	רַבּוֹת	with many	Adj	ܣܓܝܐܬܐ.	many
935	ū-ḇā	וּבָא	and he shall enter	Verb	ܘܢܥܘܠ	and enter
776	ḇa-'ă-rā-ṣōwṯ	בַּאֲרָצוֹת	into the countries	Noun	ܒܐܪܥܐ	Into land/ country
7857	wə-šā-ap̄	וְשָׁטַף	and shall overflow/ overwhelm	Verb		
5674	wə-'ā-ḇār.	וְעָבָר:	and invade	Verb		

S#	Translit	Hebrew	English	Morph	Aramaic	English
Daniel 11: 41						
935	û-bā	וּבָא	and He shall enter	Verb	ܘܢܡܛܐ	and reach/ come to
					ܠܐܪ	of
776	bə-'e-reṣ	בְּאֶרֶץ	land	Noun	ܐܪܥܐ	land/ country
6643	haṣ-ṣə-ḇî,	הַצְּבִי	the beautiful/ pleasant	Noun	ܐܝܣܪܐܝܠ	of Israel
7227	wə-rab-bō-wṯ	וְרַבּוֹת	and many	Adj	ܘܣܓܝܐܐ	and many
3782	yik-kā-šê-lū;	יִכָּשֵׁלוּ	shall fall	Verb	ܢܬܩܛܠܘܢ	be killed/slaughtered
428	wə-'êl-leh	וְאֵלֶּה	but these	Pro	ܘܗܠܝܢ	and these
4422	yim-mā-lə-ṭū	יִמָּלְטוּ	shall escape	Verb	ܢܫܬܘܙܒܘܢ	will escape
					ܡܢ	from
3027	mî-yā-ḏōw,	מִיָּדוֹ	out of his hand	Noun	ܐܝܕܗܘܢ,	power/ control
123	'ĕ-ḏōwm	אֱדוֹם	[even] Edom	Noun	ܐܕܘܡ	Edom
4124	û-mō-w-'āḇ,	וּמוֹאָב	and Moab	Noun	ܘܡܘܐܒ	and Moab
7225	wə-rê-šîṯ	וְרֵאשִׁית	and the chief/ finest	Noun	ܘܫܪܟܐ	and all the rest
1121	bə-nê	בְּנֵי	of the sons	Noun	ܕܒܢܝ	of sons
5983	'am-mō-wn.	עַמּוֹן׃	of Ammon	Noun	ܥܡܘܢ	Ammon
Daniel 11:42						
7971	wə-yiš-laḥ	וְיִשְׁלַח	and He shall stretch forth	Verb	ܘܢܘܫܛ	and extend
3027	yā-ḏōw	יָדוֹ	his hand	Noun	ܐܝܕܗ	arm/control
776	ba-'ă-rā-ṣō-wṯ;	בַּאֲרָצוֹת	against [other] countries	Noun	ܒܐܪܥܬܐ	into lands
776	wə-'e-reṣ	וְאֶרֶץ	and the land	Noun	ܘܐܪܥܐ	and land
4714	miṣ-ra-yim,	מִצְרַיִם	of Egypt	Noun	ܕܡܨܪܝܢ	of Egypt
3808	lō	לֹא	not	Adv	ܠܐ	not
1961	tih-yeh	תִהְיֶה	become	Verb	ܬܬܦܨܐ	be saved
					ܡܢ	from
6413	lip̄-lê-ṭāh.	לִפְלֵיטָה׃	delivered	Noun	ܐܝܕܗܘܢ,	control/ possession
Daniel 11:43						
4910	û-mā-šal,	וּמָשַׁל	but control/ dominion	Verb	ܘܢܫܠܛ	and to rule/dominate
4362	bə-miḵ-man-nê	בְּמִכְמַנֵּי	over treasures	Noun	ܒܓܙܐ	treasury
2091	haz-zā-hāḇ	הַזָּהָב	of gold	Noun	ܕܕܗܒܐ	of gold
3701	wə-hak-ke- sep̄,	וְהַכֶּסֶף	and of silver	Noun	ܘܕܣܐܡܐ	and of silver

S#	Translit	Hebrew	English	Morph	Aramaic	English
3605	ū-bə-ḵōl	וּבְכֹל	and over all	Noun	ܘܒܟܠ.	also all
2530	ḥă-mu-ḏō-w	חֲמֻדוֹת	the precious things	Verb	ܪܓ	precious
4714	miṣ-rā-yim;	מִצְרָיִם	of Egypt	Noun	ܡܨܪܝܢ	Egypt
3864	wə-lu-ḇîm	וְלֻבִים	and the Libyans	Noun	ܘܠܘܒܐ	Libya
3569	wə-ḵu-šîm	וְכֻשִׁים	and the Ethiopians	Adj	ܘܟܘܫܐ	Ethiopia/Cush
4703	bə-miṣ-'ā-ḏāw.	בְּמִצְעָדָיו׃	follow steps/at heels	Noun	ܢܗܘܘܢ	will become
					ܒܥܘܕܪܢܗ	his aid

Daniel 11:44

8052	ū-šə-mu-'ō-w	וּשְׁמֻעוֹת	But news	Noun	ܘܛܒܐ	and reports/ rumors
926	yə-ḇa-hă-lu-hū,	יְבַהֲלֻהוּ	shall disturb/terrify	Verb	ܢܒܗܬܘܢܗ	will frighten
					ܡܢ	from
4217	mim-miz-rāḥ	מִמִּזְרָח	from the East	Noun	ܡܕܢܚܐ	east
					ܘܡܢ	and from
6828	ū-miṣ-ṣā- pō-wn;	וּמִצָּפוֹן	and out of the north	Noun	ܓܪܒܝܐ.	north
3318	wə-yā-ṣā	וְיָצָא	and come/ go out	Verb	ܘܢܦܘܩ	and leave
2534	bə-ḥê-mā	בְּחֵמָא	fury/ rage	Noun	ܒܚܡܬܐ	in anger
1419	ḡə-ḏō-lāh,	גְדֹלָה	great	Adj	ܪܒܬܐ.	great
8045	lə-haš-mîḏ	לְהַשְׁמִיד	to destroy	Verb	ܠܡܚܪܒܘ	in order to destroy
2763	ū-lə-ha-ḥă-rîm	וּלְהַחֲרִים	exterminate	Verb	ܘܠܡܩܛܠܘ	and to kill
7227	rab-bîm.	רַבִּים׃	many	Adj	ܠܣܓܝܐܐ	many

Daniel 11:45

5193	wə-yiṭ-ṭa'	וְיִטַּע	shall plant/ establish	Verb	ܘܢܩܪܒ	and besiege/wage war
168	'ā-ho-le	אָהֳלֵי	the tabernacles/ dwellings	Noun	ܠܡܫܟܢܗ	toward sacred house
643	'ap-paḏ-nōw,	אַפַּדְנוֹ	throneroom	Noun	ܕܗܝܟܠܐ	of the temple
					ܕܟܝܐ.	pure/sincere
996	bên	בֵּין	between	Prep	ܒܝܬ/ܒܝܢ	between
3220	yam-mîm	יַמִּים	the seas	Noun	ܝܡܐ	the sea
2022	lə-har-	לְהַר-	mountain	Noun	ܠܛܘܪܐ	toward mountain
6643	ṣə-ḇî-	צְבִי-	glorious/ beautiful	Noun	ܘܢܛܪ	and watch/ guard
6944	qō-ḏeš;	קֹדֶשׁ	holy	Noun	ܩܕܝܫܐ	holy place
935	ū-ḇā	וּבָא	shall come/ arrive	Verb	ܘܢܡܛܐ	and reach/ come to
5704	'aḏ-	עַד-	as far as	Prep	ܥܕ	set time

S#	Translit	Hebrew	English	Morph	Aramaic	English
7093	qiṣ-ṣōw,	לֵץ	final end	Noun	ܩܨܗ.	final end
369	wə-'ên	וְאֵין	and none	Prt	ܘܠܐ	and none
					ܢܗܘܐ	will appear
5826	'ō-w-zêr	עֹזֵר	shall help	Verb	ܠܗ	for
	lōw.	לוֹ:	to	Prep	ܡܥܕܪܢܐ	helper/ aid

Bibliography

1911 Encyclopedia Britannica. (Retrieved 2016). Sabaeans. Retrieved from http://www.theodora.com/encyclopedia/s/sabaeans.html

Abib of God. (Retrieved 2014). Abib Report 2013. Retrieved from http://abibofgod.com/resources/Abib+Report+2013.pdf

Abib of God. (Retrieved 2014). Abib Report 2004. Retrieved from http://abibofgod.com/resources/abib2004.pdf

Albright, W. F. (1943). The Gezer Calendar. *BASOR*, 92.

Anderson, Sir Robert. (1894). *The Coming Prince*. London: Hodder & Stoughton.

Augustus Caesar. (Retrieved 2014). Res Gestae 8 – The Deeds of Divine Augustus. Retrieved from http://classics.mit.edu/Augustus/deeds.html

BibEnc. (Retrieved 2015). International Standard Bible Encyclopedia Online (1939). Retrieved from www.internationalstandardbible.com/J/judith-book-of.html

Bible. (1917). *(TNK) The Holy Scriptures According to the Masoretic Text. A New Translation*. Jewish Publication Society.

Bible. (1946, 1952, and 1971). *(RSV) The Revised Standard Version of the Bible*. Division of Christian Education of the National Council of the Churches of Christ in the United States of America.

Bible. (1901). *(ASV) The Holy Bible, Containing the Old and New Testaments, Translated out of the Original Tongues, Being the Version Set Forth A.D. 1611, Compared with the Most Ancient Authorities and Revised A.D. 1881-1885, Newly Edited by the American Revision Committee A.D. 1901, Standard Edition*. New York: Thomas Nelson & Sons.

Bible. (1960, 1962, 1963, 1968, 1971, 1972, 1973, 1975, 1977, 1995).

(NASB) New American Standard Bible®. The Lockman Foundation.

Bible. (1973, 1978, 1984). *(NIV) Holy Bible, New International Version®, NIV®*. Biblica, Inc.™.

Bible. (Retrieved 2014). (KJV) Holy Bible, King James Version. Retrieved from www.bibleprotector.com

BibleHub.com. (Retrieved 2016). Bible Hub Online Bible Study Suite. Retrieved from www.biblehub.com

Biltz, Mark. (Retrieved 2009). 2014/2015 Eclipses at Feasts. Retrieved from http://www.elshaddaiministries.us/video/eclipsecharts.html.

Bloomfield, Arthur E. (1971). *Before the Last Battle*. Minneapolis: Bethany Fellowship, Inc.

Brenton, Lancelot C. (1851). *The Greek Septuagint Version of the Old Testament according to the Vatican edition, together with the real Septuagint version of Daniel and the Apocrypha including the fourth book of Maccabees and an historical introduction*. London: Samuel Bagster and Sons.

Bright, John. (2000). *A History of Israel, Fourth Edition*. Westminster John Knox Press.

Caesar, Stephen. (Retrieved 2014). A Brief comment on the Census in Luke 2. Retrieved from http://www.biblearchaeology.org/post/2008/10/16/A-Brief-Comment-on-the-Census-in-Luke-2.aspx

Compton, Jared. (2009). Once More: Quirinius's Census. *Detroit Baptist Theological Journal*, Fall 2009.

De Sola, D.A., Raphall, M. J. (1843). *Eighteen Treatises from the Mishna*. London: Sherwood, Gilbert, and Piper, Paternoster Row.

Edwards, Jan Editor. (2010). *ProCrop Barley Growth & Development*. NSW Government - Industry & Investment.

Espenak, Fred. (Retrieved 2016). Eclipses and the Saros. Retrieved from http://eclipse.gsfc.nasa.gov/SEsaros/SEsaros.html

Evans, Craig A. (1998). *Introduction: An Aramaic Approach Thirty Years Later*. Peabody: Hendrickson Publishers.

EWB. Encyclopedia of World Biography (2008). (Retrieved 2014). Dionysius Exiguus.. Retrieved from Encyclopedia.com

Fear, A. T. (2010). *Orosius: Seven Books of History against the Pagans*. Liverpool University Press.

Feldman, W. M. (1931). *Rabbinical Mathematics and Astronomy*. London: M. L. Cailingold.

Galil, J. and Eisikowitch, D. (1968). FLOWERING CYCLES AND FRUIT TYPES OF FICUS SYCOMORUS IN ISRAEL. *New phytology*, 67.

Goldstein, Bernard R.. (2001). Astronomy and the Jewish Community in Early Islam. *Aleph*, 2001, 1.

Green Cover Seed, Nebraska, USA. (Retrieved 2015). Green Cover Seed. Retrieved from greencoverseed.com

Greenspahn, Frederick E.. (2002). *Beyond Babel: A Handbook for Biblical Hebrew and Related Languages:Aramaic*. Society of Biblical Literature.

Grove, George. (1900). *The Bible Atlas of Maps and Plans 6th Edition*. London:Society For Promoting Christian Knowledge.

Hall, Isaac H. (1915). *Syriac New Testament. Translated by James Murdock. Appendix II*. Boston: H.L. Hastings & Sons.

Hasel, Gerhard. (1992). New light on the book of Daniel from the Dead Sea scrolls. *Bible and Spade*, Spring 2011.

Heath, Thomas. (1913). *Aristarchus of Samos:The Ancient Copernicus*. Oxford: Clarendon Press.

Hebrew Union College - Jewish Institute of Religion. (Retrieved 2016). (CAL) Comprehensive Aramaic Lexicon Project. Retrieved from cal1.cn.huc.edu/index.html

Hicks, R.D. (1972 (First published 1925)). *Lives of Eminent Philosophers. Diogenes Laertius*. Cambridge: Harvard University Press.

Hoehner, Harold W. (1975). Chronological Aspects of the Life of Christ Part VI: Daniel's Seventy Weeks and New Testament Chronology. *Bibliotheca Sacra*, Volume 132.

Humphreys, Colin J., Waddington, W.G. (1992). The Jewish Calendar, A Lunar Eclipse And The Date Of Christ's Crucifixion. *Tyndale Bulletin*, 43:2.

Instone-Brewer, David. (2011). Jesus of Nazareth's Trial in the Uncensored Talmud. *Tyndale Bulletin*, 62.2.

Jamieson, Robert; Fausset, A.R.; Brown, David. (1871). *Commentary Critical and Explanatory on the Whole Bible, Volume 1*. Glasgow: William Collins.

Josephus, Flavius. (1895). *The Works of Flavius Josephus. Translated by. William Whiston, A.M*. Auburn and Buffalo: John E. Beardsley.

Jouon, Paul; Muraoka, T. (2011). *A Grammar of Biblical Hebrew*. Gregorian & Biblical Press.

Levin, Christoph (translated by Margaret Kohl). (2005). *The Old Testament:A Brief Introduction*. Princeton University Press.

Lister,Diane L.;Thaw, Susan; Bower, Mim A.; Jones, Huw; Charles, Michael P.; Jones,Glynis; Smith, Lydia M.J.; Howe, Christopher J.; Brown, Terence A.; Jones, Martin K.. (2009). Latitudinal variation in a photoperiod response gene in European barley: insight into the dynamics of agricultural spread from 'historic' specimens. *Journal of Archaeological Science*, 36.

Migowski, C. (2001). *Untersuchungen laminierter holozänerSedimente aus dem Toten Meer: Rekonstruktionenvon Paläoklima und -seismizität*. GeoForschungsZentrum.

Molnar, Michael R. (1999). *The Star of Bethlehem: The Legacy of the Magi*. New Jersey:Rutgers University Press.

Murdock, James. (1915). *Syriac New Testament Translated into English from the Peshitto Version. 9th Edition*. Boston: H.L Hastings & Sons.

Parker, Richard A. And Dubberstein, Waldo H. (1956). *Babylonian Chronology 626 BC – AD 45*. Chicago: The University of Chicago Press.

Peshitta. (Retrieved 2015). Dukhrana Biblical Research. Retrieved from http://www.dukhrana.com

Peterson, Stephanie Bowers. (2006). *The Cult of Dushara and the Roman Annexation of Nabataea* . Thesis. McMaster University.

Porter, Stanley E. (1991). *The Aramaic of the Gospels In: The Language of the New Testament Ed. Stanley E. Porter* . JSOT Press: Sheffield Academic Press.

Roberts, Alexander; Donaldson, James (editors). (1885). *Ante-Nicene Fathers. Volume 1. The Apostolic Fathers, Justin Martyr, Irenaeus* . Christian Literature Company.

Sachau, Dr. C. Edward. (1879). *The Chronology of Ancient Nations: An English Version of the Arabic Text of the Athar-ul-bakiya of Albiruni or "Vestiges of the Past"* . London: W. H. Allen & Co.

Stern, Sacha. (2001). *Calendar and Community* . Oxford University Press.

Strabo. (Retrieved 2016). Geography. Retrieved from http://data.perseus.org/text/urn:cts:greekLit:tlg0099.tlg001

Tertullian. Edited and translated by Ernest Evans. (1972). *Tertullian:Adversus Marcionem* . Oxford University Press.

Torrey, Charles C. (1933). *The Four Gospels: A New Translation* . New York: Harper & Brothers Publishers.

Torrey, Charles C. (1991). *The Aramaic of the Gospels In: The Language of the New Testament Ed. Stanley E. Porter* . JSOT Press: Sheffield Academic Press.

Wallace, Daniel B. (2004). The Problem of Luke 2:2 'This was the first census taken when Quirinius was governor of Syria'. , .

Walvoord, John F. (1971). *The Key to Prophetic Revelation* . Chicago: Moody Press.

Williams, Jefferson B.; Schwab, Markus J.; Brauer, A.. (2011). An early first-century earthquake in the Dead Sea. *International Geology Review*, DOI:10.1080.

Wong, Dale. (2006). *The Ancient 360 Day Year* . Charleston, South Carolina: Advantage.

Wright, R. Ramsay (translator). (1934). *The Book of instruction in the elements of the art of astrology Written in Ghaznah, 1029 AD*

Reproduced from Brit. Mus. MS Or. 8349 Abu'l-Rayḥān Muḥammad Ibn-Aḥmad al-Biruni. London. Luzac & Co..

Young, Robert. (1898). *Young's Literal Translation*. Grand Rapids:Baker Book House.

Index

70 Weeks prophecy 2, 3, 7, 67, 75, 97, 98, 109, 140, 159, 173, 206, 209, 213, 236, 259, 266
abib 12, 14, 18-20, 26, 31, 42, 43, 62, 63, 216, 220, 232, 233, 237, 238, 244-247, 263, 265, 275
abomination of desolation 124, 134-136, 280
Abraham 82, 161, 164, 167
Al-Biruni 22, 27, 34-36, 40, 62, 63, 156-158, 173, 175, 179
Anno Alexandri 173, 174
Anno Mundi 33, 36, 38
Antiochus Epiphanes 81, 120, 121, 134, 136
Arabia 162-167, 170, 171
Aramaic 2, 82-85, 89-91, 97, 125, 126, 130, 131, 136-138, 140, 141, 153-156, 165, 168, 169, 183-186, 193, 194, 196, 281, 283, 289, 296
Artaxerxes 71-73, 96, 114, 115, 117, 158, 249
Assyrian 68, 106, 244
Assyrians 27
astronomy 2, 13, 40, 44, 171
Babylon
    Babylon 2, 14, 27, 31, 35, 37, 38, 40, 62, 63, 68, 74, 82, 98-102, 106, 116-118, 154, 157, 158, 171, 243-245, 247, 269-273, 275, 276, 278
    Babylonian 2, 14, 31, 35, 37, 38, 40, 62, 63, 68, 74, 82, 99, 102, 116, 157, 243, 244, 269, 270, 275

Babylonians 27
barley 17, 19, 20, 26, 32, 34, 40-43, 62-64, 176, 192, 197, 216, 232, 233, 238, 263, 265
blood moons 213, 215, 233
Chorasmia 35, 157
Creation Week 11, 13, 24, 204, 250, 251
Crucifixion 72, 73, 175, 178, 187, 190, 192, 195, 199, 200, 204, 205, 239
cycles 1, 12, 13, 15, 24, 30, 31, 36, 37, 64, 239, 240, 252, 292
Darius 96-98, 103, 106, 249
Day of Atonement 211, 282
eclipse event sign 207, 216, 218, 220, 221, 224, 227, 229, 232, 234, 235, 238, 240, 243-247, 250, 252, 258, 259, 265, 271, 276, 290
Era Adami 35, 36
Era Alexandri 36
Exodus 7, 14, 17-19, 21, 22, 24, 30, 32, 34, 137, 204, 242, 278
Feast of Firstfruits 20, 211
    Firstfruits 18-20, 43, 192, 197, 211
Feasts of the LORD 18, 182, 204, 211
Firstfruits 18-20, 43, 192, 197, 211, 287
Gabriel 3, 65, 68, 69, 91, 92, 109-111, 114, 138, 140, 141, 158, 259, 278
Good Friday 180, 205
Gregorian 16, 37, 44, 45, 62, 73, 74,

146, 266
Hillel 33, 40, 62
intercalation 27, 31, 35-38, 40, 57, 60, 62-64, 216, 232, 233, 263, 265, 275
Jeremiah 1, 68, 82, 98, 99, 101, 106, 110-112, 140, 245, 247, 269-272, 276
Jerusalem 1, 2, 28, 36, 58-60, 68, 70-72, 76-78, 91, 95-100, 102-104, 108-112, 114-122, 132, 134, 138, 141, 145, 154, 158, 159, 173, 176, 181, 195, 199, 227, 236, 242, 247, 249, 270, 271, 273-275, 290
Jesus 2, 3, 71, 72, 115, 119, 130, 134, 136-138, 143, 145-147, 153, 157, 173-180, 183, 185-190, 192, 193, 195-197, 199, 204, 205, 235, 236, 240, 251, 253, 259, 282, 292, 293
Josephus 32, 117-120, 134, 135, 151, 181, 201, 286
Julian calendar 36, 57, 73, 74, 266
Magi 27, 38, 81, 146, 153-161, 166, 168, 170-172
Mahzor 35-37
Masoretic 79-81, 84, 136
Messiah 2, 32, 70, 72, 76, 93-95, 204, 236, 275
metonic cycle 31, 33, 36-38, 63
Mishnah 188, 189
Nebuchadnezzar 68, 99-101, 110, 112, 154, 244, 245, 269-273, 278
Nehemiah 15, 71, 73, 114-118, 120, 141, 249
New Moon 13, 14, 16, 19, 24, 28-30, 44, 57-60, 63, 182, 186, 200, 204, 251, 268, 284
Parthian 159, 161
Passover 18, 19, 21-23, 26, 32, 72, 137, 175, 176, 178, 180-182, 185, 187-190, 196, 197, 199, 200, 204, 211, 242, 266, 275, 287
Persia 27, 35, 37, 68, 71, 72, 95-97, 99, 112, 115, 117, 157, 171, 244, 247
Peshitta 2, 82-84, 97, 136, 154, 183-185, 193, 194, 196, 281, 283
Preparation Day 30, 188, 190, 195
Ptolemy 171, 172
Sabbath 13, 14, 20-22, 30, 101, 102, 180-182, 185, 186, 188-193, 211
Sanhedrin 28, 30, 31
Seir 163, 164, 170
Sheba 15, 103, 163, 165-168
Sinai 21, 163
Table of Kebioth 36
temple 28, 32, 71, 95, 103, 117, 120-123, 125, 132-137, 145, 188, 240, 246, 249, 270, 271, 276, 278, 290
Tertullian 152
tetrad 213-216, 226, 227, 265
Unleavened Bread 12, 18-20, 182, 189, 191, 192, 195, 196, 211, 287
Vernal Equinox 31, 32, 42, 45, 62, 63

www.ingramcontent.com/pod-product-compliance
Lightning Source LLC
Chambersburg PA
CBHW071649090426
42738CB00009B/1465